Literary Obscenities

Literary

OBSCENITIES

U.S. CASE LAW AND NATURALISM AFTER MODERNISM

Erik M. Bachman

The Pennsylvania State University Press
University Park, Pennsylvania

Library of Congress Cataloging-in-
Publication Data

Names: Bachman, Erik M., 1981—author.
Title: Literary obscenities : U.S. case law and natu-
    ralism after modernism / Erik M. Bachman.
Other titles: Refiguring modernism.
Description: University Park, Pennsylvania : The
    Pennsylvania State University Press, [2018] |
Series: Refiguring modernism | Includes bibli-
    ographical references and index.
Summary: "Examines U.S. obscenity trials in the
    early twentieth century and how they framed a
    wide-ranging debate about the printed word's
    power to deprave, offend, and shape behav-
    ior"—Provided by publisher.
Identifiers: LCCN 2017045208 | ISBN
    9780271080055 (cloth : alk. paper)
Subjects: LCSH: Sex in literature—History—20th
    century. | Pornography in Literature—
    History—20th century. | Obscenity
    (Law)—United States—History—20th century.
    | Naturalism in literature—History—20th cen-
    tury. | Lewis, Wyndham, 1882-1957—Criticism
    and Interpretation. | Caldwell, Erskine,
    1903—1987—Criticism and interpretation. |
    Smith, Lillian (Lillian Eugenia), 1897—1966—
    Criticism and interpretation.
Classification: LCC PN56.S5 B33 2018 | DDC
    809/.933538—dc23
LC record available at https://lccn.loc.gov
    /2017045208

Published by The Pennsylvania
State University Press,
University Park, PA 16802-1003

The Pennsylvania State University Press is a
member of the Association of University Presses.

It is the policy of The Pennsylvania State University
Press to use acid-free paper. Publications on
uncoated stock satisfy the minimum requirements
of American National Standard for Information
Sciences—Permanence of Paper for Printed Library
Material, ANSI Z39.48–1992.

To Walter and Kathryn Bachman,

who merrily have yet to be called

to account for their own manifest

tendencies to deprave and corrupt

Contents

Acknowledgments

This book would not have initially come into being without the midwifery of Robert H. Birkby, Susan Gillman, Jody Greene, and Christine Hong.

It would not have grown into what it has since become without the folksy acumen and friendship of H. Marshall Leicester, Jr.

It likewise would not have been fit to see the light of day without the mentorship, singular exemplarity, and unstintingly generous aid of Tyrus Miller.

It is written with my ideal readers in mind: James Bachman (who is not just my ideal copyeditor), Nicholas Gaskill, Aliyah Khan, Christine Lupo Montgomery, Shane Elsa Marie Sweeting, and Evan Calder Williams.

An earlier version of chapter 2 appeared in *Textual Practice* 28, no. 3 (May 2014): 427–51, doi: 10.1080/0950236X.2013.848925. See www.tandfonline.com.

An earlier version of chapter 4 appeared in *Studies in American Fiction* 42, no. 2 (Fall 2015): 191–217. Copyright © Johns Hopkins University Press.

Introduction

During the first half of the twentieth century, the ability of writing to make unruly claims on our bodies preoccupied judges, jurists, authors, and critics involved in debates over ongoing revisions to the definition of and tests for legal obscenity in the United States. At the same time that modernist writing was challenging fiction and poetry as they had been created hitherto, state and appellate courts began undermining the grounds on which books could be prosecuted for their corruptive moral influences and salacious bodily appeals. Putting into dialogue obscenity case law's crisis of legitimation and modernism's crisis of representation, *Literary Obscenities* argues that "obscene modernism" helps us to account for the cultural logic of a period in which the meaning, identity, and very existence of obscene writing itself seemed to be evaporating. "Modernism," it should be noted, does not refer to fundamentally subversive, shocking, or disruptive texts here. Instead, it encompasses a widely dispersed set of discursive practices that are marked by concerns regarding the conditions of possibility for art as such. At the same time that these practices contributed to major formal innovations and to a further widening of aesthetic sensibilities, long-held certainties about legal obscenity began to wither under closer examination, and efforts to explain how books could be judged obscene appeared to become more and more Sisyphean with each passing year. In short, the expansion of what potentially counted as a text worthy of artistic or literary judgments under modernism coincided with the contraction of what could possibly be deemed proscribably obscene in a U.S. court of law. At issue in these obscenity cases was nothing less than the capacity of mute words to get off the page and affect readers formation of their civic comportments and social identities. Depending on which precedents a given judge cited from the case law, however, obscene books either posed too much of a threat or no threat at all. Accordingly, proscribed writers such as Wyndham Lewis, Erskine Caldwell, and Lillian Smith responded to contemporary obscenity trials by interrogating the power of words to take on embodied dimensions even as they continued to grapple with the manner in which human interests, capacities, and self-knowledge nevertheless get fostered or distorted by the affecting appeals made by putatively obscene texts.

Furthermore, ambivalence regarding what constituted obscenity in the first place extended to the realm of social relationships affected by it. Obscenity trials and the texts prosecuted in them were perennial news items and topics of debate in this period, as were the evolving standards for what constituted obscenity, which oftentimes shifted year to year, state to state, and court to court. Just as the definition of obscenity was up for grabs, so too were its broader effects on readers, who were variously depicted in case law at this time as children requiring parental oversight, women in need of male protectors, or adults able to determine what was or was not good for them. However, even those judges who treated readers of obscenity like grown-ups still did not fail to assign them a common social role: that of consumers in a market economy. I contend that all of this was not accidental, as obscenity was a conspicuously contested field through which writers and judges addressed other, even more socially pervasive aspects of writing's effects. As *Literary Obscenities* demonstrates, the struggle to account for the libidinal efficacy of writing prominently figured in a number of period disputes, such as those concerning the manipulative use of behaviorist-informed advertising practices, shifts in cultural hierarchies between print and visual materials, and activist strategies for desegregating the Jim Crow South before the 1950s.

Just as lascivious writing carried the weight of some enormously important cultural issues, a survey of the case law on obscene books shows that the more frequent targets of obscenity prosecutions in the early twentieth-century United States were not modernist novels but literary naturalist texts such as those of Caldwell, Smith, and James T. Farrell. In this study I understand "literary naturalism" to refer to fiction that, in the words of György Lukács, "describes" life rather than "narrates" it.[1] That is to say, it is fiction in which expansive descriptions are tacitly organized and fixed in place by the findings and methodologies of contemporary sociology, psychology, physiology, criminology, and evolutionary biology rather than by the (realist) impulse to model typical human characters and nascent forms of dynamic social action. Because early naturalist writing tended to rely heavily on these fields of scientific inquiry, many of its initial critics in the United States claimed it was robbing fiction of its own authentically literary forms, functions, and narratives. Moreover, by putatively adopting some form of determinism to present their characters as the objects of the social and natural forces investigated by these same discourses of human knowledge, naturalist texts were widely believed to have reduced men and women to "human insects," to use Malcolm Cowley's expression, insofar as they reliably depicted a world in which people were more "done to" than "doing."

Notable scholarly work of the past few decades, however, has moved our discussions of U.S. literary naturalism beyond warmed-over debates about the two cultures (literary vs. scientific) or about the coherence of determinism as a philosophy and its broader implications as a worldview. The attention devoted to literary naturalism by many notable critics aligned with New Historicism in the 1980s, for instance, shifted our focus to the ways in which U.S. naturalist fiction called into question the autonomy of literature with respect to the institutions and discourses in or alongside which it circulated. As a result, "co-optation" has increasingly replaced "determinism" as a keyword in studies of literary naturalism, and the result has been greater attention paid to complicitous relationships in naturalist works rather than to determinist subsumption pure and simple. In keeping with this, scholars and critics have since developed more nuanced conceptions of how subjectivity, will, and agency become informed (rather than wholly overmastered) by the tremendous social and natural forces set forth by naturalist fiction.

Emblematic here remains Jennifer Fleissner's work on compulsion, which has broadened our conception of how U.S. literary naturalist texts exemplify their embodied reception in readers by representing worlds in which embodiment as such reliably takes the form of repetition, habit formation, and failure. For Fleissner, subjectivity and agency are not abolished by the routine behaviors encrusted onto the bodies to which they are attached in naturalist fiction, nor are they canceled out by the conspicuous inability of this fiction to offer shapely narratives of triumph or tragedy. Instead, literary naturalism forces us to situate such subjectivity and such agency ever and always in terms of mundane, nonlinear habits and recurring motions (e.g., those involved with cleaning or lovemaking) that do not eventuate in a sense of mastery or completion so much as they do in bodily experiences of repetition and disappointment that nevertheless constitute the only path available to us in naturalist fiction that can still perhaps lead (beyond the frame of the text itself) to mastery and completion eventually. In short, failure in the present does not foreclose the possibility of different outcomes in the future, though according to Fleissner what distinguishes naturalism from other modes of writing is that it locates this future in our bodies (where self and world interface and become meaningfully entangled), and in women's bodies in particular.

In many respects, then, what my calling attention to the literary naturalistic qualities of early twentieth-century obscenity in the United States entails is that we reckon more expansively with failure, by which I refer both to the recurrent failure

3

of courts at this time to formulate adequate tests for obscenity and to the ultimate failure of fiction to be deemed proscribably obscene, even though the works by Smith, Caldwell, and Lewis examined here were indeed proscribed in courts of law for their obscenity. I would also note that this preoccupation with failure is already encoded in the title of the first chapter—"Getting Off the Page"—in which the key propositions aimed at by its wordplay are only somewhat felicitously expressed. The salacious implications of the idiomatic "get off" are easily discernible, but they badly need a preposition to make it clear that it is a prospective reader who is sexually gratifying him- or herself *on* (or by means of) a book rather than the leaves of the book itself that are somehow being sexually satisfied by the reader. Despite the possibility of conjuring forth bizarre visions of readers clumsily jerking off or going down on or otherwise illicitly stimulating a book somehow, someway, I have nevertheless opted to omit the preposition, not simply because "Getting Off on the Page" is a less euphonious title but more importantly because "Getting Off the Page" nevertheless does indeed succinctly express the core preoccupation of this book, which has to do with how obscenity has more or less ceased to be something readily predicable of written texts of fiction in a court of law in the United States. In this less idiomatic sense, then, obscenity in this period ceased to get off the page in the ways expected by courts hitherto (namely, by having untoward effects on the bodies and behaviors of readers in the world) and started to get off the page entirely by leaving books behind and moving on to other media (primarily visual ones), with which it is more credibly associated now than it is with writing as such. While this is an outcome that did not become codified until the end of the Supreme Court's repeated efforts to work up a suitable set of new standards for obscenity during the second half of the twentieth century, *Literary Obscenities* locates formative (and, up to now, largely overlooked) sources for this eventual result in the period, cases, and works of fiction examined here.

This approach thus distinguishes itself from significant critical work on law, literature, and obscenity carried out by both literary critics and jurists, for whom quite different concerns and questions have guided much recent scholarship. On the one hand, obscenity has tended to provide many of those working in the New Modernist Studies an opportunity to reassert the subversive potentials of certain modernist texts that were creatively vivified by the tussles their respective writers had with obscenity laws and the various institutions enforcing them. On the other hand, some have used "obscene modernism" to express a deep and abiding skepticism about these transgressive potentials by drawing our attention to the ways in which such writing nonetheless ended up embodying the very sorts of interdictions and proscriptions it nominally sought to flout. For legal scholars, in contrast, questions of principle (Is obscenity even an instance of speech in the first place? Is obscenity law equipped to address the problem of moral harm that would potentially justify the proscription of obscenity if such a thing were indeed an instance of speech?) and practice (Are obscenity prosecutions a wise use of limited institutional resources? Are the conceptions of art and literature offered in obscenity law really in line with how those two things are actually performed or created today?) have tended to predominate over the more historical and evaluative pursuits of those working in the New Modernist Studies.

The aim of this book is therefore to offer an alternative angle of vision onto early twentieth-century writing and obscenity, one that orients itself more around states of development in the reformulation of legal obscenity in this period than around the retroactive credentialing of literary modernism as either a dependably subversive or regrettably compromised set of innovative texts and compositional practices. Likewise, I am not all that interested in reading law in/as literature or literature in/as law. Instead, my concerns are with assessing the consequences of treating proscribably obscene fiction in the early twentieth century not simply as an object of obscenity case law but more importantly as its respondent, as texts that answer to the conditions and limits placed on literary writing's efficacy by the disparate accounts and appraisals made by judges themselves in this period. In particular, what this closer attention to case law makes salient about the relationship between writing and obscenity in the United States throughout much of the past century is twofold. First, the proscription of obscenity in this period usefully indexes major shifts in contemporary cultural hierarchies that were then in the midst of slowly but surely prioritizing visual texts over written ones, a point I most fully expound in the chapter on Caldwell. When viewed from afar, the large-scale narrative of U.S. legal obscenity in the twentieth century is decidedly not a story of censorship forces heroically overcome by an elite group of modernist pioneers; instead, the tale forced on us by history is a decidedly more ambivalent one that foregrounds the wholesale neutralization of the claims that books can potentially make on bodies, and it is the U.S. literary naturalist texts of this period (rather than modernist works) that offer us a means of conceptualizing the end of book obscenity not so much as a timely victory over censorship forces but rather as the emergent recognition of the sobering and troubling possibility that reading books can no longer affect us in ways that are worth proscribing. Ever since the Supreme Court's decision in *Miller v. California* (1973), after all, it is always okay *not* to masturbate when we read.

This brings up the second point made apparent by the story of obscene writing in the United States when it is first focalized through case law: when the libidinal potentials of books were indeed being neutralized in U.S. courtrooms in the twentieth century, this tended to be carried out by positing art and literature as autonomous modes of human expressivity, along with the aesthetic conceptions of value typically associated with those two things. Hence, the nearly century-long

5

effort to deproscribe obscene books in this country principally entailed the efforts of liberalizing judges, jurists, writers, publishers, and academics to separate the "literary" from the properly obscene in the eyes of judges, juries, post office employees, police officers, and customs officials. In this view, literary writing could not and cannot be obscene because truly obscene writing was not and is not properly literary, a state of affairs pithily summed up in present-day obscenity statutes exempting prurient and patently offensive books from proscription so long as they possess "serious literary value," which, since *Miller*, has been implicitly extended to all fiction. As the first chapter shows, modernist writing and its critical reception provided the immediate occasions for the expansive aesthetic arguments offered in defense of obscene writing in the early twentieth-century United States. As indicated earlier, however, even though such aesthetic considerations now allow previously objectionable books to be disseminated to adult readers without state interference, this does not signify a triumph of enlightened liberal attitudes toward salacious and unruly writerly practices but rather a diminution of writing's effective power in the field of social representation. Ironically, liberalization of this sort reflects a judgment over writing that has already fallen "before the law": the demotion of writing's capacity to affect our bodies with the sort of unsettling immediacy that various other media—such as television, film, photography, videogames, the internet, and so forth—still seem to possess with all the self-evident force of a publicly lewd man.

Consequently, if books no longer appear to affect us in the eyes of the law in the United States, then that is due in no small part to their successful neutralization on aesthetic grounds provided by modernism and its critical reception. In the twentieth century, obscene books became simply "literature," which itself raises new terminological issues that raise all sorts of skeptical responses, beginning with the obvious question, "Well, what *is* literature, and what does it *do* anyway?" Yet despite brass-tacks questions such as this, the matter remains fairly settled for all that. We live in an age in the United States in which Stein-ese may be the best idiolect with which to convey how writing both expresses and yet holds in check its potential to make unmanageable libidinal or behavioral appeals: "Obscene books should be written and read since obscene books are literature and literature should be written and read because literature is literature is literature and there is a difference between obscenity and literature in the character of their quality to be written and read and literature can be and ought to be written and read while obscenity cannot be read because it cannot be written anymore so it is literature that is different from obscenity anyway, meaning obscene books are not obscenity anymore just literature." Alternatively, much like the attempts of various early twentieth-century avant-gardes to intervene violently into and qualitatively transform contemporary life, the abilities of obscene books to do much of anything in the world appear to have become a matter of historical and antiquarian interest—matters for professors and collectors of rare books—but not anything we would want our overstuffed court system to squander its time considering.

Disenchantingly, then, the overmastering imperative in telling the story of legal obscenity, modernism, and the dull persistence of literary naturalism in the early twentieth-century United States is not to make it new, but to make it *neutral*. Accordingly, in place of the familiar "obscene modernism" story of transgressive modernist writing practices and their wildly successful repurposing of a variety of censorship discourses, I want to put forward instead a highly recursive narrative that looks a lot like *Invasion of the Body Snatchers*, an ungainly story of textual identities and readerly bodies secretly compromised, evacuated, and replaced from the inside out through shadowy interactions between obscenity case law and early twentieth-century writing that are best described in an uneasy, equivocal middle voice. One day we woke up to find our offensive, foulmouthed, philandering neighbors had become reputable suburban members of the community; books that were once dirty had been reborn as literature. This volume's response is to elaborate how proscribed salacious writing in this period neither actively neutralized its own capacities to make unmanageable claims on readerly bodies, nor was it expressly deprived of its abilities to make such claims by heteronomous social forces. Instead, this overarching process of failure and cooptation is one in which English-language writing in the twentieth century *got itself neutralized* of the potential to deprave, corrupt, make prurient appeals, patently offend, or make libidinal claims of any consequence on human bodies. Whether writers and judges were ascribing too much power to the ability of printed words to ineluctably arouse the bodies of readers and incite them to action (as Lewis, Smith's early writings, and the judges of the Massachusetts Supreme Court certainly did), or whether they were calling into question the ability of written language to do anything of note in an age increasingly suffused with and informed by visual representations instead (as Caldwell and Judge Curtis Bok did), literary obscenity was an occasion for *naturalizing* obscene literature: proscribably obscene writing in the early twentieth-century United States became something we could both take for granted and eventually disregard (it had become second nature, as it were, to accept that the obscenity of a book did not make it simply an obscene book) because much of that writing had situated its own unmanageable bodily appeals in terms of existing forms of human knowledge that helped us to articulate them descriptively rather than to reexperience them narratively (it had become second nature by way of literary naturalism). If modernism gives us the means of accounting for how aesthetic and literary exceptions to obscenity got articulated by judges in the early twentieth century, then literary naturalism offers us a way of conceptualizing how proscribed writing of this time got itself neutralized of the ability to act obscenely.

7

I would further note that two interrelated concerns have informed my selection of the obscenity cases and proscribed works discussed in the chapters that follow. First of all, I have chosen decisions and texts that exemplify the uneven and peculiar history of U.S. obscenity case law in the early twentieth century, a period in which obscenity was primarily a lower court (rather than a Supreme Court) concern. Hence, there is little sense of definite progress in the labile definitions of and tests for obscenity put forward by these lower courts between 1917 and 1950. Instead, judges seemed to be stuck returning to the same issues and precedents with little certain or lasting effect. Even District Judge John M. Woolsey's famous holistic test for obscenity in *United States v. One Book Called "Ulysses"* (1933) did not mark an advance in the deproscription of obscene books insofar as the Massachusetts Supreme Judicial Court had no problem using his standard to find *God's Little Acre* (1933) and *Strange Fruit* (1944) obscene more than a decade later. Thus, it would be wrong to interpret the legal battles surrounding *Ulysses* (1922) as the end of something. Woolsey's decision and Augustus Hand's affirmation of it in the appellate case that took place the following year are instead part of a much longer sequence of trials in which reproscribing and deproscribing tendencies are often hard to distinguish from each other when looked at up close. Consequently, the chapters on the proscribably obscene works of Lewis, Caldwell, and Smith do not organically follow from each other so much as they recursively work through the same legal precedents and deterministic processes over and over as issues connected with behaviorism, voyeurism, and racial identity formation, respectively, come to the fore in each case. In other words, as in a naturalist novel, there is no shapely overarching narrative to be told here, only the variously failed efforts of judges, writers, and jurists to come to terms with the problems named by obscenity as they reappeared in different times, places, and texts.

Second, my choice of cases and literary texts spotlights the belatedness of literary obscenity in the United States at this time. I mean "belated" in two senses. First, it was not the muckraking literary naturalism from the turn of the century that proved to be the primary target of obscenity prosecutions in this period but rather literary naturalism *after* modernism. With the exception of Dreiser's *An American Tragedy* (1925), the literary naturalism being proscribed for obscenity in the years covered by this study was not comprised of the figures (Crane, Norris, London, Cahan) familiar to many of us from the customary surveys of U.S. literature. Instead, the texts that were targeted belong to what I refer to here as literary naturalism "after modernism," with "after" doing double duty. On the one hand, it serves as an indication of imitative facility: modernist styles, techniques, concerns, and problems were available to be mimicked or "taken after," either with great gusto, as in the early fiction of Caldwell, or ambivalently, as in the work of Smith. On the other hand, "after" serves as a marker of temporal priority: the event of modernism had already happened by the time Farrell, Caldwell, Smith, and others commenced their careers. This is not to say that modernism was a neatly contained phenomenon that had already run its course by the early 1930s. Much valuable work on periodizing modernism (into its late modernist and, more recently, its metamodernist strands) of course attests to the ways in which it subsequently unfolded and continues to ramify down to the present. Instead, my point is simply that the proscribably obscene naturalist writers looked at here took up writing after modernism's horizons of legibility had already been disclosed both to a broader public and to (at least a few) judges. I develop this point at length in the chapter on Lewis, who is the token modernist here and whose legal troubles with obscenity in the 1910s afford us a chance to reflect afresh on how courts of law in the United States dealt with modernism before aesthetic and literary justifications for its jarring formal features and (at times) *outré* contents became matters of course. I would also underscore for my readers that it is this principle of selection that has justified the otherwise conspicuous exclusion of Dreiser, *An American Tragedy*, and *Commonwealth v. Friede* (1930) in this study.

The belatedness of literary obscenity is also a preoccupation here because this period does indeed mark the beginning of the end of proscribably obscene books, if not their end as such. That is to say, despite the lack of clarity and agreement among many state and appellate courts during these decades, efforts like those of the Massachusetts Supreme Court to proscribe obscene books well into the middle of the twentieth century certainly did comprise *derrière-garde* actions in light of what the U.S. Supreme Court accomplished with its obscenity cases between the late 1950s and the early 1970s. However, the chapters that follow resist the temptation to present the course of obscenity case law at this earlier contested time in a teleological fashion, not least of all because the beginning of the end of legally obscene books was a period marked by *too much* (rather than too little) obscenity law, as the first chapter shows. *Literary Obscenities*, then, is partly an effort to excavate and re-present the forgotten detours, byways, and dead ends that obscenity case law took in these critical and contentious years.

In chapter 1, "Getting Off the Page," I demonstrate how literary criticisms of naturalism illuminate debates around book obscenity in early twentieth-century U.S. case law. On the one hand, judges who wanted to continue to proscribe books for obscenity often resorted to drawing a distinction between works with redeeming "literary" value and those without it. In view of their literary qualities having been disputed since the late nineteenth century, naturalist texts proved to be a prominent target for proscriptive forces. On the other hand, the ways in which literary naturalism was believed to divest characters of agency also relate to a number of legal arguments about how obscene books deprive readers of the willpower to resist their aroused sexual or immoral urges. Objective social forces and subjective

9

compulsions thus hazily overlap in obscene books and literary naturalism, just as they did in the debates occasioned by both, a point I develop through a close reading of James T. Farrell's *Studs Lonigan* (1932–35). As obscenity case law unfolded across the century, however, this view of the relationship between readers and salacious texts became more vexed. Instead of taking for granted the obscene efficacy of writing, tests for obscenity today tend to assume that books no longer possess any such force. Much like a character in a naturalist novel, obscene writing over the past century has gotten itself deprived of the capacity to get off the page and transgress in the world, such that novels like Samuel R. Delany's *Through the Valley of the Nest of Spiders* (2012) appear on bookstore shelves rather than on court dockets. *Literary Obscenities* ventures an account of how this naturalistic muting of writing's libidinal effectiveness took place across different modes of fictional writing (the short story and the novel) and in a variety of publication formats (little magazines, deluxe limited-edition hardcover books, and mass-market trade paperbacks) that circulated among an emblematic range of readers, from small literary coteries to the mass audiences of best seller lists.

Chapter 2, "How to Misbehave as a Behaviorist (if You're Wyndham Lewis)," reveals that what the New York District Court found so troubling about "Cantleman's Spring-Mate" in the October 1917 issue of *The Little Review* was its preoccupation with representing obscenity not as a quality intrinsic to a text but rather as a set of culturally produced reading habits. Lewis's World War I narrative connects a young British soldier's ludicrously overheated readings of Thomas Hardy's *The Trumpet-Major* (1880) to his wartime milieu, in which distinctions between man and animal appeared to be breaking down altogether. Comparing Lewis's culture critiques of the 1920s and 1930s to the work of John B. Watson as a behaviorist psychologist and later as a successful advertising executive, I claim that for Lewis the bodily responsiveness of a reader to the printed word indexed a broader social trend whereby consumers everywhere were being reduced to well-oiled stimulus-response mechanisms by the twinned forces of behaviorism and modern advertising. "Obscenity," in his view, was a by-product of cultural training—of a widely inculcated "art of being ruled"—not a primary datum of either "obscene works" or "depraved readers." "Cantleman's Spring-Mate" therefore demonstrates Lewis's hypothesis through a fictional provocation to which, as it happened, the judiciary proved adversely responsive in the 1910s, though the legal and cultural absorption of modernist writing's practices over the next decade or so would ultimately start to change that.

Chapter 3, "Erskine Caldwell, Smut, and the Paperbacking of Obscenity," examines how the fiction of Erskine Caldwell undermines Lewis's basic assumptions. For Caldwell, obscenity was no longer something writers could take for granted by the 1930s, because books were quite possibly henceforth unable to elicit a bodily response at all. Instead, Caldwell's novels in this decade addressed their doubtful capacity for salaciousness through the calculated, repeated experience of mirthful frustration. Evaluating such an experience in light of Judge Bok's ruling in *Commonwealth v. Gordon et al.* (1949), which absolved *God's Little Acre* of obscenity in the state of Pennsylvania, I approach both the novel and legal case as indicative of contemporary shifts in the cultural hierarchies existing between visual media and print texts. According to Bok, *God's Little Acre* was not obscene because it failed to present its readers with the erotic allurement of a publicly lewd man, the clear and present danger of which he assumed as given. I then go on to consider more closely the roles played by frustration in Caldwell's fiction, particularly in his representations of visuality, by comparing the indeterminacies and gaps in Caldwellian voyeurism to the sorts of frustrating experiences elicited by the illustrated covers of the paperback reprints of his books in the late 1940s. In the concluding section of this chapter, I discuss both of these frustrations—verbal and visual—in connection with the concept of "smut" elaborated by Sigmund Freud in *Jokes and Their Relation to the Unconscious* (1905). For Freud, when smutty language does not lead to sexual acts, it can become an autonomous pleasure, albeit one thereafter primed to transmute into action with a change in circumstances. Smut, I contend, is a way of conceiving the linkages between erotic allurements, bodily experiences, and the various frustrations intervening between the two in Caldwell's fiction and in writing more generally. Caldwell in turn opens up the possibility that the failure of words to seduce readers may nevertheless constitute a technique of "weak" seduction or salacity beyond the purview of proscriptive judges.

Chapter 4, "Sin, Sex, and Segregation in Lillian Smith's Silent South," returns to the assumptions subtending Lewis's position by showing that for Smith obscenity was indeed an overpowering result of a cultural training that hailed a specific kind of social identity. In particular, I contend that the essays, fiction, and little magazine publications of this civil rights activist in the 1930s and 1940s consistently presented the Jim Crow South as a region organized by obscene words that enacted racial difference through the dangers said to be presented by particular forms of sexual desire. Just as certain body parts were off-limits to Southern youth, so too were certain groups of people, and Smith's work from this period comprises an attempt to account for the ways in which sin, sex, and segregation mutually reproduced and overdetermined the efficacy of the social, cultural, and political institutions of the region. In fact, in *Commonwealth v. Isenstadt* (1945) the Massachusetts Supreme Judicial Court criticized—and in part proscribed—*Strange Fruit* because of its artful capacity to make such linkages not only known but also overwhelmingly felt by its readers. According to the opinions in *Isenstadt*, whether panderingly attractive or unduly repellent, words in that novel did in fact move beyond the limits of what language ought to do to people. Far from being the biased observations of a group of robed censors, however, these opposing perspectives on the efficacy of Smith's language—its ability to push and pull its readers—were shrewdly attentive to the somatic functions her texts almost ceaselessly ascribe to words. In *Strange Fruit*, in particular, Smith sought to demonstrate how segregation had turned the early twentieth-century South into the nation's closet, whereby symptomatic inconsistencies and incoherence in a community's sexual knowledge could act as guarantor for discriminating laws, behaviors, and folkways that trumped any rational appeals a reformer might hope to make to her community.

The work of Lewis, Caldwell, and Smith accordingly typify the response of fiction to the evolving standards for obscenity in this period. From within the unfolding process that eventually delivered writing to its present-day neutral zone, Lewis's essays and creative writing still assume that mere words on the page can hyperbolically affect readers in the world, though his account of obscene embodiment as something that can be performatively contradicted suggests that bodily sensations can be made to mean something other than what they in fact are: just because a woman in a Thomas Hardy novel gives a character in "Cantleman's Spring-Mate" an erection does not mean that Lewis would have us understand this character to be aroused by her. What Lewis instead insists upon time and time again is that the body and its reactions to stimuli can be transformed into rhetorical gestures, into ironic expressions emanating from a dubious self barely subsisting just below the surface. The work of Smith provides a surprisingly complementary instance of an author from this period who also subsumes bodily arousal under a broader web of signification, although her focus is on allegory rather than irony. For Smith, obscenity does not so much offend as discriminate against, especially by corporeally marking and enforcing otherwise unstable black-white divides. Ultimately, she responds to this dilemma by subjecting obscene words (and their inexorable efficacy in hailing racialized bodies) to an allegorical philosophy of history in which the problems posed by obscenity become null in the face of the evaporation of racial divisions in a projected future where being a human means acting collectively and cooperatively for the good of all. Between Lewis's ironic embodiment of obscenity and Smith's allegorical disembodiment of it, Caldwell's fiction opens up a parenthesis in which an aroused bodily response to writing need not (indeed, probably will not) occur. Caldwell's writing alludes time and time again to voyeuristic scenes of salacity but refuses to evoke them visually, leaving his reader-viewers to wait and *not* see as they stare expectantly through a peephole looking out onto a void space that will not be filled, though it is said to remain engrossing all the same. Unlike the works of Lewis or Smith, Caldwell's fiction problematizes the medium of obscenity rather than the fact of obscene embodiment itself. In sum, then, whereas Lewis has the bodily response evoked by book obscenity take the form of a performative contradiction, and whereas Smith, following the proscription of *Strange Fruit*, spends the remainder of her career trying to allegorically efface the obscene human body out of existence altogether, Caldwell cussedly doubts that such obscene efficacy is even possible in the case of books anymore.

Finally, when we consider the history of legal obscenity and writing in the first half of the twentieth century, the story that fitfully emerges is not simply the naturalist one of failure but also the *Body Snatchers* tale of usurpations, howsoever improbable they may appear at first glance. We therefore come upon a contrarian Wyndham Lewis who displaces the renowned James Joyce at the center of *The Little Review*'s legendarily outsized ordeals with obscenity; a know-nothing Erskine Caldwell, whose Southern legion of minimalist hick voyeurs cudfully dislodges D. H. Lawrence's secular apostles of the flesh; and a decently indecent Lillian Smith, whose early determinist visions of the Jim Crow South and later evolutionary cosmologies supplant the more expressly tragic subjectivities explored in the proscribed writings of William Faulkner. In short, this book is all about modernism's tardy cuckoos, the presumptive might-have-beens who never quite managed to make it and thus ended up being left behind in the discard pile among the never-weres, the preterite of "obscene modernism." *Literary Obscenities* is for the scumbags, smut peddlers, and closet cases who populated the literary landscape towered over by the modernist giants we love to study, criticize, and esteem. More often than not, however, this thing called "obscenity" was produced by men and women as unprepossessing and downright disreputable as these bottom dogs.

13

1. Getting Off the Page

If you look into a textbook of chemistry for a definition of *lithium*, you may be told that it is that element whose atomic weight is 7 very nearly. But if the author has a more logical mind he will tell you that if you search among minerals that are vitreous, translucent, grey or white, very hard, brittle, and insoluble, for one which imparts a crimson tinge to an unluminous flame, this mineral being triturated with lime or witherite rats-bane, and then fused, can be partly dissolved in muriatic acid; and if this solution be evaporated, and the residue be extracted with sulphuric acid, and duly purified, it can be converted by ordinary methods into a chloride, which being obtained in the solid state, fused, and electrolyzed with half a dozen powerful cells, will yield a globule of a pinkish silvery metal that will float on gasolene; and the material of *that* is a specimen of lithium. The peculiarity of this definition—or rather this precept that is more serviceable than a definition—is that it tells you what the word *lithium* denotes by prescribing what you are to *do* in order to gain a perceptual acquaintance with the object of the world.

—CHARLES PEIRCE, "SYLLABUS," CA. 1902

To say, "I know a sea lion when I see one," is to report that one can identify a sea lion but not that one is now doing so.

—B. F. SKINNER, *ABOUT BEHAVIORISM*, 1974

I

Given that one of the places twentieth-century U.S. obscenity case law almost ended up was somewhere in the parking lot to B. F. Skinner's Sea World ("But I *know* it when I *see* it!"), it ought to be remembered at the outset that this was not always so, nor is it now the case. In fact, if the statutory and case law involving obscenity could be understood to have tacitly developed its own theory of meaning by the beginning of the last century, then that theory looked a lot more like Charles Peirce's famous definition of lithium than it did Skinner's reports of visual certainty. For one thing, the first modern standard for obscenity in British and U.S. jurisprudence framed the problem much more tentatively and operationally than did Supreme Court Justice Potter Stewart's notorious assertions regarding hard-core pornography in *Jacobellis v. Ohio* (1964).[1] According to Lord Chief Justice Alexander Cockburn in *Regina v. Hicklin* (1868), the test for obscenity involved simply the determination of "whether the tendency of the matter charged as obscenity is to deprave and corrupt those whose minds are open to such immoral influences, and into whose hands a publication of this sort may fall."[2] Commenting critically on this test more than eighty years later in *Commonwealth v. Gordon et al.*, Judge Curtis Bok of the Philadelphia County Common Pleas Court complained that, "strictly applied, this rule renders any book unsafe, since a moron could pervert to some sexual fantasy to which his mind is open the listings in a seed catalogue. Not even the Bible would be exempt."[3]

As Bok's flippancy suggests, this British case from the Victorian era persisted as a much-contested touchstone for obscenity law in the United States well into the twentieth century.[4] In fact, it was not until the Supreme Court's decision in *Roth v. United States* (1957) that Cockburn's test was definitively overturned in this country because it unconstitutionally restricted First Amendment rights.[5] To be sure, this is a manifestly strange career for a judgment that could not have been produced in a more irreducibly British setting. After all, Cockburn formulated his infamous test for obscenity in response to *The Confessional Unmasked* (1836), an anti-Papist pamphlet that was being clandestinely sold as pornography and had been implicated in several riots in the United Kingdom. Sectarian strife, public unrest, and the hazy boundaries between obscenity and acceptable propagandistic writing informed the most pressing concerns in the *Hicklin* decision. Nevertheless, an attention to the circumstances under which Cockburn put together his test for obscenity does not belie the fact that it quickly migrated far beyond Britain. Within eleven years *Hicklin* was being invoked approvingly by U.S. circuit court judges, and by 1896 the Supreme Court further solidified its applicability to obscenity law here in *Rosen v. United States*.[6] By 1913 District Judge Learned Hand was forced to admit that "[the *Hicklin*] test has been accepted by the lower federal courts until it would be no longer proper for me to disregard it," even though Hand's opinion made it abundantly clear how much he wished he could do precisely that.[7] Consequently, assessing the impact of *Hicklin* on U.S. obscenity case law requires we do to it what state and appellate courts did: take it out of its British context.

While *Hicklin* proved to be an easy target for the derision and satirical animus of liberalizing jurists and proscribed writers in the United States for much of the twentieth century, it is nevertheless worthwhile to consider briefly the latent sophistication of its conditional propositions. Implicitly conceived of in *Hicklin* both as a matter of poetics (of a making, a producing) and a matter of aesthetics (of a sensing, a receiving), obscenity is comprised of a virtual experience activated in a certain kind of encounter with a certain kind of text by a certain kind of reader. In particular, Cockburn's opinion poses it as a convergence of two immoral inclinations: that of the text ("to deprave and corrupt") and a complementary one in the reader or viewer ("whose minds [and presumably bodies as well] are open to such immoral influences"). A property neither of a person nor of a text alone, obscenity in *Hicklin* refers us to a troubling heightening of the commerce between subjects and texts such that the two become morbidly intertwined in a mutual perversion. Obscenity accordingly presents us with a situation in which the singular quirks and kinks of individual readers get identified with the socially undesirable effects latent in salacious texts. Obscenity thus possesses a radical sort of exemplarity, whereby the contingent personal desires of readers blur together with the thoughts, behaviors, and impulses of the characters being depicted in a given obscene text. Perhaps not surprisingly, since obscenity is granted such a hyperbolically effective power to jumble distinctions, Cockburn's test also implies an intention to manage vulnerable populations through the proscription of obscene texts. After *Hicklin*, in any case, the prosecution of obscenity in both the United States and Britain often seemed to provide judges, jurists, and lawmakers with a means to carry out any number of governmental, public health, and educational policies targeting a variety of marginalized demographic groups (women, children, adolescents, lower socioeconomic classes) euphemistically covered by the vague advertence to "those whose minds are open to such immoral influences, and into whose hands a publication of this sort may fall."[8]

Of course, the administration of obscenity law in both countries was quite different. Whereas authorities in Britain targeted printers, publishers, and booksellers, obscenity prosecutions in the United States primarily focused on distribution and the use of the mails. The relevant British statute in *Hicklin* was the Obscene Publications Act 1857, which had empowered magistrates with the authority to seize and destroy material they found to be obscene.[9] Conversely, the closest analogues to this in legislation passed by the U.S. Congress at the time were the Comstock Laws (1873, amended 1876), which made obscene materials nonmailable. As these laws and their interpretations developed over the coming century, different concerns and institutional authorities respectively came to the fore. In the twentieth century,

17

extralegal civic agencies and ministerial departments such as the Home Office increasingly took the reins in the regulation of obscene publications in Britain.[10] By contrast, the Customs Bureau and the Post Office Department were the primary enforcement agencies alongside the police at the local, state, and federal level in the United States.[11] An even more significant difference, however, is the fact that during the twentieth century the closer scrutiny of the grounds for regulating obscenity was most conspicuously undertaken by courts in the United States, whereas this role fell chiefly to Parliament in Great Britain.[12] Notwithstanding these different institutional arrangements and proscriptive foci, however, what the elaborations of *Hicklin* in Britain and the United States nevertheless share are a preoccupation with protecting obscenity's prospective receivers, howsoever they may be defined.

Yet Cockburn's single sentence leaves many things unspecified regarding what one has to do in order to create an obscene book or to produce either an obscene experience or an obscene reader. On its own, *Hicklin* offers no ramified account equivalent to Peirce's experimental methodology concerning the trituration of a particular kind of mineral with lime or witherite rats-bane. Publishers, writers, and laymen could not categorically know how to make—or avoid making—books the occasions for obscenity. What Cockburn's protopragmatic enframing of obscenity eventually did make possible, however, were a number of interactive cultural and legal processes that have been unfolding for well over a century. Legislators, judges, jurists, publishers, writers, artists, and cultural critics have ended up, howsoever intentionally or inadvertently, putting a lot of time into fleshing out those missing intermediary steps, be it in the interest of re- or deproscribing obscene books. As an example of where all of this collaborative effort has settled for the time being as far as the legal status of obscenity in the United States is concerned, here is the precept for the "obscene" as it is currently defined in the state of Tennessee's criminal statute, which in turn closely follows the most recent federal standard for obscenity devised by the U.S. Supreme Court in *Miller v. California*: "'Obscene' means: (A) The average person applying contemporary community standards would find that the work, taken as a whole, appeals to the prurient interest; (B) The average person applying contemporary community standards would find that the work depicts or describes, in a patently offensive way, sexual conduct; and (C) The work, taken as a whole, lacks serious literary, artistic, political, or scientific value."[13] In short, obscenity today in Tennessee and throughout the country is processual rather than substantive, as it has arguably been since *Hicklin*.[14] A number of conditions must be experimentally established before obscenity can be legitimately proscribed. A judge or juror has to put the charged object through a threefold test according to which (1) that object's potentially lascivious solicitations are assessed as a whole in light of an imaginary run-of-the-mill person's grasp of imagined local norms and customs; (2) this imaginary run-of-the-mill person then makes use of these same imagined local community norms and customs to determine whether or not the charged object's representations of sex boldly give offense; and (3) the work itself gets holistically evaluated according to all sorts of heteronomous value judgments, deriving from the sciences, politics, art, and literature.

Consequently, it appears that for both Peirce and an obscenity-defining U.S. juror or judge in the early twenty-first century, meaning itself has come to encompass expansive descriptions (the Tennessee statute goes on to define "patently offensive," "sadomasochistic abuse," "sexual conduct," and "sexual excitement," among various other words and phrases), nonlinguistic embodied doing (according to later sections of the statute, graphic representations of sexual conduct can indeed lead to actual sexual excitement), and an awful lot of conditional thinking (*if and only if* all three prongs of the Tennessee precept for the "obscene" are present, then so is obscenity itself).[15] To recur to an earlier, much more famous Peircian definition of what "meaning" means, obscenity in U.S. statutory and case law comes down to a text's effects and what our notions of that text's effects happen to be. Or as Peirce himself limpidly puts it in "How to Make Our Ideas Clear" (1878): "Consider what effects, that might conceivably have practical bearings, we conceive the object of our conception to have. Then, our conception of these effects is the whole of our conception of that object."[16] Although it leaves open a space for taking into account the literary or artistic qualities of a text, legal obscenity in the twenty-first-century United States continues to privilege issues and questions pertaining to a text's efficacy in evoking prurient and patently offended reactions among its prospective receivers.

19

Of course, one must nevertheless concede that a rather big difference exists between Peirce's steps for producing floating specimens of lithium and U.S. law's thought experiments about the production, dissemination, and reception of obscene texts. If, for a pragmatist like Peirce, meaning involves what everyone has to do to have a perceptual relationship to objects in the world at all, then for our hypothetical obscenity-assessing juror or judge the meaning of obscenity concerns what *someone else* has to do to orient him- or herself obscenely with respect to the various potentially salacious texts out there in the world. The quality of this other person may, it is true, have shifted in the century and a half since *Hicklin* from an amorphously conjured obscene reader to that shadowy statistical entity denoted by the Tennessee statute's "average person." Still, the sorts of operations Cockburn intimated in his decision remain very nearly the same today. For you, the trier of fact, obscenity is a matter of what happens to *other people's bodies* that you presume not only to speak for but also in the place of. Moreover, you insist on this presumption even if your own sensoria and habituated modes of reading occlude the kinds of experiences occasioned by the potentially obscene texts upon which you are called to judge. To be sure, the substance and medium of obscenity can be quite variable:

U.S. statutes and case law on obscenity since the 1860s have prosecuted a wide range of materials—from books, newspapers, pamphlets, and magazines to photographs, films, and advertisements. Nevertheless, the grounds for proscribing these texts have consistently required judges and juries to approach them with impressive speculative scope, particularly in terms of the various contemporary social pressures that inform mass identity itself, whether these pressures tend to dissociate the masses from traditional moral standards, as they did in *Hicklin*, or influence them through dangerous alternative norms, as they do in *Miller*. Obscenity in these instances pertains less to objectionable or possibly harmful objects than to the governance of a variety of public and private experiences, particularly as these relate to moral, social, and aesthetic self-formation. Not simply the freedom of expression and the potential for its suppression are at issue in the modern legal concept of obscenity but also the manner in which human interests, moral capacities, and self-knowledge get shaped by restrictions placed on the behaviors, techniques, and dispositions modeled in putatively obscene works. In short, the issue of legal obscenity raises multiple questions about what sorts of social identities and interpersonal practices obscene texts foster and disseminate within historically changing circumstances.

For contemporary literary critics whose conceptual lexicon is replete with libidinal apparatuses, affects, jouissance, performativity, and confessional depictions of sexuality as they relate to cultural context and artifacts of all sorts, such claims will hardly appear earth-shattering. After all, we have become well accustomed to recognizing and making effective use of the tools of the trade that late twentieth-century literary theory has bequeathed us to interpret bodies, texts, images, narratives, and identities. More surprising, however, is to uncover congruent sorts of moves and concepts within autonomously developed legal discourses that were compelled to account for the unruly claims that twentieth-century books might make on readers' bodies and self-formation. Yet it is indeed the case that the U.S. case law on obscene books since *Hicklin* constitutes a repository of more or less sophisticated attempts to come to terms with what happens when words printed on a page uncontrollably arouse or affect the readers into whose hands they happen to fall.

This need not be a crude way of suggesting that obscenity law is a straightforward reflection of contemporaneous developments in modern literary studies, despite the prominent use of a number of New Critics and academics from university English departments as "experts" in obscenity trials in the middle of the last century.[17] It simply means that more is to be made of obscenity case law and the texts proscribed by it than has necessarily been registered in recent work by legal scholars, for whom the questions and problems that obscenity law continues to raise (particularly as it relates to literature and art) have provided the occasions to do one of four things: (1) argue that we deprioritize the prosecution of obscene works altogether on the grounds that such prosecutions entail an unwise use of limited institutional resources,[18] (2) account for the ways in which obscenity law is or is not equipped to handle the problem of moral harm it nominally seeks to address,[19] (3) debate whether or not obscenity and pornography are indeed instances of speech in the first place,[20] and (4) disclose how the third prong in the *Miller* test tacitly codifies a view of what counts as literature and art (namely, works possessing "serious" literary or artistic value) that no longer seems to apply to the literature and art actually being produced and consumed today.[21]

In reassessing the relationship between early twentieth-century law, writing, and culture in the United States, I wish to emphasize instead the interactions of all three of these fields in mutually defining this thing called "obscenity." Just as obscenity in *Hicklin* is dynamically a matter of texts, readers, and experiences, so too here it ought not to be understood simply as the reified object of legal thought. Obscenity, rather, is the collaborative, mutable product of overlapping cultural, literary, and legal positions concerned with a wide variety of works. Only through close attention to their interaction can we begin to understand the assorted processual grounds given for justifying or refuting the proscription of salaciously offensive texts.

Moreover, early twentieth-century obscenity in the United States should likewise be interpreted through relevant statutory and case law *without* recourse to censorship logics or concepts, no matter how nuanced these may have become in much of the recent work produced on obscene writing by scholars in the New Modernist Studies.[22] It bears repeating that there is a lot more to obscenity in the early twentieth century than censorship forces and their artful subversion by a stylish canon of modernist innovators, be they ever so high (James Joyce) or late (Vladimir Nabokov). To be sure, this particular narrative of a "bad modernism" is credible as far as it goes, but it is easy to overlook all of the ways in which it insinuates that modernism's badness here is perhaps not something peculiar to modernism as such insofar as it betrays latent affinities of English-language obscene modernist books to various literary and artistic movements (particularly decadence) of the 1800s, during which ignobility, ugliness, decay, and disorder increasingly became the preoccupations of texts that did not necessarily cast these things in an unflattering light.[23] In this respect, it is useful to refer to the ambivalent reception of "modern literature" in the work of Lionel Trilling, for whom early twentieth-century modernism was merely the "apogee" of a period that began "in the latter part of the eighteenth century."[24] Notably, in place of the more celebratory views of "bad modernisms" often offered in the New Modernist Studies, Trilling's engagement with "modern literature" tended to foreground misgivings about the effects of the embrace of adversary cultures, nonethical forces, and anticivic comportments that he believed to be essential to such literature. For Trilling, these misgivings were most apparent when it came to teaching works of "modern

21

literature," for which merely formal analysis "went against the grain of [modern] authors themselves—structures of words they may indeed have created, but these structures were not pyramids or triumphal arches, they were manifestly contrived to be not static and commemorative but mobile and aggressive, and one does not describe a quinquereme or a howitzer or a tank without estimating how much *damage* it can do."[25] Two things are worth noting. First, Trilling's anticipation of New Modernist Studies' "bad modernisms" already read them like U.S. case law was disposed to read works of obscenity: in terms of their (potentially harmful) efficacy on readers. Second, "obscene modernism" is shown here to be a misnomer only so far as it blinds us to the ways in which the obscene writing undertaken by canonical modernist writers is part of a longer historical continuum and vaster range of literary-artistic movements than are customarily encompassed by "modernism" when it is posed as a phenomenon neatly contained between the late nineteenth century and the early twentieth century. In any case, we as modernist scholars and critics have gotten too used to telling just one kind of story about modernism and obscenity, and that story remains doggedly rooted in an assumed background of puritanical suppression, which in turn allows us to assumptively esteem modernism for its singular transgressivity.[26]

To be sure, in the hands of its best recent expositors, this narrative of transgression and subversion tactfully abstains either from making visionary heroes out of prosecuted modernist writers or from allocating to social purity movements, the British Home Office, and the U.S. Post Office the cartoonish role of hypocrite, philistine, or villain. Instead, most scholars working on early twentieth-century writing and obscenity have been quite attentive to heeding the lessons learned from both the "end of obscenity" free-speech movement in the 1960s and the far-reaching critiques of pornography made by second-wave feminists such as Kate Millett, Catharine A. MacKinnon, and Andrea Dworkin in the following two decades. Gingerly skirting the fraught political dimensions of obscenity that proved so explosive to its prospective feminist censors and its freedom of (bodily) expression spokespersons, the story of modernist transgression that we tell and retell ourselves instead tends to focus on the largely formal properties and reassuringly historical problems posed by early twentieth-century obscene books. Neither the revolutionary activation of new communal sensoria nor the reliably patriarchal means of violently dispossessing women of their agency and access to authentic subjective experiences, obscenity has instead become just another evocative modern phenomenon, like advertising or fascism or fashion or speed or little magazines, attachable to canonical modernist texts seemingly in need of more and more recovered historicist content, which critics, scholars, and teachers have been supplying at an impressively rapid clip in recent decades. Obscenity has thus made visible a variety of hitherto occluded networks, archives, material objects, institutions, and figures. Armed with these, we have been able to undertake the meritorious intellectual labor of resituating literary modernism in terms of actually existing censorship forces and their uneven influences on the genesis of indisputably important modernist texts such as *Ulysses*, *Lady Chatterley's Lover* (1928), or *Orlando* (1928), to take but three notable examples. We have freshened up the hoary old narrative of modernism's implicit transgressivity by elaborating upon the ways in which "obscene modernism" incorporated and transformed various censorship discourses (both official and unofficial) through an analyzable set of sociocultural relationships and compositional procedures.

Celia Marshik's *British Modernism and Censorship* (2006), for instance, makes a strong case for understanding literary modernism in Britain as having devised a number of its most familiar formal features—self-reflexivity, fragmentation, irony, and satire—in response to the institutionalized pressures of censorship forces.[27] For Marshik, the encounters that Virginia Woolf, James Joyce, and Jean Rhys respectively had with censors required these particular writers to negotiate between the claims of total expressive freedom and the sorts of resistance actually evinced by all kinds of offended readers, such that the texts produced by each of these eminent modernists were qualitatively impacted by these encounters. In many instances, the repressiveness of early twentieth-century censorship practices threw a number of major contemporary writers back on their heels and forced them to make ever more complicated texts in order to get around the looming threat of their potential suppression, either in seats of governmental power or in the offices of their own publishers. Consequently, the censorship of obscenity did not merely proscribe books; it also helped to shape the dense formal structures of many canonical modernist texts along with the estranging compositional methods used by seminal modernist authors either to conceal or exacerbate the offensively prurient qualities of their writing. Obscenity censorship, in other words, played an important role in the creation of difficult works, long prized as a determinate characteristic of most Anglo-American modernist writing.[28]

From this perspective, therefore, censorship's repressive measures all proved to be creatively—if no less improbably—generative, suggesting that accounts such as Marshik's owe more than a little to Leo Strauss (in terms of shared interpretive framework at least, if not political commitments). In *Persecution and the Art of Writing* (1952), after all, Strauss argued that there can be no such thing as censorship if we understand that term to refer us to the absolute silencing of free expression, because the persecution of writing "cannot prevent independent thinking. It cannot prevent even the expression of independent thought."[29] According to Strauss's provocative rereadings of the works of preeminent medieval Jewish philosophers such as Moses Maimonides and Baruch Spinoza, the effect of censorship on writing simply leads to the development of a variety of compositional strategies that make any given text by

23

a persecuted author more elaborate and obscure: "For the influence of persecution on literature is precisely that it compels all writers who hold heterodox views to develop a peculiar technique, the technique which we have in mind when speaking of writing between the lines."[30] It does not seem much of a stretch, therefore, to observe that for most recent literary modernist scholars, like Marshik, the impulse informing the story we tend to tell about "obscene modernism" has been precisely this Straussian one of reading between the lines of exemplary modernist texts, both to find the more or less deeply buried traces of censorship forces and to disclose the artful subversion of those same forces by these definitively modernist—and, correlatively, difficult—works. In this widely shared view, the novelties of form and content in so much proscribed British and U.S. modernist writing betoken the creative functions indirectly served by nominally repressive forces, whether they were to be found in social purity movements, commercial publishing houses, printing presses, or branches of national governments themselves.

Notable recent attempts to deviate from this mode of reading do little more than invert the Straussian paradigm. For instance, according to Florence Dore's *The Novel and the Obscene: Sexual Subjects in American Modernism* (2005), sexually graphic modernist fiction did not overcome censorship logics and forces so much as it performatively enacted them: "American modernists do represent divergent forms of desire, I argue, but only in castrated subjects—their desire construed as a prohibitive, negative aspect of civic identity."[31] "For American modernism," Dore goes on to contend, "bodily coherence requires participation in a social order—the very social order these authors seek to challenge in their explicit opposition to obscenity law. The discovery of phallic logic in these laws and in these novels suggests that we should continue to cultivate skepticism wherever the body appears to have at last been revealed."[32] What the difficulties of modernist writing continue to disclose for Dore is not creative ingenuity so much as the disciplining omission of non-phallocentrically sexualized bodies, leading her to demand of modernist novels over and over again: *Habeas corpus!*

Thus, in the favored story we tell ourselves about obscenity and early twentieth-century English-language writing, all roads invariably start with and lead unerringly back to literary modernism. Modernist writers and what they wrote always win, while the organizations that tried to be modernism's censors always end up playing invaluable (if involuntary) parts in its victory. As a result, historical censorship forces have been consistently made to pay their obeisance to a modernism triumphant in the image projected by its own champions and the beliefs that these same champions have compensatorily generated of social and cultural resistances not only confronted but also epically overcome. Conversely, even when a more glum reckoning is required, as in Dore's bracing work, modernist prejudices still carry the day. For instance, according to *The Novel and the Obscene*,

Theodore Dreiser, Willa Cather, and Richard Wright are all modernist writers. In a single introductory paragraph, an entire century of criticism that has posed them as canonical *naturalist* writers gets effaced willy-nilly because Dore "takes modernism as a general term encompassing—and emphasizing overlap among—the distinct literary movements of the twentieth century. . . . If 'social criticism' began as a naturalist goal, it came to fruition as a modernist presumption."[33] For Dore, if it is an early twentieth-century book published in the United States that is still worth reading and thinking about today, then it is best approached in terms of literary modernism. In sum, all of the attention we modernist scholars have lately been devoting to obscenity seems to have demonstrated but one thing: much like Supreme Court Justice Potter Stewart, we know literary obscenity when we see it in and as an exemplary instance of literary modernism.[34]

II

Instead, U.S. case law ought to be calling the tune when it comes to the study of book obscenity. Such a shift in orientation has several merits, starting with the fact that it foregrounds a number of obscene works and writers not often considered by the more exclusive canons of either "obscene modernism." A comparative study of the cultural, literary, and legal contexts of modern U.S. obscenity law reveals that modernism's centrality in the narrative of twentieth-century obscenity is, for all of its popular and scholarly appeal, historically unwarranted. Embarrassingly persistent expressions of literary naturalism, much more so than emergent or consummate articulations of "modernism" per se, comprised the primary book targets for obscenity prosecutions in the United States well into the middle of the last century. In the legal realm, one might say, modernist obscenity is derivative from, or even parasitic upon, the cultural work done by naturalist provocations against community norms.

While a complete list of such proscribed works is probably impossible to compile without inadvertently omitting some texts, and while a number of important obscenity cases from this period were unreported, it is worth considering the following list of books that were prosecuted on grounds of obscenity in the United States and resulted in court opinions between 1900 and 1950:[35]

1909	Voltaire, *The Works of Voltaire* (1901)	*St. Hubert Guild*, 118 N.Y.S. 582
	Elinor Glyn, *Three Weeks* (1907)	*Buckley*, 200 Mass. 346
1913	Daniel Carson Goodman, *Hagar Revelly* (1913)*	*Kennerley*, 209 F. 119
1915	Margaret Sanger, *Family Limitation* (1914)[36]	*William Sanger*, 154 N.Y.S. 414
1918	Theodore Dreiser, *The "Genius"* (1915)*	*Dreiser*, 171 N.Y.S. 605

1920	Théophile Gautier, *Mademoiselle de Maupin* (1835)	*Halsey*, 180 N.Y.S. 836
	Anonymous, *Madeleine, the Autobiography of a Prostitute* (1919)	*Brainard*, 183 N.Y.S. 452
1922	Théophile Gautier, *Mademoiselle de Maupin* (1835)	*Halsey*, 234 N.Y. 1
	James Branch Cabell, *Jurgen* (1919)[37]	*People v. Holt, McBride and Company et al.*, Court of the General Sessions of the Peace in and for the County of New York, October 19, 1922
1924	Arthur Schnitzler, *Casanova's Homecoming* (1918)	*Seltzer*, 203 N.Y.S. 809
1929	Radclyffe Hall, *The Well of Loneliness* (1928)	*Friede*, 233 N.Y.S. 565
1930	Arthur Schnitzler, *Reigen* (1900/1903)	*Pesky*, 243 N.Y.S. 193
	Mary Ware Dennett, *The Sex Side of Life* (1919)[38]	*Dennett*, 39 F.2d 564
	Theodore Dreiser, *An American Tragedy* (1925)*	*Friede*, 271 Mass. 318
	D. H. Lawrence, *Lady Chatterley's Lover* (1928)	*DeLacey*, 271 Mass. 327
1931	Marie Stopes, *Married Love* (1918)	*One Obscene Book Entitled "Married Love,"* 48 F.2d 821
	Marie Stopes, *Contraception* (1923)	*One Book Entitled "Contraception,"* 51 F.2d 525
1933	James Joyce, *Ulysses* (1922)	*One Book Called "Ulysses,"* 5 F. Supp. 182
	Erskine Caldwell, *God's Little Acre* (1933)*	*Viking Press, Inc.*, 264 N.Y.S. 534
1934	James Joyce, *Ulysses* (1922)	*One Book Entitled "Ulysses,"* 72 F.2d 705
	Donald Henderson Clarke, *Female* (1934)	*Berg*, 272 N.Y.S. 586
1935	Gustave Flaubert, *November* (1842)	*Herman Miller*, 279 N.Y.S. 583
1936	André Gide, *If It Die* (1924/1926)	*Gotham Book Mart, Inc.*, 285 N.Y.S. 563
1940	Maurice Parmelee, *Nudism in Modern Life* (1927)	*Parmelee*, 113 F.2d 729
1944	D. H. Lawrence, *The First Lady Chatterley* (1944)	*Dial Press*, 182 Misc. 416
1945	Paul Bowman Popenoe, *Preparing for Marriage* (1938)	*Walker*, 149 F.2d 511
	Lillian Smith, *Strange Fruit* (1944)*	*Isenstadt*, 318 Mass. 543
1946	Serge G. Wolsey, *Call House Madam* (1942.)	*London*, 63 N.Y.S.2d 227
1947	Serge G. Wolsey, *Call House Madam* (1942)	*Rodd*, 165 F.2d 54
	Edmund Wilson, *Memoirs of Hecate County* (1946)[39]	*Doubleday*, 71 N.Y.S.2d 736;, and *Doubleday*, 297 N.Y. 687
	Calder Willingham, *End as a Man* (1947)	*Vanguard Press, Inc.*, 84 N.Y.S.2d 427

1948	Kathleen Winsor, *Forever Amber* (1944)	*The Book Named "Forever Amber,"* 323 Mass. 302
	Edmund Wilson, *Memoirs of Hecate County* (1946)	*Doubleday*, 335 U.S. 848
	Charles O. Gorham, *The Gilded Hearse* (1948)	*Creative Age Press, Inc.*, 79 N.Y.S.2d 198
1949	William Faulkner, *Sanctuary* (1931)	
	James T. Farrell, The *Studs Lonigan* Trilogy (1932–35)*	
	Erskine Caldwell, *God's Little Acre* (1933)*	
	James T. Farrell, *A World I Never Made* (1936)*	
	William Faulkner, *Wild Palms* (1939)	
	Calder Willingham, *End as a Man* (1947)	
	Harold Robbins, *Never Love a Stranger* (1948)	*Gordon*, 66 Pa. D.&C. 101, aff'd sub nom. *Feigenbaum*, 70 A.2d 389
1950	Erskine Caldwell, *God's Little Acre* (1933)*	*The Book Named "God's Little Acre,"* 326 Mass. 281
	James M. Cain, *Serenade* (1937)	*The Book Named "Serenade,"* 326 Mass. 324

27

This inventory helps make clear at least two things. First, the prosecution of obscene books in the first half of the twentieth-century United States was often a recursive undertaking. Just because a text got off clean on obscenity charges in one state in one year (as Erskine Caldwell's *God's Little Acre* did in New York in 1933) did not mean that it was thereafter exempt from prosecution in another state (as in fact happened to Caldwell's novel in Pennsylvania in 1949 and then again in Massachusetts the following year). Therefore, the legibility of potentially obscene books was not always punctually linked to the date of original publication, and the legal strategies for re- or deproscribing them from state to state or year to year were variably responsive to evolving sociocultural forces. For instance, as we will see later, the belated attempts to proscribe *God's Little Acre* in the 1940s have as much to do with the contemporary boom in mass-market trade paperbacks as they do with the caricatural organ grinding of Caldwell's Walden family. Furthermore, this recursivity is a built-in feature of Western legal systems insofar as the proscription of obscene books in lower courts is almost always appealable, which accounts for the multiple appearances on this list of Edmund Wilson's *Memoirs of Hecate County*, a novel that was deemed obscene in two New York appellate courts in 1947 before it later led to a split decision in the U.S. Supreme Court. (Justice Felix Frankfurter recused himself from participating in the deliberations concerning the book due to his friendship with Wilson, and the court went on to affirm the lower court decisions in its curt two-sentence opinion the following year.)

This list also makes visible the degree to which canonical works of English-language literary modernism (e.g., the exhaustively studied examples of *Ulysses* or the various proscribed novels of Lawrence and Faulkner) recede into the background while other modes of writing come to the fore. The collected works of Voltaire, erotica (Glyn and Wolsey), contraception and sex health manuals (Sanger, Dennett, Stopes, and Popenoe), autobiographies (*Madeleine* and Gide), works of fin de siècle Viennese decadence (Schnitzler), a historical romance (Winsor), a work of lesbian realism (Hall), an ornate comic allegory (Cabell), a fictional exposé of the book publishing industry (Gorham), pseudoscientific nudist propaganda (Parmelee), a popular collection of satirical short fiction on sex in suburbia and New York City (Wilson), an account of sadism at a Southern military academy (Willingham), and pulp fiction (Clarke, Robbins, and Cain) were all prosecuted for obscenity in this period, and all (with the exception of Flaubert's juvenilia and Gide's memoir) are not easily subsumable within existing modernist frames of reference. Even more saliently, however, works of literary naturalism appear over a longer period of time than any other single genre, mode, or type of writing on this list (see the starred [*] entries above). Far from indexing the startling innovations of subversive modernist writing practices, obscenity case law presents us instead with the unruly, salacious, and offensive appeals evoked by the obstinate remainders of a nineteenth-century mode of writing often assumed to have been surpassed by literary modernism itself. In short, if we take en masse the kinds of books most often proscribed by obscenity case law as a useful archive from which to draw our generalizations, then early twentieth-century book obscenity in the United States would seem to persist in rubbing our faces in the lower depths noisesomely explored by works of literary naturalism, a mode that likewise faced obscenity prosecutions as it spread throughout Europe in the late nineteenth and early twentieth centuries.[40] What we have here, then, are not modernism's naughty self-reflexive monoliths so much as a naturalist preserve of sorts.

By recognizing literary naturalism's rival claims to primacy as an object of concern for U.S. courts in this period, we fundamentally readjust the accepted understanding of modernism's relationship to legal obscenity. Far from being the typical or exemplary target of obscenity prosecutions in the early twentieth century, modernism instead should be more precisely understood to comprise a variably articulated cultural field in early twentieth-century Europe, Britain, and the United States, according to which past modes and forms of art were subjected to various negative procedures (cancellation, allegorization, negation, irony) in order to pose art as a problem to itself. In countless interpretations of the art and cultural objects of this period, the delaying, discrediting, and negating of preexisting genres, modes, and forms in a particular work of art have long persisted as one of the key identifying features for both modernism and the historical avant-garde. While pathbreaking early twentieth-century visual artists were in the midst of calling into question the significance of rules of perspective through a belabored emphasis on the flattened surface of the canvas, and while inventive composers were unsettling the values usually assigned to fundamental compositional elements such as tonality, a similar project of literary innovation through critical self-reflection sought to upend the coherence of inherited realist narratives and (in some cases) narrative altogether. At their most extreme, the more properly avant-garde of these practices—such as the assault that Duchamp's ready-mades waged on art exhibition in the second decade of the century—could call into question the very possibility of art altogether, such that at the end of his life Theodor Adorno was still credibly able to observe that art, in order to survive, "must turn against itself, in opposition to its own concept, and thus become uncertain of itself right into its innermost fiber."[41] By the beginning of the twentieth century, art could no longer afford to ignore its own "impossibility" as it came to be increasingly governed by heteronomous forces and arrangements in which the art-object's claims to exceptional status with respect to market relations and dominant modes of social organization looked more and more like the mutterings of a lyrically dissolute basket case. At the very least, such was the polemical thrust of the frame narrative in F. T. Marinetti's "The Founding and Manifesto of Futurism" (1909), in which the pointedly decadent trappings of the opening paragraph (replete with filigreed mosque lamps and "opulent oriental rugs") get exuberantly discarded (*goodbye to all that!*) in favor of automotive sprees that end in collisions with muddy, womb-like ditches.[42]

29

Understandably, then, the words most often used to describe the highly stylized and deforming compositional maneuvers carried out by innovative early twentieth-century writers on realist narratives and on narrative itself tend to circle around procedures characterized by negation or negativity. Perhaps the most prominent English-language expositor of such a position, Fredric Jameson has more than once in his career disputed the novelty of modernist fiction by describing that writing instead as "rather something like a canceled realism, a realism denied and negated and *aufgehoben* in genuinely Hegelian fashion."[43] Analogizing it to the relationship of consumer capitalism to classical capitalism, Jameson posits that modernism was not the demiurgic expression of unfettered creative self-reflexivity unleashed upon an unsuspecting mass culture so much as it was a second-order articulation of an older and long-accredited mode of narrative (realism) with which early twentieth-century writers and critics had simply become tired. Blanket boredom—not a feat of superhuman originality or the inspiration of a singular genius—is said by Jameson to comprise the fountainhead of modernist writing, which in the main sought to liven up the old realist way of telling stories by making nearly illegible the representational codes on which such narratives had usually tended to rely. According to this influential account, the strange and off-putting surfaces that modernist fiction presents to the world obfuscate the continued existence of realist narrative structures somewhere beneath the superficial pyrotechnics and hyperstylizations of such writing. All that the cancellation of realism did was simply move realism from text to subtext, as it were, in modernist novels and short stories.[44] In Jameson's disenchanted readings, the transgression of convention and its reaffirmation remain inextricably affiliated activities. As a result, we ought not be too easily impressed by the subversive claims that authors and critics have happened to make on modernist writing's behalf, because realism still persists as the operative norm or measure. In departing from realist systems of representation, modernist writers could not help but continue to feed off of them.[45]

Seen in this light, "obscene modernism" is better suited not to account for the primary objects of early twentieth-century obscenity prosecutions but rather to describe a period in which the value, identity, and very existence of obscene books themselves became subjected to protracted, inconclusive arguments between judges, jurists, and writers. In this view, modernism refers us to a broad set of dispositions painfully marked by doubts about the possibility for art and writing as these had been traditionally undertaken. Crucial for any interpretation of the relationships between modernism and obscenity, in turn, is the corollary recognition that similar doubts manifested themselves as well in the case law on the obscene writing of this period. Keeping this in mind, consider the following remarks on and definitions of obscenity produced by U.S. judges in the period between 1896 and 1950:

Swearingen v. United States (1896)
> The words "obscene," "lewd" and "lascivious," as used in the statute, signify that form of immorality which has relation to sexual impurity, and have the same meaning as is given them at common law in prosecutions for obscene libel.[46]

United States v. Kennerley (1913)
> I hope it is not improper for me to say that the rule as laid down [in *Hicklin*], however consonant it may be with mid-Victorian morals, does not seem to me to answer to the understanding and morality of the present time, as conveyed by the words, "obscene, lewd, or lascivious."[47]

> If there be no abstract definition, such as I have suggested, should not the word "obscene" be allowed to indicate the present critical point in the compromise between candor and shame at which the community may have arrived here and now?[48]

> To put thought in leash to the average conscience of the time is perhaps tolerable, but to fetter it by the necessities of the lowest and least capable seems a fatal policy.[49]

Anderson v. Patten, Postmaster (1917)

Few would, I suppose, doubt that some prevention of the mailing of lewd publications is desirable, and yet no field of administration requires better judgment or more circumspection to avoid interference with a justifiable freedom of expression and literary development.[50]

I have little doubt that numerous really great writings would come under the ban, if tests that are frequently current were applied, and these approved publications doubtless at times escape only because they come within the term "classics," which means, for the purpose of the application of the statute, that they are ordinarily immune from interference, because they have the sanction of age and fame, and usually appeal to a comparatively limited number of readers. It is very easy, by a narrow and prudish construction of the statute, to suppress literature of permanent merit.[51]

Halsey v. New York Society for the Suppression of Vice (1922)

No work may be judged from a selection of such paragraphs alone. Printed by themselves they might, as a matter of law, come within the prohibition of the statute. So might a similar selection from Aristophanes or Chaucer or Boccaccio or even from the Bible. The book, however, must be considered broadly as a whole.[52]

United States v. Dennett (1930)

An accurate exposition of the relevant facts of the sex side of life in decent language and in manifestly serious and disinterested spirit cannot ordinarily be regarded as obscene.[53]

United States v. One Obscene Book Entitled "Married Love" (1931)

In Murray's Oxford English Dictionary the word "obscene" is defined as follows:
"Obscene—1. Offensive to the senses, or to taste or refinement; disgusting, repulsive, filthy, foul, abominable, loathsome. Now somewhat arch.
"2. Offensive to modesty or decency; expressing or suggesting unchaste or lustful ideas; impure, indecent, lewd."[54]

United States v. One Book Called "Ulysses" (1933)

The meaning of the word "obscene" as legally defined by the courts is: Tending to stir the sex impulses or to lead to sexually impure and lustful thoughts. Whether a particular book would tend to excite such impulses and thoughts must be tested by the court's opinion as to its effect on a person with average sex instincts—what the French would call *l'homme moyen sensuel*—who plays, in this branch of legal inquiry, the same role of hypothetical reagent as does the "reasonable man" in the law of torts and "the man learned in the art" on questions of invention in patent law.[55]

United States v. One Book Entitled "Ulysses" (1934)

It is settled, at least so far as this court is concerned, that works of physiology, medicine, science, and sex instruction are not within the statute, though to some extent and among some persons they may tend to promote lustful thoughts. We think the same immunity should apply to literature as to science, where the presentation, when viewed objectively, is sincere, and the erotic matter is not introduced to promote lust and does not furnish the dominant note of the publication. The question in each case is whether a publication taken as a whole has a libidinous effect.[56]

Parmelee v. United States (1940)

Probably the fundamental reason why the word obscene is not susceptible of exact definition is that such intangible moral concepts as it purports to connote, vary in meaning from one period to another. It is customary to see, now, in the daily newspapers and in the magazines, pictures of modeled male and female underwear which might have been shocking to readers of an earlier era. An age accustomed to the elaborate bathing costumes of forty years ago might have considered obscene the present-day beach costume of halters and trunks. But it is also true that the present age might regard those of 1900 as even more obscene.[57]

Commonwealth v. Isenstadt (1945)

A book is "obscene, indecent or impure" within the statutory prohibition if it has a substantial tendency to deprave or corrupt its readers by inciting lascivious thoughts or arousing lustful desire. It also violates the statute if it "manifestly tends to corrupt the morals of youth."[58]

Commonwealth v. Gordon et al. (1949)

I assume that "obscenity" is expected to have a familiar and inherent meaning, both as to what it is and as to what it does. It is my purpose to show that it has no such inherent meaning; that different meanings given to it at different times are not constant, either historically or legally; that it is not constitutionally indictable unless it takes the form of sexual impurity, i.e. "dirt for dirt's sake" and can be traced to actual criminal behavior, either actual or demonstrably imminent.[59]

32

A book cannot be a present danger unless its reader closes it, lays it aside, and transmutes its erotic allurement into overt action. That such action must inevitably follow as a direct consequence of reading the book does not bear analysis, nor is it borne out by general human experience; too much can intervene and too many diversions take place.[60]

Attorney General v. The Book Named "God's Little Acre" (1950)

Viewing the book as a whole we find ourselves unable to agree with the conclusion of the trial judge that the book was not obscene, indecent, or impure as those words have been defined in our decisions. The book abounds in sexual episodes and some are portrayed with an abundance of realistic detail. In some instances the author's treatment of sexual relations descends to outright pornography. Nothing would be gained by spreading these portions of the book on the pages of this opinion.[61]

What these various definitions of obscenity in this selection from relevant case law over half a century should make clear is that it is anything but simple to negate a received tradition. It proved as tricky for a liberalizing judge eager to deproscribe book obscenity once and for all as for a modernist artist responding critically to an inherited set of forms, narratives, and generic conventions. Thus, in the years between 1930 and 1950, we end up with a number of attempts either to reaffirm or to do away with Cockburn's notorious processual account of obscenity in *Regina v. Hicklin*. On the one hand, book obscenity in these two decades is said to be both too amorphous and too unreal to warrant legal oversight or restriction anymore. On the other hand, as described in those Massachusetts cases where precedential continuity was more explicitly valued, obscenity in this same span of time is what Cockburn always said it was—depraving and corrupting—even if new considerations have entered the picture since 1868, such as the concession that books ought to be judged now "as a whole" and that the readers most in need of protection belong to youth demographics. As with Jameson's modernist "cancellation" of realist narratives, the very legal postulates being canceled by later rulings linger as norms long after they were supposed to have been overcome or surpassed.

In this view, then, what modernist literary studies meaningfully contribute to critical work on legal obscenity in the early twentieth-century United States is attention to negative processes rather than to singular events or acts of negation. This period confronts us not with the end of book obscenity (that had to wait until the U.S. Supreme Court's decision in *Miller v. California* in 1973) but rather with the *beginning* of the end of book obscenity, the undertaking of a protracted labor of negation. Consequently, Woolsey's much-mythicized opinion in the *Ulysses* case was part of a much longer sequence that both started well before 1933—his redefinition of obscenity in terms of holistic interpretations was first expressed by Judge William S. Andrews in *Halsey*, a 1922 case involving Théophile Gautier's historical romance from the previous century, *Mademoiselle de Maupin*—and unfolded across decades of further litigation well after him. In fact, following Woolsey's revisions to Cockburn, there began a forty-year period in the United States in which there was *too much obscenity law*. Before the early 1930s, the Cockburn test in *Hicklin* did effectively comprise the obscenity law of the land; after Woolsey, new tests (some slightly different, others extremely so) started to appear, making determinate assessments as to what constituted legal obscenity in the United States more and more of a rebarbative task. The Supreme Court itself soon enough realized this when its 1957 opinion in *Roth v. United States* set off a cavalcade of new decisions, tests, and opinions on obscenity over the next fifteen years.[62]

What this means for the comparative study of law and literature is that any attempt to coordinate a modernist frame of reference with early and mid-twentieth-century obscenity case law must stress a provisional open-endedness. We should be cautious not to read backward from the achieved end of book obscenity so as to conclude that the complicated twists and turns of the case law were leading inevitably toward greater freedom. Instead, there were books, opinions, and justifications along the way that startlingly impeded, detoured, and sometimes even effaced this long-term trajectory. For instance, both Lillian Smith's *Strange Fruit* and Erskine Caldwell's *God's Little Acre* were proscribed in 1944 and 1950, respectively, *because of* the direct application of Woolsey's *Ulysses* test. Moreover, we would do well to resist the temptation to interpret these later applications of Woolsey's decision as misappropriations of his widely admired standard. If anything, our modernist frame of reference in this instance should put us on the lookout for how subsequent proscriptive uses of the *Ulysses* test reveal the ways in which that standard—much like literary modernism itself with respect to realism—continued to rely upon Cockburn's much-reviled and supposedly suspended definition of obscenity in *Hicklin*. Taking the modernism of legal obscenity in this period seriously demands nothing less.

III

The negative processes slowly unfolding across the early twentieth century in literary texts and courtrooms also sensitize us to the anxieties evoked by obscene texts and "provocative" literary naturalist ones, both of which straddled the shifting boundaries between literature and paraliterature. Cockburn, it will be remembered, quite pointedly demurred from making an exception on behalf of works of high literary value in his test for obscenity in *Hicklin*. Just because an obscene text possessed literary merit did nothing to detract from or otherwise qualify its capacities to deprave and corrupt those whose minds were open to such influences and into whose hands such a work might have happened to fall. Fittingly enough, then, throughout this period books frequently found themselves proscribed on grounds of obscenity alongside religious pamphlets, advertising circulars, photographs, contraception guides, sex manuals, nudist magazines, and instruments of abortion, among other apparently nonliterary objects of legal disapproval.

The first effective legal challenge to this lack of distinction between obscene works and literary ones did not take place in the United States until 1894, when Anthony Comstock, the head of the New York Society for the Suppression of Vice, opposed the sale of a collection of books as part of the assets of the recently insolvent Worthington Company. Included among these assets were Jean-Jacques Rousseau's *Confessions* (1782–89), Henry Fielding's *The History of Tom Jones, a Foundling* (1749), the collected works of Rabelais, Boccaccio's *The Decameron* (circa 1353), and Ovid's *The Art of Love* (1 C.E.)—all of which Comstock claimed were examples of "immoral literature" that were so far beyond the sanction of New York state law that they could not be offered for sale within its borders.[63] The members of the New York Supreme Court, however, were ultimately unconvinced by Comstock's bold assertions:

35

> It is very difficult to see upon what theory these world-renowned classics can be regarded as specimens of that pornographic literature which it is the office of the Society for the Suppression of Vice to suppress, or how they can come under any stronger condemnation than that high standard literature which consists of the works of Shakespeare, of Chaucer, of Laurence Sterne, and of other great English writers, without making reference to many parts of the Old Testament Scriptures, which are to be found in almost every household in the land. The very artistic character, the high qualities of style, the absence of those glaring and crude pictures, scenes, and descriptions which affect the common and vulgar mind, make a place for books of the character in question, entirely apart from such gross and obscene writings as it is the duty of the public authorities to suppress. . . . A seeker after the sensual and degrading parts of a narrative may find in all these works, as in those of other great authors, something to satisfy pruriency. But to condemn a standard literary work, because of a few of its episodes, would compel the exclusion from circulation of a very large proportion of the works of fiction of the most famous writers of the English language.[64]

Tacitly calling into question not only the scope of *Hicklin*'s test but also its methods of proscribing entire texts on the basis of brief or isolated passages, *In re Worthington*

Company set an important precedent for taking into account the literary merit of a charged book by defending the classics and "standard literary work[s]" against obscenity prosecutions in the state of New York.

While the Woolsey test articulated in *United States v. One Book Called "Ulysses"* in 1933 may be the most famous instance of a lower court judge extending this carefully observed distinction between legal obscenity and literature to a contemporary book, it was Judge Augustus Hand's affirmation of Woolsey's opinion and ruling in *United States v. One Book Entitled "Ulysses"* the following year that even more trenchantly expressed the growing sense among liberalizing judges and jurists that whatever obscenity may have once consisted of, it was probably not going to include the literary anymore: "We think the same immunity should apply to literature as to science, where the presentation, when viewed objectively, is sincere, and the erotic matter is not introduced to promote lust and does not furnish the dominant note of the publication. The question in each case is whether a publication taken as a whole has a libidinous effect. The book before us has such portentous length, is written with such evident truthfulness in its depiction of certain types of humanity, and is so little erotic in its result, that it does not fall within the forbidden class."[65] At least two things are worth noting here. First, because it was (on the whole) long-winded, frank, and not very titillating, *Ulysses* was almost certainly a specimen of literature, meaning that it was not to be mistaken for an instance of obscenity since literature was literature and obscenity was obscenity. Second, the immunity prospectively extended to literature by Hand was expressly modeled after exceptions made earlier on behalf of scientific works, thus securing the recognition of literature as its own field by way of the immunity already granted to a wholly different one. The story of literary value in U.S. obscenity case law, therefore, should not omit the interdisciplinary pressures exerted by science on literature and vice versa. Given the foundational appeals to "scientific" values in naturalism—starting with Zola's programmatic essay, "The Experimental Novel" (1880)—a shift in focus from the texts of modernism to those of literary naturalism becomes all the more exigent.

Although the literary value test broached here would ultimately win out forty years later in *Miller v. California*, the 1930s and 1940s were hardly a period in which this view ended up getting seamlessly ratified court by court and state by state. For instance, in the notoriously censorious Commonwealth of Massachusetts, which made "banned in Boston" a household phrase, an especially subtle appropriation of holistic tests occurred in the 1940s, albeit with the important difference that questions of literary merit ended up being evaluated in an entirely different way. In *Commonwealth v. Isenstadt*, for instance, the Massachusetts Supreme Judicial Court argued that literary value was not all that relevant to determining whether or not a given text was proscribably obscene: "It is possible that, even in the mind of the general reader, overpowering sincerity and beauty may sometimes entirely obscure or efface the evil effect of occasional questionable passages, especially with respect to the classics of literature that have gained recognized place as part of the great heritage of humanity. The question will commonly be one of fact in each case, and if, looking at the book as a whole, the bad is found to persist in substantial degree alongside the good, as the law now stands, the book will fall within the statute."[66] In proscribing Lillian Smith's naturalist antilynching novel, *Strange Fruit*, the Massachusetts Supreme Judicial Court reminded judges, jurists, and writers everywhere that obscenity was indeed not *not* literature, because it was impossible to distinguish salacious literature from the claims of indecency, impurity, and corruption effectively mounted by obscene works more generally. In fact, if anything, the beauty and sincerity of good writing provided authors with the means of camouflaging the unruly claims of their obscene passagework, making certain parts of their texts all the more indecent, impure, and corrupt. The literariness of literary works potentially made them more, not less, obscene.

Since the late nineteenth century, however, literary naturalism in the United States had provided reliable occasions to doubt the self-sufficiency of "literature" as a meaningful category in the reception of fiction. Just as Stephen Crane's *Maggie: A Girl of the Streets* (1893) had presented itself as being of a piece with the urban ethnographic and psychological analyses inaugurated by Jacob Riis's *How the Other Half Lives* (1890), Theodore Dreiser quite self-consciously described his early fiction as metaphoric reappropriations of Herbert Spencer's materialist metaphilosophy, particularly as it was expressed in *First Principles* (1862).[67] Likewise, in the return of naturalist fiction in the interwar period, sociological and eugenic discourses came more to the fore, particularly in the novels of James T. Farrell and Erskine Caldwell, respectively.[68] More recently, Christopher L. Hill has made the compelling case that this confusion of literary naturalism with other "non-literary genres of social knowledge" was indispensable to its development not only in the United States but also in other countries: "The rise of naturalist schools around the world was the result of the circulation of multiple genres, literary and otherwise, through distinct paths whose intersections were enormously varied but mutually reinforcing in the aggregate. Naturalist fiction would have been unlikely to travel so widely without these other genres, or they without it or each other."[69] Not purely literary by nature, literary naturalism has always constituted itself as an alloyed mode of writing in which sociological, psychological, evolutionary, physiological, criminological, and other extraliterary discourses have been adopted and transformed by self-identified naturalist writers the world over.

Following the attacks mounted against it in the first half of the century and the structural analysis that it subsequently underwent, literary naturalism fittingly enough became a privileged object of study for the New Historicism. After all, the interpretive procedure of structural homology, most forthrightly put into practice

37

in Walter Benn Michaels's *The Gold Standard and the Logic of Naturalism* (1987) but also implicit in June Howard's *Form and History in American Literary Naturalism* (1985), is predicated upon a refusal of context: nothing is background because everything is foregrounded. For instance, nothing in Caroline Meeber's milieu or situation "explains" her in *Sister Carrie* (1900). Instead, everything about her, her milieu, and her situation can be transformed into everything else.[70] Consequently, the same entanglement plays itself out again and again in New Historicist criticism: "literature tries to distinguish itself with respect to other social and cultural formations and fails."[71] Not revolt, but cooptation is the paradigmatic story told by New Historicism, and the fact that literary naturalism already collapses the literary and the social into one messy heap meant it was a ready-made venue for critics in the 1980s to explore—rather than traduce—the ramifications of this unconsoling worldview.[72]

Among many early twentieth-century critics, however, U.S. literary naturalism's uncomfortably close associations with nonliterary discourses were cause for disdain rather than for doubts about the possibility of adopting an oppositional stance in the first place. A notable expression of this is Malcolm Cowley's "Naturalism in American Literature" (1950), which poses the tradition of naturalist writing in the United States—from Frank Norris, Crane, and Dreiser through to Farrell, John Steinbeck, and Richard Wright—as one bound together principally by a spirit of rebellion against gentility and orthodoxy.[73] Glumly assessing the pseudoscientific objectivity of naturalist writing in terms that emphasize its fundamental misapprehension of scientific materials and methods, Cowley contends that one of the manifest shortcomings of the naturalist tradition in the United States has been its tendency "always to explain the complex in terms of the simple: society in terms of self, man in terms of his animal inheritance, and the organic in terms of the inorganic. The result is that something is omitted at each stage in this process of reduction. To say that man is a beast of prey or a collection of chemical compounds omits most of man's special nature; it is a metaphor, not a scientific statement."[74] By confusing figural language with the presentation of facts and the procedures used to test the validity of those facts, naturalism manages to evacuate literature of its own authentically literary forms, functions, and effects, including—most troublingly in Cowley's estimation—the ability to tell credible tragic narratives:

> This scientific weakness of naturalism involves a still greater literary weakness, for it leads to a conception of man that makes it impossible for naturalistic authors to write in the tragic spirit. They can write about crimes, suicides, disasters, the terrifying, and the grotesque; but even the most powerful of their novels and plays are case histories rather than tragedies in the classical sense. Tragedy is an affirmation of man's importance; it is "the imitation of noble actions," in Aristotle's phrase; . . . for the naturalists, however, men are "human

insects" whose brief lives are completely determined by society or nature. The individual is crushed in a moment if he resists; and his struggle, instead of being tragic, is merely painful or ironic, as if we had seen a mountain stir itself to overwhelm a fly.[75]

A year before "Naturalism in American Literature" appeared, Philip Rahv voiced a similar dissatisfaction with the lack of tragic potentials in literary naturalism: "The world of naturalist fiction is much too big, too inert, too hardened by social habit and material necessity, to allow for that tenacious self-assertion of the human by means of which tragedy justifies and ennobles its protagonists."[76] Not the protagonists but the social and natural worlds themselves were the real heroes of naturalist writing, and with this dehumanizing displacement of agency from character to setting, in Rahv's view, tragedy had been well and truly lost to U.S. fiction for a time.

According to Cowley, from beneath the thin conceptual protection provided by its pseudoscientific cover story, literary naturalism had thus spent the past half century traducing the dignity of humanism. People in naturalist fiction were little more than abstractly composed formulae, "the blind result of conditions, forces, physical laws, or nature herself."[77] Therefore, literary naturalist authors may indeed have deserved credit for having "immensely broadened the scope of American fiction" by integrating materials, social classes, and subject matter hitherto marked off-limits.[78] However, in doing so they had relied far too much on "the meanest of everything they describe," with the result that this widening of subject matter likewise represented a watering down of U.S. fiction.[79] When mankind as a whole was not being thoroughly proletarianized in the pages of a naturalist novel, it was undergoing a grotesque ordeal of devolution and degeneration before the reader's very eyes, of which Frank Norris's *Vandover and the Brute* (1914) still provides the most famous (but by no means the only) example: "All in an instant [Vandover] had given way, yielding in a second to that strange hallucination of that four-footed thing that sulked and snarled. Now without a moment's stop he ran back and forth along the wall of the room, upon the palms of his hands and toes, a ludicrous figure, like that of certain clowns one sees at the circus, contortionists walking about the sawdust, imitating some kind of enormous dog."[80] For Cowley and most other mid-twentieth-century critics, the overmastering preoccupation of such naturalist writing with the bestial and the brutish betokened not a serious reflection upon species-being so much as it did an act of juvenile delinquency on the part of the guilty naturalist writers, who could be seen to be gleefully doing the dirty on mankind's self-image in the name of a mechanistic and filth-obsessed materialism that could only be called, in the words of Oscar Cargill, "pessimistic determinism."[81]

To be sure, not all literary critics at the time were so quick to view naturalism's representations of the world quite so reductively. For one thing, as Charles Child

Walcutt hastens to point out in *American Literary Naturalism: A Divided Stream* (1956), the deterministic philosophies so comprehensively excoriated by contemporaries such as Cargill and Cowley do not have to be taken at face value. Just because the ideology espoused by the narrator or by a character in a given naturalist work appears to be mechanistic in the extreme does not necessarily indicate that this same novel is bereft of the means of contradicting or otherwise inflecting this overly simplistic account of the world. In other words, apathy and "mass insensibility" are not the ineluctable results of our reading a novel whose ethos is supposedly consistent with that of literary naturalism.[82] Instead, according to Walcutt, the naturalist novel in the United States constitutes a complex linguistic artifact informed both by progressive idealism and scientific determinism, the two currents that make up the divided stream of his book's title.[83]

Due to this animating antagonism between intuition and empirical investigation, naturalist fiction in this country is said to have insinuated itself into all sorts of extraliterary discourses, running the gamut from pure speculative science to the social sciences and on to public policymaking. The result of this scrambling of discourses and institutional authorities is that any sufficient reading of a given naturalist text first has to evaluate the claims and appeals being made by that work within its various interdisciplinary and social contexts. In other words, if a naturalist novel rather conspicuously deprives characters of agency or will, then that deficit is probably being made up for somewhere else. In particular, Walcutt argues that in so graphically denying volition and effective intentionality to the subjects it sets forth, naturalist fiction more often than not ends up transferring intentionality and volition from its characters to its readers and—correlatively—to society itself. If a given work of literary naturalist fiction is in fact correct about the situations it so implacably and gloomily depicts, then society and readers of naturalist fiction are now in a better position to do something about it. Much like Peirce's processual account of lithium, in which the act of defining lithium gets equated with the activities one has to undertake in order to produce real existing specimens of lithium, naturalist novels in Walcutt's view have the potential to self-reflexively elaborate the steps by which naturalist milieus and characters get themselves produced off the page and in the real world. Therefore, unlike the pitiless machinations of fate, naturalism's gruesomely reductive determinisms need not bar the possibilities for amelioration or even revolutionary transformation. Not only mortified but also *edified* at the sight of the impending mountain, Cowley's poor fly could, in a collective effort with other like-minded flies, potentially overwhelm *it* instead: "The more helpless the character [in naturalist writing], the stronger the proof of determinism; and once such a thesis is established the scientist hopes and believes that men will set about trying to control the forces which now control men. . . . Thus can the scientists' 'optimistic' purpose be served by a 'pessimistic' novel."[84]

In this way, the antihumanist cul-de-sac condemned by Cargill, Cowley, Rahv, and many other mid-twentieth-century critics of U.S. literary naturalist fiction could be meaningfully transformed by bringing out the incipient activist, reformist, and humanist impulses underlying the violence, brutishness, and implacability in all sorts of naturalist works.

Despite the ingeniousness of his reading, however, Walcutt never quite convinces himself that naturalist fiction actually works this way. Instead, he goes on in *American Literary Naturalism: A Divided Stream* to insist that "whatever its ultimate social intent, naturalist fiction does not exhort the reader to action."[85] As he quite disenchantedly points out: "If some of Zola's best novels are still read it is because of their logical, integrated, relentless movement toward disaster—not that *L'Assommoir* will discourage drunkenness, or *Germinal* usher in the Revolution, or *Nana* apprise us of the evils of sexual license in a decadent society."[86] For Walcutt, therefore, the implicit contradiction between a faith in human progress and a commitment to mechanical determinism in literary naturalist fiction is less an index of unquestioned social optimism through unfolding scientific processes than it is an expression of "a profound uncertainty as to whether science liberates the human spirit or destroys it."[87] Offering in effect a protodeconstructive interpretation of literary naturalism's relationship to its putative first principles, Walcutt's book seeks not merely to undermine the operativity of deterministic philosophies and science in naturalist novels but also to explore the affective terrain on which such things could be erected. According to Walcutt, U.S. literary naturalism's foundations were originally constructed on fear and doubt in the face of the disturbingly ambiguous effects that modern science was having on human existence at that time. Consequently, once these same scientific developments had successfully started to make inroads into everyday life and even into the subjective interiorities of the masses, the matrix of uneasy affects that had made naturalist writing possible in the first place ceased to exist: "When science has brought us to a moral relativism that substitutes therapy for personal responsibility, the last trickle of the stream of idealism has disappeared, and the divided stream of naturalism has lost a vital half of itself."[88]

Walcutt's book accordingly argues that the popularization of science is responsible for the end of naturalism. Inadvertently echoing Wyndham Lewis's attacks in the 1920s on the utility of cutting-edge scientific research as a means of ideological warfare in the relativization of social, moral, and cultural values, Walcutt contends that the most widespread insights of early twentieth-century science—from the Oedipus complex to the theories of general and special relativity—had become elements of general culture by the first decade of the Cold War, with the result that there no longer seemed to be absolutes on which the doubts and fears of literary naturalism might continue to corrosively act. Instead, existentialism and orthodox

41

Christianity were now the more timely expressions of the persistence of an idealist faith in nature.[89] Correlatively, now that its affective wellspring had been depleted, literary naturalism in the 1950s was said to be "[spread] out so far that it covers the whole literary landscape—but very thinly."[90] Naturalism no longer existed as an independent mode of writing, though that did not belie the likelihood that all U.S. fiction would continue to bear a naturalistic impress for some time.

As a result, the problem for critics was increasingly that of recognizing literary naturalism when they saw it. Every writer and critic of naturalism in this period appeared to have his or her own sense of how to define it, and no consensus seemed to be evolving from this clash of informed opinions. Arguably the best expression of literary naturalism's elusiveness as a concept at this time is to be found in an audio lecture recorded by Erskine Caldwell entitled "Naturalism and the American Novel" (1953). Using the talk mostly to get in some jabs at the same literary critics who had spent the past decade calling into question his worth as a writer of fiction, when they were not simply ignoring him altogether, Caldwell starts by admitting that the "critical man of letters" is "by reason of heritage, birth, and environment, . . . a man far superior in mind and morals, and a man who can outtalk a mere writer of fiction anytime, anywhere." Consequently, as "a mere writer of fiction," Caldwell himself must be whatever it is these men of letters say he is. Unfortunately, it seems that these vastly superior men of morality and knowledge cannot quite make up their minds as to what to do with him: "Some critics have called me a realist, and I came to believe them. Other critics have called me a romanticist, and I came to believe them too. Now, if I am to be called a naturalist, I shall no doubt believe that as well, but I can't be all things, and until the question is resolved for once and for all, I would be content to remain just what I thought I was: a writer of fiction, a storyteller from Georgia."[91] Despite the sarcasm here, however, Caldwell is emphatically not content to remain a Georgian teller of tales, because the charge of being a naturalist has gotten under his skin like a hookworm, leading him to go on in this audio essay to determine just what "the meaning of such a term as 'naturalist fiction'" might credibly be.[92]

Caldwell's principal stalking horse throughout his lecture is *American Idealism* (1943), in which Floyd Stovall ranged U.S. writers under four headings: Idealists (Ralph Waldo Emerson, Walt Whitman, and Thomas Wolfe), Romantic Realists (Willa Cather, Ellen Glasgow, Edna Ferber, Sinclair Lewis, Steinbeck, and John P. Marquand), Sometimes Naturalists or Realists (William Dean Howells, Crane, Hamlin Garland, Norris, John Dos Passos, and Ernest Hemingway), and Undisputed Naturalists (Jack London, Dreiser, Faulkner, Farrell, and Caldwell).[93] Discovering himself placed among the "Undisputed Naturalists," Caldwell claims to be "somewhat surprised and well-taken-back too." Whatever naturalism happened to be ultimately, its widespread use as a label of disapproval among most contemporary critics in the United States leads the world-famous author of *Tobacco Road* (1932) and *Gods Little Acre* to quip, "I find that all comfort and peace of mind has been taken from me."[94]

The remainder of Caldwell's lecture attempts to cope with this satirically presented dark night of the soul by shifting the shortcomings of literary naturalism from the texts of naturalism to the critics of naturalism themselves. Instead of agreeing with the Cargills and Cowleys of the world in finding literary naturalism to be an unduly pessimistic mode of writing, Caldwell calls the definitional efforts of these same scholars to be "pessimistic to an extreme." Not naturalist fiction itself but interpreters of naturalism such as Cargill are to blame for its supposed cynicism, doubt, and gloom. Similarly, Cowley is singled out for propagating the erroneous notion that naturalism somehow constitutes the subtraction of all human responsibility from fiction in the United States. Consequently, it is the detractors—and not the writers—of literary naturalism who are said to be proceeding far too deterministically, irresponsibly shutting down the kinds of experiences and ideologies that naturalist fiction can be made to embody or represent in the act of reading itself. According to Caldwell's lecture, the violent and the ugly, as well as the poverty and class conflicts of life, often exist side by side with "spasms of laughter, the horseplay of humor, and the enjoyment of living" in literary naturalist fiction like his own. Therefore, instead of approaching literature as a "laboratory frog to be sliced, pickled in a jar, and labeled *this, that,* and *the other thing,*" literary critics in this country in the mid-twentieth century would better serve their reading communities by treating creative writing as if it were "an untamed, rampaging creature ranging the land" and in need of guidance perhaps but not the proscriptions or finicky classifications of a group of men wholly out of touch with the world. Naturalist archetypes thus end up mediating Caldwell's cheeky account of contemporary writing and the burgeoning Cold War industry of academic literary criticism. Whereas fictional texts are said to constitute the Jack London–esque wolves shiftily roaming the literary landscape in this country, its critics are apparently unprepared to confront or otherwise account for these undomesticated beasts because they are too much like Zerkow, the miserly rag-and-bone man of Norris's *McTeague* (1899), fussily coveting and hoarding those objects that have long outlived their use: "Next to a dull novel," Caldwell observes, "I don't know anything more depressing than a critic who has mewed himself up from the world, and especially a naturalistic critic."[95]

IV

These thematic problems and issues raised by U.S. literary naturalism for its mid-century critics ought to make more salient the degree to which the period's arguments over the criminally libidinal appeals of writing encompassed more than

43

just the relationships embodied by chance between mute words and their presumably lewd readers. Literary naturalism was no more depraved, corrupt, offensive, or prurient than any other contemporary mode of writing, though its constitutive incorporation of extraliterary forms of social knowledge and its attention to the impact of societal forces upon personal identity made it better suited than most to reflect upon the putative uses—normal and aberrant—to which writing's effective force could be put. If early twentieth-century readers really were so in thrall to their somatic responses that books needed to be prohibited for their illicit solicitations, then the threats evoked by the potential manipulability of irrational consumers went well beyond masturbatory gratification.

This concern over the embodied subsumption of identities gets trenchantly thematized throughout the three volumes of James T. Farrell's *Studs Lonigan*, which details the deleterious impact of mass urban life in the early twentieth-century United States on historical consciousness, particularly that of its titular protagonist. In fact, as the frightening exemplification of these effects, William "Studs" Lonigan has "no language and no experience, whether societal, personal, or physical, which he can genuinely call his own."[96] Depicting modernity in the first decades of the last century as an impoverishment not just of language but of experience, *Studs Lonigan* again and again calls into question the operativity of literature as an autonomous sphere of human activity by ranging *all* writing within the context of mass culture, the nature and functions of which prove to be far from affirmative.

Frequently, the anxieties and concerns evoked by this get expressed in satirical episodes like the mission sermon described in the twenty-first chapter of *The Young Manhood of Studs Lonigan* (1934), where Father Shannon declaims against a number of writers on the grounds that their books are "vile," as are the sins to which they tend to lead their readers:

> And if I met the authors of the books I shall mention, I should tell them to their faces (his voice rose, almost to a shout): "Your books are vile. In order to make a sale for them, you fill them with spiritual poison, with all the resources of your filthy and putrid minds. For thirty pieces of silver, you sign your names to oozing immorality. You are worse than dogs! You are the vilest of the vile, the most vicious of the vicious, lower than snakes, you rats who write books to rob youth of its shining silvered innocence!"[97]

And just who are these Judas-like "rats who write books"? Father Shannon singles out Sinclair Lewis, whose novel *Elmer Gantry* (1927) is said to make a mockery of "the most sacred profession that man can enter"; Judge Ben Lindsey, whose *Companionate Marriage* (1927), "like the anarchistic, atheistic Bolshevists in unhappy Russia, says (his arms flung out in a gesture): 'Away with the holy bonds of Matrimony!'"; H. L. Mencken, whose articles spread the gospel of nihilism and blasphemy to American youths who thereafter "think themselves (sneering) smart"; H. G. Wells, whose popularization of evolutionary outlooks marks him out as an egotist and materialist of the lowest kind; and the various propagandizing writers of birth control pamphlets, who do nothing but instigate a lack of sexual continence throughout the United States (*SL*, 437–40). Suitably, the result of all these bad influences—together with "Filthy movies. Newspapers. The doctrines in universities aimed to destroy morality" (*SL*, 441)—threatens nothing less than the end of the United States of America because "vile" books such as these are said by Father Shannon to be leading not just good Catholic men and women but in fact all Americans toward "that drastic, terrible fate which befell the proud and mighty empire of Rome" (444). Since they appear to be especially efficacious instruments of a degrading mass culture, books are therefore more than an affront to Catholic or American morals; more importantly, they are also potentially a mortal threat to *all* nations, no matter the time or place.

As shrill as Father Shannon's attacks on "vile" books manifestly are, it would nevertheless be a mistake to read Farrell's cunning pastiche of the fire-and-brimstone histrionics of the retreat described in the third chapter of James Joyce's *A Portrait of the Artist as a Young Man* (1916) as a straightforward send-up of the overwrought fears of crumbling religious and moral orders in a modern secular society. For one thing, Father Shannon's attacks on mass culture get complicated by the fact that his fellow clergymen are in the midst of successfully co-opting various media outlets of contemporary mass culture itself. In the final volume of the trilogy, *Judgment Day* (1935), Father Moylan hosts a popular radio program in which he casually throws around Red-baiting quips and obliquely anti-Semitic references as if he were a bona fide demagogue. At one point, Studs Lonigan's father asks him, "What does Father Moylan say? He tells what the bankers are doing. Loaning American money to Europe. If they had kept American money in America where it belongs, there wouldn't be any depression" (734). Unpacking Father Moylan's views a bit more fully, his father goes on to observe:

> America was a fine country. And all these foreigners came here to take jobs away from Americans who have a right to them. And now we got too many men for the jobs we got. Well, I know what we ought to do. Put all the foreigners we got taking jobs away from Americans, pack them in boats, and say to them, "Now, see here, America belongs to Americans. You get back where you belong." And if we did that, we wouldn't have these Reds here agitating to overthrow the government. Say, you know what those dirty Reds are doing now? They're exciting the niggers down in the Black Belt, telling them they're as good as white men and they can have white women. I tell you, Bill, some day

45

American people have got to wake up and take things into their own hands. (734–35)

It is presumably because of bigotries and xenophobic insights such as these that Studs Lonigan's father can then claim that Father Moylan is "one of the finest and smartest men in America, and he tells the people what's what" (735). Furthermore, it is because of demagogic appeals such as these that Ann Douglas has been able to demonstrate how the social and spiritual functions of Catholicism are inextricably linked to those of mass culture throughout *Studs Lonigan*: "At best, Studs' parents and their friends go to church in much the same spirit Studs and his gang go to the movies, to have their prejudices reinforced and their discontent siphoned off in fantasy."[98]

As *Judgment Day* also reveals, however, Father Shannon's complaints about mass culture are not simply reactionary or hypocritical; they are, it seems, quite well founded. At the beginning of the tenth chapter, Studs kills time by aimlessly walking around an urban street while erratically trying to distract himself from thinking about a fight he has recently had with his fiancée, Catherine. After getting hassled by a cop for looking like "a suspicious character," Studs wanders off down a street and overhears a bit of music from "Piccolo Pete" (*SL*, 659–61): "Radios all over. And he hated that damn song. But women, now, they never did seem to know their own minds, or what they wanted, so how could a guy know it? Even so, and even if he was in the right, still, he needn't have been so goddamn mean to her. Yes, he was kind of sorry about it." Unable to make up his own mind because the women in his life cannot seem to make up *their* minds, Studs moves farther on down the street and "stopped at a window of a book store and rental library, looking from a stack of greeting cards to books piled up and spread around the window, with their bright jackets, reading the titles, *Lumber*, *Jews Without Money*, *The Women of Andros*, *The Crystal Icicle*, *Iron Man*, *The Mystery of Madame Q*, *Bottom Dogs*, *Arctic Quest*. Sometime he might rent one or two of the books they had and do a little reading, he reflected, turning away from the window" (*SL*, 661). Instead of doing a little reading, however, Studs starts to admire some young women ("not at all bad on the eyes") passing by him before he moves on to a corner drug store (*SL*, 662). In the drug store, he almost calls Catherine's home, but ends up deciding against it:

He laid the slug on the counter, picked up his nickel, stopped by the magazine rack near the door and thumbed through a copy of an art magazine, looking at the pictures of naked and veiled women. Hot babies, but why the hell didn't it show them in different positions to give the whole works. He set the magazine back and selected a copy of *True Confessions*, opening it at a photograph of a dishevelled girl. Her dress was torn down one shoulder as she gripped a door knob, her face trapped in fear, with a man looking beastly, lurching toward her, his shirt torn, his face scratched and bleeding. Studs quickly skipped through the story, written in the first person, coming upon the scene represented in the paragraph where the girl was attacked. He hoped the fellow would succeed, and it would be described. But she escaped, and his eagerness sapped away.

Now, I learned my lesson.

The clerk stared at him with cold suspicion. He replaced the magazine and left the drug store. Girls weren't always so lucky as the gal who'd written the story.

Glaring "idly and half-interestedly" at the headlines of the papers displayed at a nearby newsstand, Studs decides finally to go home for lunch and figure out just what the hell it is he is going to do with the rest of his day (*SL*, 663). After all, maybe Catherine has left a message for him with his folks.

As he certainly is throughout the remainder of the trilogy that bears his name, Studs Lonigan in this passage proves to be unduly responsive to the conflicting stimulations and cues provided to him by his surroundings, with the result that he is never really quite sure how he comes to do the things he finds himself doing. The books glimpsed through the window of the bookstore and rental library, for instance, catch his eye not so much for the words they contain as for "their bright jackets," which lead to the short-lived notion that he really ought to get around to "do[ing] a little reading" sometime soon. Rather than check out a book or two, however, he eventually finds himself inside a drug store skimming through magazines. The sight of the books gets intermingled with his ogling of passing women on the street in such a way that both impulses get displaced onto another activity that combines the two in the drugstore, where Studs can critically appraise the "naked and veiled women" in an art magazine before being deprived of the rape he wants to see verbally depicted in the issue of *True Confessions* (1922–present). The supposedly "vile" desires once satisfied by the "vile" books described in Father Shannon's mission sermon are now apparently more readily fulfilled by nonliterary means: visual culture and the luridly exhibitionistic moralism ("*Now, I learned my lesson*") of early twentieth-century confessional magazines.

As pictures, movies, illustrated book covers, and (later) comic books increasingly supplanted the libidinal appeals of mere words on a page as the primary targets of criminal prosecution and legislative oversight in the United States, writing itself gradually became an outmoded way of delivering salacious or patently offensive experiences to prospectively obscene consumers, for whom books seemed to be little more than supplements to the supposedly more provocative and immediate stimulation provided by their paperback covers.[99] Appropriately enough, therefore, the interest of Studs in this particular confession in this particular confessional magazine hinges upon the "photograph of a dishevelled girl" that accompanies

47

it. Very much a seeker after the sensual and degrading parts of a narrative, Studs hastily shuffles through the woman's story to the paragraph that seems most like the caption to the photo. Regrettably, to his mind at least, it does not follow through on the rape fantasies this image first stimulated in him.

In effect, then, the reading habits of Studs Lonigan in the 1930s would mark him out as a prototypically obscene reader in the estimation of the Massachusetts Supreme Judicial Court in the 1940s. For Studs, words on a page are not to be read consecutively as a whole but instead are just a series of holes, of more or less suggestive lacunae either to be manically skipped over or to be scrutinized lasciviously.[100] Whereas the judges in 1894's *In re Worthington* and in the two *Ulysses* cases of the early 1930s were quite certain that literary books reliably tended to call forth the properly literary modes of reading them, the notoriously proscriptive opinions in Massachusetts countered that there were in fact no innate linkages between literary texts and literary reading practices. Instead, putatively literary books could in fact be read obscenely—that is to say, selectively, with an eye and a body attuned to maximizing self-arousal at the prospect of graphic descriptions and actions isolated from the unitary frames or forms put around them in a text.

Studs Lonigan thus helps to call into question the holistic prejudices of Woolsey's test (obscene works are obscene as a whole) and to muddy the distinction between literary and obscene texts. For instance, an issue of *True Confessions* may not have been "literary" the way *Ulysses* eventually was in the minds of its contemporaries, but it was no less deserving of being read as a whole than Joyce's novel happened to be. Writing in the 1950s, George Gerbner assessed the social functions performed by U.S. confessional magazines—including *True Confessions* and Bernarr Macfadden's *True Story* (1919–present)—and concluded that despite the garishness of most of the "true" narratives published in them, these confessions ultimately served moralistic functions when read as a whole:

> The social appeal of the confession story pivots around the heroine's human frailties in a bewildering and punitive world she cannot fully understand. The "truth" of this world is brought home through the inevitable encounter and the final coming to terms—resigned and tragic—with the code of society. The dynamic power of respect and sympathy for confused victims struggling in a web they cannot avoid or escape, or really comprehend, is harnessed to the cause of individual restraint. The flame of rebellion is first kindled, then controlled in scope or divorced from its broader social context, and then doused in jet streams of remorse, sacrifice, and compromise.[101]

While Studs Lonigan's salacious reading of a *True Confessions* story briefly alludes to this tendency toward restraint and self-control in such types of periodicals ("*Now, I learned my lesson*"), the moral of his own encounter with the confession of this particular "dishevelled girl" appears to be that there are reading practices that not only show a complete lack of self-control or restraint but also nullify whatever restraint or self-control a text may be immanently claiming for itself through either its contents or forms. In other words, if Studs ever really did get around to checking out Edward Dahlberg's *Bottom Dogs* (1929) or Mike Gold's *Jews Without Money* (1930), then he would likely not be reading them for their plot or ideological consistency so much as skimming through them rapidly for the naughty, juicy bits. Similarly, one readily imagines that Gerty MacDowell might have caught Studs's eye and imagination as one hot babe as well, should a copy of *Ulysses* have ever fallen into his hands before his premature death from heart failure in the last volume of the trilogy bearing his name.

Furthermore, the separability of text from social context gets undermined altogether in *Judgment Day* because by the end of the tenth chapter in that book, Studs finds himself within a real unfolding *True Confessions*–style narrative. After losing money on every horse race at the gambling establishment run by his brother-in-law, a luckless housewife solicits Studs and three other men to come back to her apartment for sex. Studs agrees, and after lots are drawn, he gets to go first:

> Grinning foolishly, Studs walked down the hall, opened the bedroom door. "All right?" he asked.
>
> "Come in," she said.
>
> He entered the small, neat bedroom and saw her, naked, her black hair falling down her back, reclining on a high poster bed, with feminine clothes and a copy of *True Stories* magazine on a chair beside it.
>
> "Well, I suppose we better get started," she said coldly. (*SL*, 679–80)

With a confessional magazine in place beside the bed to recursively mark the culturally mediated nature of his imminent sexual encounter, Studs is presumably in a position to realize the sort of ending he sorely felt the lack of in the *True Confessions* narrative he skimmed through earlier in the day. Now, he himself is cast as the relentless sexual predator, while the housewife plays the role of the "dishevelled girl" who ought not to have been quite as lucky as she ended up being.

Instead of being jubilant following this opportunity to enact his rape fantasies, however, Studs "was disappointed, because it had all happened so quickly." Leaving the woman's apartment, he is altogether confused as to how to account for what he has just done or how he feels about it:

> All over so quickly. He wanted more, but she'd said no encores without another two and a half [dollars]. And he'd rather go back alone some morning than now with the others there.

49

He felt lazy, too, and he thought of how when he went back it would be better. She was nice, and he remembered her naked on the bed when he'd entered the room. But a married woman and mother who'd do such a thing, lower than a snake. What was the difference between her and a whore? None. And what a chump and a sap of a husband she must have.

Catherine didn't know about it, and what she didn't know wouldn't hurt her. If she wanted to be tough, as she had last night, let her, and then she could see what she was going to lose. Lighting a cigarette, he thought that this was a just revenge on her. (*SL*, 680)

The street was alive with people, women rushing through their last-minute marketing, people coming home from work. Suppose one of these men coming along was George Jackson. Nice surprise for Georgie.

And now that the day was finished, he had to get through the night. Christ, things sometimes got dull for a guy.

But maybe [Catherine would] call up after supper, and he'd go over and see her. He thought she would. She really cared for him. Maybe when he got home there would already be a message for him from her. (*SL*, 681)

An overgrown lab rat traversing a maze with no goal, center, or exit, Studs Lonigan reacts to his own "true story" in ways that closely follow the well-worn habitual grooves embedded deep within his body and mind by the world around him. After leaving open the prospect of an encore performance with the housewife on some future morning, he immediately refers back to Father Shannon's mission sermon in the previous volume of the trilogy. Like Sinclair Lewis, Judge Ben Lindsey, H. L. Mencken, and H. G. Wells before her, the housewife is said to be "lower than a snake," which makes evident yet again the impoverishing quality of Studs Lonigan's experiences. After all, the very language he uses to make sense of his encounters in the world around him is made up largely of citations he unreflectively produces on the spot in response to present or recent stimuli. A button is pressed, and other people's words start to spool out of his mouth or to cycle through his head.

Unfortunately for Studs, however, these reactions tend to overlap and frequently contradict one another, leading him to carry out a series of conflicting responses that leave him endlessly deferring either an assertion of willpower or the actualization of an intention. The housewife is desirable and should probably be pursued by him again sometime later. Then again, the housewife is a cuckolding whore, and her husband a sap. On the one hand, Catherine does not need to know about what Studs and the housewife-whore did together. On the other hand, even if Catherine were to find out somehow, it would serve her right because she would only be getting what she has coming to her. George Jackson, the housewife's husband, sure is a sap. Maybe Catherine has left a message with Studs Lonigan's folks so that they can make up and he can put this enervating day behind him by spending the night out with her instead. Much like the heroines of early twentieth-century confessional magazines analyzed by Gerbner, Studs Lonigan is a confused victim struggling in a web he cannot avoid, escape, or really comprehend. Unlike them, however, there is no final reconciliation with existing social codes in his future, just a premature death.

No doubt, John B. Watson would have found Studs Lonigan to be an excellent case study for why societies, governments, and businesses badly needed behaviorists to take the reins in educating men, women, and children if human beings were ever going to start realizing their evolutionary potentials as a species. Both professionalizing and transforming the study of psychology by grounding it in physiologically observable behaviors, habits, and reactions, this "founder" of behaviorism popularized the notion in the early twentieth century that humans were little more than complexly arranged stimulus-response mechanisms that could be streamlined and made to run more effectively once comparative psychologists had experimentally determined the protocols by which we all functioned: "In a system of psychology completely worked out," Watson wrote, "given the response the stimuli can be predicted; given the stimuli the response can be predicted."[102] Accordingly, Watson went on to submit that behaviorism

> ought to be a science that prepares men and women for understanding the principles of their own behavior. It ought to make men and women eager to rearrange their own lives, and especially eager to prepare themselves to bring up their own children in a healthy way. I wish I could picture for you what a rich and wonderful individual we should make of every healthy child if only we could let it shape itself properly and then provide for it a universe in which it could exercise that organization—a universe unshackled by legendary folklore of happenings thousands of years ago; unhampered by disgraceful political history; free of foolish customs and conventions which have no significance in themselves, yet which hem in the individual like taut steel bands.[103]

Without this unshackling of human behaviors from irrational—but no less resilient—customs, and without correlatively transferring governmental control from democratic institutions to the oversight of behaviorist scientists themselves, contemporary social environments would continue to produce subjects with erratic behaviors as well as unreliable response mechanisms. No business or governmental agency would ever be able to effectively anticipate or control the actions of such mass populations, because the individuals making up these populations would be too much like Studs Lonigan.

From this point of view, then, English-language book obscenity at this time brought out the degree to which words on a page were potentially reducible to mechanical stimulation and the reader to an unduly responsive automaton. As a result, to insist that readers were not really just creatures of habit and that literature was actually separable from obscenity implied that literary writing was without sensory content, a claim that behaviorists, illiberal judges, and I. A. Richards alike were rather reluctant to grant.[104] In the mid-1920s, Richards conducted a famous experiment with his Cambridge students (mostly undergraduates) in which he asked them to write "protocols" in response to thirteen decontextualized poems. The students knew nothing about each work's author, title, or date of publication beforehand; all they had to go on were the words in the poem itself.

In part, Richards's purpose in undertaking this study was to carry out "a piece of field-work in comparative ideology" that would be of use to those seeking to improve pedagogical methods and to elucidate obstacles to proper literary criticism.[105] Among the obstructions expansively itemized and analyzed in *Practical Criticism* (1929) were the "stock responses" found throughout the written protocols his students produced. Stock responses, according to Richards, "have their opportunity whenever a poem seems to, or does, involve views and emotions already fully prepared in the reader's mind, so that what happens appears to be more of the reader's doing than the poet's. The button is pressed, and then the author's work is done, for immediately the record starts playing in quasi- (or total) independence of the poem which is supposed to be its origin or instrument" (*PC*, 15–16). For example, in one of the protocols responding to the most disliked of the thirteen assigned poems, Henry Wadsworth Longfellow's "In the Churchyard at Cambridge," Richards discovered that a student found "again only stock material and stock treatment." According to this anonymous student, "the poet has attempted to *describe* a quiet contemplative mood. He has not felt it. These are *just a few commonplaces about Death the Leveller* uttered with an ill-feigned naïvete which cannot pass for sincerity. The poem is like the oft-delivered sermon of a preacher who knows what he *ought* to say. Hence all its conventional tricks—'a lady of high degree,' 'vanity and foolish pomp,' 'Christian charity,' 'failings, faults and errors'—he might have added 'trespasses'—and *above all 'the village church-yard,' the conventional setting* for ruminations upon death" (emphasis original). Although the student actually went to the trouble of quoting from the poem, he cited these passages mostly as proof of what he already assumed was the case with the poet and his intentions or state of mind. Like a hypocritical preacher, this shabby poet had merely used ready-made conventions to sham sincerity in the descriptive expression of "*a few commonplaces about Death the Leveller*," leading

Richards to voice "doubt [as to] the closeness of [the student's] reading" insofar as this protocol revealed more about the student's stereotyped expectations than it did about the meanings of the assigned poem (*PC*, 164).

Despite the negative connotations of calling responses such as these "stock," it ought to be kept in mind that Richards did not view such reactions as simply "wrong" or "bad" in and of themselves. For one thing, humans unquestionably require a vast store of stock responses if they are to function effectively in the world. In particular, according to Richards, "unless an awkward misfit is going to occur, we may agree that stock responses are much better than no responses at all. Indeed, an extensive repertory of stock responses is a necessity. Few minds could prosper if they had to work out an original, 'made to measure' response to meet every situation that arose—their supplies of mental energy would be too soon exhausted and the wear and tear on their nervous systems would be too great." The problem for Richards then became that of determining the contexts in which such reactions would be most appropriate and in response to what kinds of stimuli these reactions would tend to be most apt:

> Clearly there is an enormous field of conventional activity over which acquired, stereotyped, habitual responses properly rule, and the only question that needs to be examined as to *these* responses is whether they are the best that practical exigencies—the range of probable situations that may arise, the necessity of quick availability and so forth—will allow. But equally clearly there are in most lives fields of activity in which stock responses, if they intervene, are disadvantageous and even dangerous, because they may get in the way of, and prevent, a response more appropriate to the situation. These unnecessary misfits may be remarked at almost every stage of the reading of poetry, but they are especially noticeable when emotional responses are in question. (*PC*, 241; emphasis original)

Richard therefore contended that stock responses in the reading of good poetry deformed it because such poetry always betrayed itself by forcing readers to dispense with many of their expected emotions or accustomed reading habits: "Nearly all good poetry is disconcerting, for a moment at least, when we first see it for what it is. Some dear habit has to be abandoned if we are to follow it" (*PC*, 254).

Notably, however, *Practical Criticism* indicated that the obstacles and dangers that stock responses presented to literary interpretation were not really marked by class, gender, educational, or political differences. In fact, these stereotyped reactions seemed to be affecting pretty much all of Richards's protocol writers, few of whom liked having their responses labeled "stock" by their teacher and mentor:

53

If we wish for a population easy to control by suggestion we shall decide what repertory of suggestion it shall be susceptible to and encourage this tendency except in the few. But if we wish for a high and diffused civilisation, with its attendant risks, we shall combat this form of mental inertia. In either case, since most of the protocol writers would certainly regard themselves as belonging to the few, rather than the many, were such a division to be proposed, we shall do well to recognise how much of the value of existence is daily thrust from us by our stock responses, necessary though a substratum of stable and routine mental habits may be. (*PC*, 314)

For Richards in *Practical Criticism*, this propensity to respond to a diverse batch of poetic stimuli in a limited number of ways was both an asset to governments, businessmen, and educators wishing to behavioristically standardize the repertoire of mass behaviors and a threat to those who did not want to be so easily susceptible to such suggestive lures. For both the many and the few, however, reading at the time was little more than habituation and predictable reaction, free of conscious reflection and certainly free of the tendency to seek out new and unusual meanings. Remarkably, Richards described this reduction of contemporary reading practices to stimulus-response relationships in terms that anticipate Ann Douglas's assessment of mass culture's effects on Studs Lonigan: "If we consider how responses in general are formed, we shall see that the chief cause of ill-appropriate, stereotyped reactions is *withdrawal from experience*" (*PC*, 246; emphasis original).

Nevertheless, the manifest shortcomings of the interpretations offered by Watson, Richards, and illiberal judges alike principally involve their certainty that particular stimuli reliably elicit equivalent responses. All three tended to be unduly deterministic in their outlooks on the capacity of the sensory content of words to have directly observable effects in the world. If deproscribing judges like Woolsey and Augustus Hand could be taken to task for assuming that literary texts necessarily called forth literary reading methods, then so could the Massachusetts Supreme Judicial Court for insisting upon the obscene efficacy of obscene texts or obscene parts of obscene texts on an imagined obscene reader. Similarly, U.S. literary naturalism was itself no less an object of scorn for early twentieth-century literary critics who, like so many stock responsive automatons themselves, found themselves censuring naturalist fiction for its overly mechanistic representations of the world and the incapacity of its characters to exert any meaningful agency.

However, at least one cogent way out of the apparent determinist impasses of naturalist (and, I submit, obscene) writing and reading has recently been put forward by Jennifer Fleissner. In *Women, Compulsion, Modernity* (2004), she contends that all of the critical attention devoted to parsing the determinist philosophies in literary naturalism over the past century has covered up the remarkable degree to which U.S. naturalist fiction at this time approached the relationship between human beings and the forces that shape them in a much more open-ended way. In particular, Fleissner argues that nineteenth-century and early twentieth-century conceptualizations of compulsion better account for how nature and society affect characters and their intentionalities in naturalist texts. Compulsion, for Fleissner, "has the potential to name an understanding of agency in which individual will and its subjection to rationalizing 'forces' appear as more deeply intertwined. More specifically, to the extent that nature appears not as the presocial wilderness in these texts but as an important feature *within* human social life, various everyday rituals taking place around the fact of embodiment (sex, birth, death, illness, cleanliness, etc.) take on new interest, to these novelists just as to the era's anthropologists, psychologists, historians, and sociologists."[106] Far from gloomily depicting the implacable dominion of heteronomous forces over subjects without agency, naturalist texts instead continue to present their readers with a more nuanced—if no less totalizing—vision in which nature, society, and individual agency all mutually constitute each other through the habitual forms that embodiment happens to take. Furthermore, the compulsive features of these habit formations foreground nonlinear, repetitive narratives as opposed to the shapely arcs of triumph or decline so commonly ascribed to naturalist novels, suggesting that these novels never really end so much as defer the possibility of closure as such. In effect, Fleissner has attempted to open the black box around the mind that Watson said could not be opened and to elaborate the various ways in which cognition somehow manages to get embodied in naturalist fiction, despite the failure of its deterministic cover stories to be totally in control. In this view, U.S. literary naturalism's representational breakdowns—and not its intended, predetermined outcomes—end up telling us a great deal about what it actually could (and does) achieve.

Such failure happens to be a hallmark not only of naturalist fiction but also of legal obscenity itself at this time. The difference, of course, is that whereas the study of U.S. naturalist fiction has been revitalized by this shift in emphasis away from determinism and toward compulsion, the collapse of determinist ways of describing obscenity between the 1930s and the 1950s altogether undermined the legitimacy of book obscenity in the opinions of many liberalizing judges. For instance, in *Commonwealth v. Gordon et al.*, which refused to deem *Studs Lonigan, God's Little Acre, Sanctuary, Wild Palms*, and three other novels obscene, Judge Curtis Bok insisted that legally obscene books could only be proscribed if they posed a clear and present danger to the community. While readily conceding that public lewdness and seditious speech presented just such a danger, he went on to express his misgivings about lumping books in with these more obvious threats. According to Bok's opinion, mere words on a page no longer seemed to have as much affective force as did a treasonous public address or the genitalia of a man exposing himself to passing women and children on a city street. The problem with allegedly obscene books was that they did not reliably elicit an observable reaction—good or bad—from their readers.

In short, obscene books were simply not obscene enough to meet Bok's pseudo-behaviorist criteria, insofar as they so often failed to "get off the page" and into the "real" world in any sort of clear-cut way. The lack of an immediate deterministic relationship between an erotic stimulus in an obscene book and a lewd response in its obscene reader thereby called into question whether obscenity itself ought to exist any longer as a criminal offense. According to Bok, hereafter a book could only be credibly charged with obscenity "where there is a reasonable and demonstrable cause to believe that a crime or misdemeanor has been committed or is about to be committed as the perceptible result of the publication and distribution of the writing in question: the opinion of anyone that a tendency thereto exists or that such a result is self-evident is insufficient and irrelevant. The causal connection between the book and the criminal behavior must appear beyond a reasonable doubt."[107] As Bok made clear earlier in his opinion, however, such a causal connection with respect to book obscenity "does not bear analysis."[108]

Bok's doubts regarding literary obscenity later informed the reasoning of many lower court judges who were themselves ever more skeptical about the legitimacy of proscribing books. For instance, in *Bantam Books, Inc. v. Melko* (1953), New Jersey Superior Court Judge Sidney Goldmann held that the prosecution of Vivian Connell's *The Chinese Room* (1942) "violated the constitutional guarantee of freedom of the press," but not before he discussed at great length the troubles he was experiencing with legally defining obscenity in the first place:[109]

> The problem is to discover, if possible, what "obscene" means. It has been suggested that the word comes from *ob* and *scena*—done off the scene or off-stage, and hence furtively. *Webster's New International Dictionary* (2d ed. 1943) gives the derivation as *obs* (*ob*) and *caenum*, filth, and then goes on to define "obscene" as:
>
> "Offensive to chastity of mind or to modesty; expressing or presenting to the mind or view something that delicacy, purity and decency forbid to be exposed; lewd; indecent["]; 2 *Bouvier's Law Dictionary*, *Rawle's Third Revision*, *page* 2396 (*8th ed.* 1914) gives the definition:
>
> "Something which is offensive to chastity; something that is foul and filthy, and for that reason is offensive to a pure-minded person. That which is offensive to chastity and modesty." These and similar reference works provide no objective standard or formula for determining when obscenity exists. The definitions all lead to the dead-end of a subjective determination. To paraphrase

Samuel Johnson, the yea or nay saying of the censor becomes the standard of the permissible.[110]

Not objectively determined processes, but subjective determinations arbitrarily arrived at were all that legal concepts of obscenity had produced over the past fifty years in the opinion of this New Jersey Superior Court judge, who went on to express doubts as to the exigency of proscribing obscene books at all anymore.

Twenty-five years earlier, Morris L. Ernst (the lawyer who defended Random House in the *Ulysses* cases of the early 1930s) and William Seagle famously began *To the Pure . . . : A Study of Obscenity and the Censor* (1928) with an equivalent claim, from which they ended up drawing very different conclusions:

> But few words are as fluid and vague in content as the six deadly adjectives—
> *obscene, lewd, lascivious, filthy, indecent* and *disgusting*—which are the basis of
> [obscenity] censorship. No two persons agree on these definitions. We shall
> see that judges differ to such an extent that courts divide by narrow margins,
> thus justifying the ironic complaint of infallible government by the odd man.
> Juries disagree with judges and the cynicisms and enthusiasms of lawyers bear
> a relation to the size of the retaining fees. Authors have to adapt their ideas to
> an unknown measure and jails invite those who cannot guess the contemporary
> meaning of obscenity.[111]

"The final refutation of criminal obscenity laws," Ernst and Seagle went on to claim in the book's concluding pages,

> lies in their futility. Even if a legal sage arose to define with precision the words
> "lewd," "lascivious," "filthy," "indecent," "disgusting," and "obscene," the ulti-
> mate logic of life would remain. Life itself has deep tendencies both toward
> elevation and corruption. None can escape such forces from the cradle to the
> grave. Even if sexual excitement were proved to be a fatally vicious influence
> we could scarcely hope to eradicate it by law or to establish ideals of asceti-
> cism by the suppression of every art. Although the censors are often accused
> of underestimating æsthetic values and the potency of the arts, their actions
> belie their words. Each assault on the printed word is a confession of a greater
> potency in art than in life.[112]

For Seagle and Ernst, all the proscriptive legal attention that writing had been receiving in the United States in the 1920s sufficed to indicate the power of artfully arranged words on a page to act on and through a world that was no longer as life-like as art itself. The tautological acrobatics of obscenity-defining judges were thus a distraction from the more consequential social dimensions indicated by the recent explosion in obscenity cases involving writing, which entailed that books—and the arts more generally—were so vital a force that they ought to be moved beyond the law's purview. In other words, the fact that there was so much criminal litigation being brought against obscene books only confirmed Ernst and Seagle in their certainty that art and aesthetics could no longer be underestimated by censors, judges, and legislators alike. Obscenity was, in their words, an "index" of writing's capacity to still shake up a politically free, intellectually open, and progressively secular society.[113]

As we have been able to see in the opinions of Bok and Goldmann, however, this hyperbolic investment in the vitalistic "potency" of books hardly carried over into subsequent U.S. case law. The difficulties encountered more and more by judges in merely defining obscenity gave rise not to mute awe in the face of writing's affective powers but rather to grave doubts about writing's capacity to do anything much of notice in the world anymore. To rephrase Ernst and Seagle, then, the final refutation of criminal book obscenity ended up having to do more with the futility of believing that obscene books could actually still instigate obscene actions than it did with the difficulty of legislators and judges in accounting for the experience of obscenity itself. After all, the U.S. Supreme Court's definition of obscenity in *Miller* persists to this day, while the prosecution of obscene books effectively does not. The eventual granting of institutionally recognized autonomy to creative writing in obscenity case law hence came about through the conspicuous *under*estimation of the effective force of the printed word, which was increasingly neutralized by the opinions of deproscribing judges and the arguments of liberalizing jurists in the decades following Woolsey's ruling in the *Ulysses* case. No buttons are pressed when twenty-first-century Studs Lonigans read today, because it is not all that clear that twenty-first-century Studs Lonigans read books to get themselves off anymore, nor is it likely that any novel, even a thoroughly depraving one, would catch their eye in the first place.

2. How to Misbehave as a Behaviorist (if You're Wyndham Lewis)

Accepted as a sort of disciple of Watson, I attracted to myself a modicum
of limelight. I had a measure of success. "How Science can be almost more
entertaining than Fiction"—you know the sort of idea. "People Behaving"
the first of these two books was called. This gave the critic of the silly
season (it is always the silly season in the "Book Pages") his opportunity, as
indeed I had calculated it would. "People Misbehaving" the cheerful ruffian
called it, with great satisfaction. This did a lot of good.

—WYNDHAM LEWIS, *SNOOTY BARONET*, 1932

With all this war stuff abaht it might do no harm to indicate that you did
in 1916 or 17 (Cantleman) what the lot of em are now cashing in on. Can't
remember whether Cantleman was suppressed or not?????? However things
have moved since.

—EZRA POUND, LETTER TO WYNDHAM LEWIS, 1930

As a matter of fact, Cantleman was suppressed, though Pound can be forgiven this lapse in memory because an awful lot was happening during the final year and a half of World War I. Leaving Harriet Monroe's *Poetry* (1912–present) in a huff, he had recently taken up foreign editorship duties for *The Little Review (1914–1929)*. Wyndham Lewis—whose work, along with that of T. S. Eliot and James Joyce, was to be Pound's most substantial contribution as editor for this quintessential modernist little magazine—had finally been deployed to the front around the beginning of June 1917 as an officer in the 224 Siege Battery of the Royal Garrison Artillery. And, around the time that the Bolsheviks were storming the Winter Palace in Saint Petersburg, *The Little Review* was being denied use of the mails by the U.S. Post Office and the United States District Court for the Southern District of New York.

Anticipating the almost mythically outsized ordeals undergone by the journal in its serialization of James Joyce's *Ulysses*, the November 1917 obscenity trial concerning the publication of Wyndham Lewis's wartime short story, "Cantleman's Spring-Mate," seemed at first glance to confirm that *The Little Review* was finally pursuing in earnest its no-quarter-given covenant between its readers and itself: "No Compromise with the Public Taste." Foreshadowing what would later happen to Joyce's text three times leading up to the "Nausikaa" trial, the District Court denied Margaret Anderson's motion to restrain the postmaster of New York. According to Judge Augustus Hand, Lewis's story addressed itself to readers' bodies in ways that could not be contained through contemplation: "The young girl and the relations of the man with her are described with a degree of detail that does not appear necessary to teach the desired lesson, whatever it may be, or to tell a story which would possess artistic merit or arouse any worthy emotion."[1] What brought Hand up short were the excessive qualities of Lewis's text. In its overmastering attention to salacious details and the striking development of those details into protracted descriptive passages, the story seemed committed to undermining the very sorts of moral and aesthetic designs to which it might otherwise lay claim. Hand thereby affirmed the postmaster's administrative judgment that "Cantleman's Spring-Mate" was in fact "obscene, lewd, or lascivious" under the terms marked out by Section 211 of the U.S. Criminal Code and therefore could not be mailed to *The Little Review*'s subscribers.[2]

"Cantleman's Spring-Mate" remains one of the minor side attractions of modernist obscenity, seldom discussed in terms other than those that would present it as a negligible dress rehearsal for the later, more consequential trials of *Ulysses*.[3] By contrast, this chapter contends that there is more to Lewis and obscenity than Leopold Bloom, Gerty MacDowell, and the Litany of Loreto. Comparing representations of animality in Lewis's story to the early popular comparative psychology essays of John B. Watson (the "father" of behaviorism), it demonstrates that "Cantleman's Spring-Mate" not only expresses behaviorist assumptions regarding obscenity considered as a reading practice but also anticipates Lewis's subsequent critical and satirical engagements with behaviorism in the 1920s and 1930s. At least since 1954, when Hugh Kenner noted the "latent contradiction" between the attacks on behaviorism in Lewis's criticism and the behaviorist premises nevertheless at work in much of Lewis's fiction, the study of this obstinate modernist's relationship to behaviorism has proven quite generative.[4] Even when they write against him, however, most critics since Kenner have tended to follow his lead and take as their focus Lewis's behaviorist novel, *Snooty Baronet* (1932).[5] Here I argue that the continuity of behaviorist preoccupations in Lewis's fiction extends much farther back than has often been assumed and that such preoccupations get expressed in his writing through the complementary experiences of animality and obscenity.

Equally important, however, "Cantleman's Spring-Mate" provided the first occasion for a United States judge to assess a modernist piece of writing in terms of legal obscenity, and as such it offers us a useful opportunity for reflecting on the horizon of legibility of modernism for its contemporaries. As this chapter demonstrates, it was clear to Judge Hand that something new and untoward was happening in Lewis's short story, but in 1917 there did not appear to be enough principled aesthetic or literary grounds on which to exempt "Cantleman's Spring-Mate" from proscription for obscenity, at least no grounds of the sort that protected the "classics" of literature at that time. Such grounds would not be forthcoming until the innovations of modernism became more intelligible to writers, readers, lawyers, and judges alike by the early 1930s, which makes Hand's interpretation of Lewis's story all the more valuable as a description of modernist writing at a historical moment in which modernism as such was far from appearing credibly artistic or literary to judges.

I

Lewis drafted "Cantleman's Spring-Mate" during the long period of waiting for his belated deployment to the front around the beginning of June 1917 as an officer in the Royal Artillery. Fittingly enough, the story focuses on waiting to go to war rather than on war itself. In fact, violent scenes of battle only intrude in the final two sentences, when the contemptuous Cantleman compares the "impartial malignity" with which he beats a Hun's brains out to the predatory sexual use he makes of his spring-mate, Stella, earlier in the narrative.[6] In fact, Stella—and *not* the brutally beaten German—comprises Cantleman's principal antagonist and scapegoat throughout the story, and in many respects Lewis's short story functions to provide a naturalistic alibi for Cantleman's impartially malign treatment of her.

The story opens with Cantleman overwhelmed by the literally steaming sexual energy given off by the animal life in the fields through which he is walking on his way back to camp. Horses are appetizingly appraising the "masses of quivering shiny flesh" of the mares surrounding them ("CS-M," 8). Female birds, though critical of the peeps and chocks making up the love songs of their partners, nevertheless admit that each of their male counterparts does indeed represent "a fluffy object from which certain satisfaction could be derived" (8). Even swine are getting in on the act:

> The sow, as she watched her hog, with his splenetic energy, and guttural articulation, a sound between content and complaint, not noticing the untidy habits of both of them, gave a sharp grunt of sex-hunger, and jerked rapidly towards him. The only jarring note in this vast mutual admiration society was the fact that many of its members showed their fondness for their neighbor in an embarrassing way: that is they killed and ate them. But the weaker were so used to dying violent deaths and being eaten that they worried very little about it.=The West was gushing up a harmless volcano of fire, obviously intended as an immense dreamy nightcap. ("CS-M," 8)

Perhaps even more so than the embarrassing expression of "this vast mutual admiration society" in terms of homicidal and carnivorous violence, the last sentence sounds the passage's jarring note, for it disrupts the salacious wildlife observations of the opening paragraph to resituate its enduring seasonal themes within a more urgent human framework. In noting Cantleman's receptiveness to the fecundating activities of the animals around him, the end of the first paragraph reveals his ambivalence toward the war in which he is about to fight, insofar as death, or rather "the prospect of death" in battle, does indeed provide the "philosophic background" for his opening "cogitation on surrounding life" ("CS-M," 8–9). Although he very well may die in action at the front, Cantleman insists that he is not naïve enough to believe that his death will thereby achieve anything like lasting significance. Far from representing an event of any historical consequence whatsoever, World War I is for Cantleman simply "a harmless volcano of fire" or "an immense dreamy nightcap" when compared to the timeless fucking, fighting, and feasting under way in the pressure-cooked fields he attentively traverses.

In short, the free indirect discourse of the opening of "Cantleman's Spring-Mate" appears to subjugate the putative nonevent of World War I and its prospects of violent death to a vaguely registered but nevertheless overmastering law of nature. Another way of putting this would be to say that the hyperbolically aroused natural life seen in "the strenuous fields" surrounding Cantleman only superficially appears to be so many anthropomorphized projections of that soldier's own spring-ignited lust ("CS-M," 8). The matter of who projects what onto whom, however, becomes a good deal more vexed as the opening paragraph unfolds. Fredric Jameson has usefully categorized the growing confusion of what constitutes cause or agency in this story as a peculiar instance of hypallage, according to which owner and property relations get scrambled by the syntactical reorientation of the adjective.[7] For Jameson, hypallage is not so much a rhetorical device in "Cantleman's Spring-Mate" as it is a stylistic modus operandi that can be found throughout Lewis's fiction: "Lewis' hypallage, where the attributes of actor or act are transferred onto the dead scenery, generates a kind of contamination of the axis of contiguity, offering a glimpse of a world in which the old-fashioned substances, like marbles in a box, have been rattled so furiously together that their 'properties' come loose and stick to the wrong places—a very delirium of metonymy of which, as we shall see, Lewis' subsequent writings provide some stunning examples."[8] If, as Jameson argues, the adjective "strenuous" seems at first glance to mismodify the noun "fields" (for surely it is the walking of Cantleman that is strenuous here), then as the paragraph develops it becomes clearer and clearer that "strenuous" is the right word after all to describe the quasi-mechanistic couplings and steamy physical exertions that in fact constitute the fields. In other words, Lewis rattles his box of marbles not to achieve new figures thereby but rather to reorder both reality itself and one's relationship to it.[9] Therefore, a preexisting affective ferment within Cantleman does not motivate his engrossed interest in the animal orgy occurring around him; his figmentary "instincts" cannot be said to have been projected onto the field. Rather, the horses, the mares, the birds, the hogs, and the sows all rub their animal instinctual responses off on Cantleman, meaning his heightened libidinal state is no innately prescripted reaction to the green fuse of spring. The story's founding move, then, is to counter Romanticism's pathetic fallacy with a rigorously pursued *anti*pathetic fallacy.[10]

As it turns out, the paradoxical and estranging goal of Cantleman's "cogitation on surrounding life" is to become something less than kin or kind to the human as such: "On the other hand, Cantleman had a little more human, as well as a little more divine, than those usually on his left and right, and he had had, not so long ago, conspicuous hopes that such a conjuncture might produce a new human chemistry. But he must repudiate the human entirely, if that were to be brought off. His present occupation, the trampling boots upon his feet, the belt that crossed his back and breast, was his sacrifice, his compliment to, [sic] the animal" ("CS-M," 10). World War I names the occasion not for a Zarathustrian flight into the wilderness but rather for a sacrifice of humanity's "meagre stream of sublimity" to the animal by hazarding one's very life (9). Nevertheless, if Cantleman has apparently developed beyond a passing youthful fancy for pseudo-Nietzschean theatrics, his disillusioned maturation still seems to have produced little more than an inverted fantasy image of Nietzsche's most enduring popular myth, for his hopes here for "a new human chemistry" are frankly more underdog than Übermensch. It must also be kept in mind, however, that Cantleman's is not a complete sacrifice, for what is said to differentiate his animalistic acceptance of a world order governed by some sort of law of nature from the assent given by swine, birds, and horses is the fact that his is consciously granted and pursued, even though consciousness is said to be the very thing that makes being human so disgusting to Cantleman: "The newspapers were the things that stank most on earth, and human beings anywhere were the most ugly and offensive of the brutes because of the confusion caused by their consciousness" ("CS-M," 9). The problem of his own consciousness notwithstanding, Cantleman's gambit remains that of stampeding recklessly and hilariously through the war *as if* he were nothing more than an animal used to dying a violent death, *as if* his consciousness did not stink like that of any other human being.

Far from being "an immense dreamy nightcap," World War I offers instead an absolute set of proving grounds for Cantleman's drastic reorganization of life, for which Stella provides something of a war game. In this case, the carnal pleasures of coupling pursued as an end in itself are Cantleman's implicit sacrifice to the animal. Moreover, he plays the part of the soldier-suitor for Stella because that is the sort of role to which she seems most susceptible. In fact, she presumably takes on the corresponding part of a game rustic mate with some alacrity: "The young woman had, *or had given herself,* the unlikely name of Stella" ("CS-M," 12; emphasis added). Though the role-playing dimensions of their spring encounters are perhaps not lost on either of them, Stella and Cantleman still materially differ in the expectations they bring to their respective parts. While her response to Cantleman's cynical gift of a ring is somewhat equivocal—"Her melting gratitude was immediately ligotted with long arms, full of the contradictory and offending fire of the spring" ("CS-M," 13)—Stella at the very least does seem to expect Cantleman to share responsibility for their child when she later begins inundating him with letters at the front regarding her pregnancy: "They came to Cantleman with great regularity in the trenches; he read them all through from beginning to end, without comment of any sort" ("CS-M," 14). Cantleman's response is effectively a nonresponse because all that Stella is to him is someone who once represented the most proximate means of partaking in the transferable libidinal intensities suggested to him earlier by the spring pursuits of the swine, birds, and horses:

> In the narrow road where they got away from the village, Cantleman put his arm around Stella's waist and immediately experienced all the sensations that he had been divining in the creatures around him; the horse, the bird and the pig. The way in which Stella's hips stood out, the solid blood-heated expanse on which his hand lay, had the amplitude and flatness of a mare. Her lips had at once no practical significance, but only the aesthetic blandishment of a bull-like flower. With the gesture of a fabulous Faust he drew her against him, and kissed her with a crafty gentleness. ("CS-M," 12)

Presenting himself to his spring-mate as if he were merely a diabolic lover cut to a ready-made pattern, Cantleman presses Stella's body to his own and feels beneath her dress not the ruse of human flesh but rather "the amplitude and flatness of a mare" as the porously contiguous world produced by the narrative achieves a delirious climax here: the rustic fields are indeed strenuous, Stella is in fact little more than a palpably blood-warmed collage of horse-bird-swine, and Cantleman's spring pursuits turn out at last to encompass so many thinly veiled acts of bestiality.

II

As drastic as this vision of the Übermensch in rout, beating a conscious retreat into the nearby sow in heat, may at first appear to be, it was no mere idiosyncrasy of Lewis's soldier. Compare, for instance, Cantleman's cogitations in an English field in the spring of 1917 with the following remarks made by a Johns Hopkins experimental and comparative psychologist in a winter 1910 issue of *Harper's Monthly*:

> The point that I would make in all this is that there is no royal road to habit and knowledge. Man gets his first steps in exactly the same way as does the animal. Studies in animal behavior, while not fulfilling the hopes of the early students of evolution in showing that animals have exalted types of intellect, nevertheless are forcing us to reconsider our extravagant notions of the all-sufficiency of the human mind. Continuity between the mind of man and brute, the idea of the early students, will still be shown to exist, not by exalting the mind of the brute, but rather by the reverse process of showing the defects in the human mind.[11]

Though he was three years away from drafting what would become *the* behaviorist manifesto ("Psychology as the Behaviorist Views It"), John B. Watson can already be found here attempting to cut the Gordian knot formed by dualist conceptions of a mind independent of a body along with the mentalist assumptions of interiority as such. In particular, Watson undercuts those of his peers who were cussedly holding on to a more anthropocentric worldview by demonstrating that the experimental study and observation of behavior, whether human or animal, was the only way to make psychology a natural science. A debasing material contiguity between the human and the animal was to be the new order of the day:

> How do we make a laboratory study of the mind of an animal? It is not possible to get into its mind and see for ourselves the drama of mental events which is taking place there, consequently how is it ever possible to get any clear insight into the workings of its mind? At first sight we seem to have here an insuperable obstacle to the study. A little reflection, however, will show that we are forever

65

debarred from studying the mind of our human neighbor in this direct way; yet surely no one in this day would be hardy enough to deny that we can and do get a very definite and scientific notion of the way our neighbor's mind works.[12]

This further exemplifies the bottom-up nature of Watson's radical reformulation of psychology in the early decades of the last century, insofar as the impossibility of studying states of animal consciousness entails not the discarding of animal psychology as a science but rather the overturning of human psychology as it had been hitherto investigated. In other words, states of consciousness were no longer the privileged objects of psychological study, because the laboratory study of animals had at last revealed consciousness itself to be the real obstacle in the way of contemporary psychological studies of human subjects. According to Watson, psychology thus had to sacrifice consciousness to see at last what ultimately binds us to animals: observable behavior. Much like Cantleman, Watson's article contemplates a momentous transvaluation of values by making the animal the measure of man rather than the obverse.[13]

Lewis's culture critiques in the 1920s and 1930s consistently anathematized behaviorism as an especially insidious factor in the mechanization of daily modern life. Yet the relationship of his fiction to contemporary versions of behaviorism is a good deal more complex than these later critical writings would seem to suggest on their face. While it would no doubt be spurious to take behaviorism, in a sort of historicist coup de main, as the "origin" of Cantleman or the "key" to his actions, I nevertheless do submit that early, exploratory formulations of behaviorism provide important contexts for assessing the obscene potentials of Lewis's narrative, particularly how he inhabits a quasi-behaviorist point of view from within by way of free indirect discourse.

This appears illogical at first sight, for interiority was precisely the sort of thing behaviorism was understood to be in the process of extirpating altogether, in psychology as in life. It was in this connection, after all, that Watson tirelessly sought to undermine the reliability and utility of the types of introspective reports influentially described and modeled by William James in *The Principles of Psychology* (1890).[14] On the one hand, Watson argued, there is no way of eliciting introspective responses from pigeons or rats experimentally. On the other hand, at a methodological level, introspection necessarily fails to achieve intersubjective agreement among scientists because of its necessary lack of objectivity. On this count, Watson reminded his peers that they need only refer to the state of psychological research on emotions at that time to see that no meaningful consensus was then possible, because the terms in which psychologists had introspectively formulated the field were arbitrary and incommensurate: whereas James divided emotions into the coarse (e.g., grief, fear, love, rage) and the subtle (e.g., the moral, the intellectual, and the aesthetic), William McDougall had taken to pairing every primary emotion with an instinct (e.g., fear was to be coupled with the instinct for flight, anger with that for pugnacity, subjection with that for self-abasement), and neither approach could be used to disprove or modify the other, because no common objective method guided either psychologist in putting together his respective schema.[15] Were this mentalist line of inquiry to be pursued for much longer, there would eventuate as many theoretical accounts of emotion as there were psychology departments. According to Watson, experimental observations of behavior would be able to fare better because such observations are refutable and accordingly subject to the sorts of comparisons and verifications that make possible the objective grounding of psychology as a natural science.[16] In thus placing the human and the animal on the shared plane of observable behavior, Watson strategically reduced the psychologist's world to one consisting entirely of observable physiological processes. That is to say, it was to be a world of surfaces behaving.

Considered simply as a methodology, then, behaviorism seems the ideal shell for Lewis's brand of literary modernism. For one thing, his culture critiques tend to appear almost surgical in their treatment of impressionistic renderings of interiorities and popular experiences, both of which Lewis operates on as if they were cancerous cysts. Perhaps the most productive structuring enmity in *The Art of Being Ruled* (1926), after all, is that of inside and outside, with Lewis relegating to the inside almost everything that he regards as an unnecessary impediment to the imminent restructuration of the world on socialist grounds, which he welcomes with more equanimity here than he was ever able to muster again for such projects. For instance, the putative impersonality of science, Bergsonian vitalism, psychoanalysis, Gertrude Stein, Henri Matisse, and "the Small Man" (or entrepreneur) of capitalist competition are all shown by Lewis to prey upon and live irrationally within "the smoking-hot *inside* of things, in contrast to the hard, cold, formal skull or carapace."[17] Each of these diverse phenomena and figures comprises a forfeiting of "objective qualities" for "more mixed and obscure issues."[18] For Lewis, this forfeiture betokens not only the confusions that follow upon the privileging of emotions but also the annihilation of intellectual activity altogether: "All the meaning of life is of a superficial sort, of course: there is no meaning except on the surface. It is physiologically the latest, the ectodermic, and most *exterior* material of our body that is responsible for our intellectual life: it is on a faculty for exteriorization that our life depends."[19] Intellect, in this view, represents the pyrrhic maintenance of minimal distinctions in our lives, for to linger upon the ectodermic is to maintain one's capacity to separate inside from outside along with subject from object. The chitinous skin-shell, in turn, functions as a shield against the outer object-world (a world increasingly difficult to differentiate from its passive consuming subjects) *and* against the affective threats posed by the intestines, by the interior and its leveling peristaltic mechanisms: "Love, as we discursively understand it, can only exist on the surface. An inch beneath, and it is no longer love, but the abstract rage of hunger and reproduction of which the swallowing of an oyster, or the swallowing of the male by the female epira, is an illustration. And it is the existence of the artist that maintains this superficiality, differentiation of existence, for us: our personal, our detached life, in short, in distinction to our crowd-life."[20] The artist in this scheme acts to foreclose mechanisms and techniques of social identification (e.g., ritualized or mimetic forms of association, role-playing), which Lewis graphically conveys throughout *The Art of Being Ruled* by images of autopsied bodies (because on the inside we are all one big gut-cramped mass of viscera and torpidly secreting glands indistinguishable from each other). Against this broad cultural and sociopolitical drift in postwar life in the West toward the corruption of subject-object relations, Lewis's antagonizing artist offers us the possibility of a world of calcified and non-interpenetrating forms. The artist's civic function, therefore, is to hold out the mere prospect of difference, or, more provocatively still, the possibility that to love and to eat are not commutative activities, despite what Cantleman's cogitations reveal to him in the spring of 1917 ("many of [the animals in the field] showed their fondness for their neighbor in an embarrassing way: that is they killed and ate them").[21]

66

Moreover, the baleful gaze of the detached, quasi-behaviorist observer endlessly preoccupied with the surface life of things constitutes perhaps *the* formative compositional perspective adopted in Lewis's satirical fiction. In fact, in the course of defending his idiosyncratic concept of nonethical satire in *Men without Art* (1934), Lewis explicitly counterposes introspective techniques to more shapely, exteroceptive forms: "To let the readers 'into the minds of the characters,' to 'see the play of their thoughts'—that is precisely the method least suited to satire. That it must deal with the *outside*, that is one of the capital advantages of this form of literary art—for those who like a resistant and finely-sculptured surface, or sheer words."[22] What disqualifies stream of consciousness or interior monologue from possessing more deliberately secondhand, ironic use in Lewis's satire is the fact that such devices tend to take subjectivity for granted, whereas *Men without Art* would insist not only that subjectivity as such has undergone a dangerous slackening in the early decades of the twentieth century but also that this reduced or dissolved subjectivity may now be said to constitute satire's chief subject matter:[23] "For what else is a character in satire but that? Is it not just because they are such *machines, governed by routine*—or creatures that stagnate, as it were 'in a leaden cistern'—that the satirist, in the first instance, has considered them suitable for satire?"[24]

If the generalized condition of man as a mimetically governed machine provides satire with its stock situation, then according to Lewis one of satire's main functions is to break up the devious standardizing forces in contemporary life by exaggerating them to the point of riant agitation:

But "men" are undoubtedly, to a greater or less extent, machines. And there are those among us who are revolted by this reflection, and there are those who are not. Men are sometimes so palpably machines, their machination is so transparent, that they are *comic*, as we say. And all we mean by that, is that our consciousness is pitched up to the very moderate altitude of relative independence at which we live—at which level we have the illusion of being autonomous and "free." But if one of us exposes too much his "works," and we start seeing him as a *thing*, then—in subconsciously referring back to ourselves—we are astonished and shocked, and we bark at him—we *laugh*—in order to relieve our emotion.[25]

The agency, autonomy, and freedom we so casually ascribe to ourselves and our respective consciousnesses in daily life are wholly illusory. The truth of this observation, Lewis argues, frequently enough gets confirmed by our fellow humans, who cannot help but fail to keep up the elevating pretenses of their own unique beings because they recurrently and inadvertently expose how thoroughly routinized their every move is. They cannot help but reveal their ludicrous susceptibility to various mimetic modes of social identification, their "works" as it were. By focusing almost exclusively on the superficiality of people and their machinic actions, by treating them as so many things, the satirist can thereby offer to his readers the only real measure of agency, autonomy, and freedom left to any of us, for it is our alleviating barks of laughter that both confirm our thingness *and* our vestigial sense of self: "And yet [our deepest laughter] is non-personal and non-moral. And it enters fields which are commonly regarded as the preserve of more 'serious' forms of reaction. There is no reason at all why we should not burst out laughing at a foetus, for instance. We should after all only be laughing *at ourselves*!—at ourselves early in our mortal career."[26]

Lewis's satire thus presents us with a kind of performative contradiction familiar to readers of literary naturalism, in which depictions of closed worlds often have a tendency to call forth antithetical responses. As I discussed in the previous chapter, the determinist networks unveiled in literary naturalist texts only appear to bar the possibility of human agency and social reform so long as one treats these texts as autonomous artifacts. Yet in principled theoretical expressions of literary naturalism, the seemingly ruthless representation of coercive social powers is often the vehicle by which these same works communicate their vested interest in intervening, through scientific and political means, into the administration of societies, bodies, and time. In addition, the apparent closures effected in works as seemingly diverse as Zola's *Les Rougon-Macquart* (1871–93), Giovanni Verga's *I Malavoglia* (1881), and Norris's *Vandover and the Brute* prove to be provisional, insofar as the reader's affective response must always be reckoned into the evaluations summoned forth by a naturalist work. Thus, the violent morcellation of satiric laughter is said by Lewis to act as a paradoxical preservative (or as an "anti-toxin of the first order") ensuring that a person yelping in hilarity is not yet completely machine-like, that he is not entirely subject to the osmotic forces of social identification that rule all.[27] As Tyrus Miller has succinctly put it, for Lewis satirical laughter represents a timely and potent rephrasing of the Cartesian thesis: "I laugh, therefore I (still) am."[28]

Satire in Lewis's work is accordingly the form that behaving surfaces take when amplified to an unqualified degree, indicating that the worlds such satire presumes are those of an infernal behaviorist utopia. Watson himself began offering a schematic Pisgah sight of such a utopia (minus the diabolism, of course) as early as 1913: "In a system of psychology completely worked out, given the response the stimuli can be predicted; given the stimuli the response can be predicted. Such a set of statements is crass and raw in the extreme, as all such generalizations must be. Yet they are hardly more raw and less realizable than the ones which appear in the psychology texts of the day."[29] For Watson, the twin goals of behaviorism were nothing less than the prediction and control of behavior.[30] Above all else, therefore, his formulations of behaviorism sought to reconstitute determinism solely as a problem of pedagogy and social management. Heredity and our genetic stock may contribute greatly to our variable ability to learn, function, or respond, but in his writings Watson was adamant in subordinating such matters to the more significant features of our environment, howsoever "natural" or constructed that environment may have happened to be: "Much of our structure laid down in heredity would never come to light, would never show in function, unless the organism were put in a certain environment, subjected to certain stimuli and forced to undergo training. Our hereditary structure lies ready to be shaped in a thousand different ways—the same structure—depending on the way in which the child is brought up."[31]

In this regard, Watson's emphasis on the importance of animal psychology for human educational development in the 1910 essay in *Harper's* becomes perhaps even more significant: "Educational systems dealing with that most precious article, the human child, are necessarily conservative, and are slow to introduce changes and to have resort to experiment. Fortunately, there is no such sentiment in regard to the courses of study prescribed for animals. We may vary the course of training *ad libitum*."[32] According to the behaviorist study of habit formation and learning under Watson, a rat potentially has more to tell us about the upbringing and educational organization of a human child than the child itself does.

Watson's behaviorist ideal ("given the response the stimuli can be predicted; given the stimuli the response can be predicted") thus affirms the technocratic aims underlying his reconstitution of psychology on behaviorist grounds, for to see and describe complex organic matter simply as a function of stimuli and responses is to become restless ultimately with mere describing and seeing. Behaviorism's real value could only be realized by treating it as an *applied* science because the behaviorist "wants to control man's reactions as physical scientists want to control and manipulate other natural phenomena."[33] One way of effecting this control in early behaviorist terms was both to study extensively and thereafter to shape the (male) role-playing of which everyday life seems to consist: "In general, we are what the situation calls for—a respectable person before our preacher and our parents, a hero in front of the ladies, a teetotaler in one group, a bibulous good fellow in another."[34] According to Watson, behaviorism presents us with the latest way of making men be what the situation called for, and it was to be behaviorists who could best guide their making and decide upon the situations calling forth the desired behaviors from the subjects thereby fabricated. As he asserts at the end of *Behaviorism* (1924; revised 1930): "For the universe will change if you bring up your children, not in the freedom of the libertine, but in behavioristic freedom—a freedom which we cannot even picture in words, so little do we know of it. Will not these children in turn, with their better ways of living and thinking, replace us as society and in turn bring up their children in a still more scientific way, until the world finally becomes a place fit for human habitation?"[35]

Watson's behaviorism thus holds out the promise of making life and its social organization not just better over time, but so much better that our current world will eventually appear to our behaviorist-shaped grandchildren as a time and place that were positively inimical to human life itself. The principal rhetorical address of Watson's *Behaviorism* is consequently interpellative: *you*, the present-day reader, can begin to ameliorate our current uninhabitable conditions by following my (Watson's) conclusions regarding the conditioning of infants, by learning to verbalize accurately your visceral behavior, by exposing yourself to stimuli contrived by behavioristically trained educators to change your personality traits for more socially desirable ones, and so forth. Watson's behaviorist ideal, therefore, is not devised to assuage men and women adrift in a universe entropically winding down; it is instead an exemplum out of a future in which everything will finally be set to rights: "I am trying to dangle a stimulus in front of you, a verbal stimulus which, if acted upon, will gradually change this universe" (*B*, 303).

III

Humans, in this view, are simply animals with complicated sets of learning schedules, reflex arcs, and repertoires of behavior. To paraphrase Lewis's *Men without Art*, they are potentially just machines governed by routine rather than ground down by thermodynamics. Consequently, any stress put upon the machine-like qualities of the (behaviorist) man in Watson's work is little more than a figural move made to reduce these organized complexities to an order digestible by an educated lay public. Watson's behaviorism often constructs machines out of humans to make a point, but such analogies are themselves not the point they so often are in Lewis's satirical fiction. For instance, when Watson describes how "the arms are levers built to permit wide excursive movements," he would seem to demote our upper limbs to mere implements in the application of force (*B*, 201). Likewise, when he depicts how the "tongue, while bearing very delicate receptors, is on the muscular side a bulk organ for rolling our food around," he apparently relegates that tissue-mass to the status of an imprecisely blunt aliment-mover (*B*, 240). In contrast, Lewis reassembles these disaggregated odds and ends into a fully functioning whole, as, for instance, happens in the final version of his postwar short story, "Bestre":

> With a flexible imbrication reminiscent of a shutter-lipped ape, a bud of tongue still showing, [Bestre] shot the latch of his upper lip down in front of the nether one, and depressed the interior extremities of his eyebrows sharply from their quizzing perch—only this monkey-on-a-stick mechanical pull—down the face's centre. At the same time, his arms still folded like bulky lizards, blue tattoo on brown ground, upon the escarpment of his vesicular middle, not a hair or muscle moving, he made a quick, slight motion to me with one hand to get out of the picture without speaking—to efface myself.[36]

Bestre's body is made up of a curious mixture of mechanical and animalistic components: he is not an ape but "a shutter-lipped ape"; he does not give his eyebrows a mechanical pull but rather a "monkey-on-a-stick mechanical pull." Yet, if his face presents the narrator, Ker-Orr, with the countenance of an ape-android, then Bestre's arms are simply "bulky lizards" resting upon his chest. The effect of the passage is not so much the effacement of Ker-Orr as it is of Bestre himself. The reduction of Bestre to ape-monkey-machine-lizard calls into question the possibility of human agency while recalling Cantleman's mimetic self-assimilation to his encompassing environment at the beginning of "Cantleman's Spring-Mate."[37]

The "Bestre" passage also evokes the behaviorist man-machine by way of the Cartesian animal. In the fifth part of his *Discourse on Method* (1637), René Descartes describes at length the ways in which animals already present us with so many "natural" automata, made up as they are of protomachinic assemblages of organs, arteries, bones, nerves, and muscles disposed to produce particular actions when placed in particular environmental arrangements. It is because of this disposition, Descartes contends, that we would be wholly unable to differentiate a real ape from an ape-android were the two displayed before us: "were there such machines exactly resembling in organs and outward form an ape or any other irrational animal, we could have no means of knowing that they were in any respect of a different nature from these animals."[38] Conversely, according to Descartes, were we to be presented with a human-android, "capable of imitating our actions as far as it is morally possible," we would nevertheless be able to detect the subterfuge because (1) such an android "could never use words or other signs arranged in such a manner as is competent to us in order to declare our thoughts to others," and (2) this hypothetical human-android would prove wholly incapable of acting from knowledge or reason because its activities would be restricted "solely [to] the disposition of [its] organs."[39] The human-android would give the game away to an observing "real" human because it would out of necessity behave exactly like an animal; in other words, it would prove itself incapable of appositely communicating with other humans just as it would finally expose itself to be "destitute of reason."[40]

Watson's behaviorism conforms to the Cartesian preoccupations within man's relationship to animal and machine even as it nominally betrays that relationship itself. In making humans and animals equivalent by way of observable behavior and patterns of habit formation, Watson no longer makes Descartes's distinctions between people and animals-machines qualitative. To argue in this way is to question the sufficiency of speech and reason as the *differentia specifica* of being human. Since Watson disregards reason, he ends up throwing mind and consciousness out with the homunculus in the bathwater, castigating all talk of them as a regrettable heritage of our savage past.[41] Against the superstitious legacy of linking mind and cogitation to metaphysics and the soul, "thought" for Watson is simply a term that encompasses the implicitly coordinated activities of the body as a whole, including visceral reactions and more organized verbal responses to stimuli.[42]

We can also note here that human speech in Watson's behaviorism represents something like an instance of economy or frugality, insofar as the principal function of words is said to consist of their capacity to act as time-saving replacements for objects. In a behaviorist world patterned after Watson, words are capable of "call[ing] out all of [the human being's] manual activity. The words function in the matter of calling out responses exactly as did the objects for which the words serve as substitutes."[43] Though they may save us a considerable amount of time in our daily lives, there is nothing all that special or ennobling about words. They remain for Watson within the realm of observable behaviors, acting as and responding to stimuli, not at all unlike an ape lifting a branch threateningly at another ape, or a monolingual American gesturally directing a Romanian nurse's attention toward a cupboard in which can be found a box of oatmeal and a matchbook.[44]

Despite these differences, however, early behaviorism certainly remained within the Cartesian framework insofar as "Nature" is always already a machine for both Watson and Descartes.[45] Watson's sole "innovation" is to take man down a notch or two and put him back in his place among his ape, rodent, and android cohort, a feature that Lewis himself discerns in the cultural and social life of postwar

73

Europe with his characteristic mixture of marvel and disgust in *Time and Western Man* (1927):

> Descartes called animals *machines*: they had not the rational spark. But men use their rational spark so unequally, and are so much machines too, that, on the face of it, that generalization is a very superficial one—one that you would expect in "the antechamber of Truth" (as Leibniz called cartesian philosophy), but not in Truth's presence. Many animals, indeed most, are more dignified, much freer, and more reasonable than men, in the conduct of their lives: and the "language habit," as the behaviourist calls it, is a servitude for those who are unable to use it, but have to be content to be used by it. It is not a thing to boast about that you *talk*, and that the elephant does not. It depends on what you say.[46]

Lewis more drastically upends Descartes's oppositions here than Watson's work ever expressly does. Descartes's positive valuation of reason, for instance, gets moved to the animal-machine column of Lewis's accounting ledger, whereas that of language stays put on the human side even as it receives a negative sign provisionally placed in front of it. In such a world as this, Descartes's casual assurance that the human as such can easily be distinguished from the android becomes entirely ungrounded, as in fact we see occurring time and time again in works such as Lewis's 1930 satire, *The Apes of God*, a novel populated with nothing but Cartesian human-androids (the titular apes), who endlessly mimic creativities and subjectivities they can never hope to embody or instantiate fully themselves. As the ever-absent Pierpont, who in the end is himself the very sort of ape he attacks, writes in his encyclical in that novel: "It is to what I have called the Apes of God that I am drawing your attention—*those prosperous mountebanks who alternately imitate and mock at and traduce those figures they at once admire and hate.*"[47] In such a book and within such a worldview, it is the "real" artist and the "real" human who would give the game away to the hypothetical objective observer, and not, as Descartes would have it, the other way round.

Yet if, as behaviorists like Watson contend, language leaves us more "done to" than "doing," then at least one tactical way of maintaining a vestigial sense of rational agency would seem to be "the dead and pulverizing silence" of a Bestre ("B," 82), Ker-Orr's most important instructor in the skirmishes waged upon the puppets of *The Wild Body* (1927).[48] Bestre's weaponry, for one thing, is strictly ocular:

> It was a matter of who could be most silent and move least: it was a stark stand-up fight between one personality and another, unaided by adventitious muscle or tongue. It was more like phases of combat or courtship in the insect-world. The

Eye was really Bestre's weapon: the ammunition with which he loaded it was drawn from all the most skunk-like provender, the most ugly mucins, fungal glands, of his physique. Excrement as well as sputum would be shot from his luminous hole, with the same certainty in its unsavoury appulsion. Every resource of metonymy, bloody mind transfusion or irony were also his. ("B," 82–83)

Idly stirring up stray animosities with his pupillary discharges, Bestre stocks these silent blasts with all the noisome resources of scatological sound. Expectorated orts, feces, and mucus ("the most skunk-like provender") unsavorily shoot out of his eyes ("his luminous hole") in an even coarser version of hypallage perhaps than "Cantleman's Spring-Mate." Aiming and shooting out the waste of his other orifices, Bestre's eyes attempt to avoid language altogether, for the mouth is no longer the organ of speech so much as it is a bronchial torpedo bay, the functions of which the eyes can perform just as well. In fact, the eyes arguably fulfill this office even better than does the mouth because Bestre's sole weakness turns out to be his regrettable tendency to use his mouth in order to boast rather than to spit and spew forth still more filth at his auditors. Ker-Orr somewhat deflatingly ends his account of Bestre by observing, "I have noticed that the more cramped and meagre [Bestre's] action has been, the more exuberant his account of the affair is afterwards. The more restrictions reality has put on him, the more unbridled is his gusto as historian of his deeds, immediately afterwards. Then he has the common impulse to avenge that self that has been perishing under the famine and knout of a bad reality, by glorifying and surfeiting it on its return to the imagination" ("B," 87). It is, in other words, as storyteller of his own silent misdeeds and antagonisms that Bestre fails ultimately to do justice to their admittedly scanty—but nevertheless, for Ker-Orr at least, exemplary—violence.

Furthermore, it is in this regard that we can begin to understand why Ker-Orr is convinced that Bestre's best last word remains his terminal offensive assault on the wife of a "pretentious peppery Paris Salon artist," to whom Bestre one day exposes the bestial expressiveness of his eye along with that of his genitals ("B," 84): "The eye was his chosen weapon. Had he any theory, however, that certain occasions warranted, or required, the auxiliary offices of some unit of the otherwise subordinated mass? Can the sex of his assailant give us a clue? I am convinced in my own mind that another agent was called in on this occasion. I am certain that he struck the death-blow with another engine than his eye" ("B," 85). Comparing this account of Bestre's silent victory with that of his subsequent defeat by way of speech and storytelling, we can see that, despite Watson's aforementioned claims, words do not in the end merely constitute substitutes for the objects they propositionally name in Lewis's fiction. A lewd man necessarily remains more lewd than a lewd story or report of that same lewd man's lewd actions. Consequently, though Lewis's far-from-silent satires may presume the operative existence of so many behaviorist worlds and utopias, the very words they use do not therefore necessarily ventriloquize the assertions of Watson's behaviorism.

IV

We must be careful, however, not to read too much of Lewis's postwar culture critiques and compositional methods back into his prewar fiction without making some effort at explanation. World War I not only interrupted Lewis's grand designs on single-handedly building up a British avant-garde culture in his own image but also left him adrift as to what to do once it ended, and he found himself among those passed over by the war itself. It was, as he points out in his first autobiography, *Blasting & Bombardiering* (1937), the great event in his generation's life, by which all previous and subsequent time was thereafter to be measured: "The War is such a tremendous landmark that locally it imposes itself upon our computations of time like the birth of Christ. We say 'pre-war' and 'post-war', rather as we say B.C. or A.D."[49] At a more personal level, Lewis used this autobiography to offer a singular and defensive view of the strange turns his life as an artist and writer had taken following the war. If he was a one-man British avant-garde unto himself before 1914, then he would have us see him now (in the *post*-postwar period) as a one-man self-advertising agency, tirelessly recasting and buffing his career on the model of a resurrection man: "I started as a novelist and set a small section of the Thames on fire. My first book *Tarr* was a novel (1918). Then I buried myself. I disinterred myself in 1926, the year of the General Strike—but as a philosopher and critic. This was considered very confusing."[50] What exactly took place between the end of the Great War and the onset of the General Strike in Britain—the bookends of Lewis's "post-war" period—is never directly confronted by him. As he remarks early in *Blasting & Bombardiering*, "1918–1926 is a period marked 'strictly private.'"[51] Instead, he only obliquely approaches this momentous interlude in his life by way of metaphors, such as the sacrilegious one he makes in comparing himself to Jesus, though Lewis would have us know that he was buried for eight years (no measly *three days* would do for him) before exhuming an utterly transformed version of himself in the mid-1920s. Should we misunderstand Lewis's impiety here as insincerity, however, we need only look at the material remainders of his transformation to disabuse ourselves: during the off-limits postwar phase of Lewis's life, almost all of his prewar literary output—including, most significantly, the stories in *The Wild Body*, the Vorticist prose drama *Enemy of the Stars* (1914/1932), and *Tarr* (1918/1928)—underwent revisions that markedly changed the style and in some cases the content of these pieces. With Lewis's new self came a new (because entirely rewritten) literary past as well.

A notable exception to Lewis's postwar revisionary frenzy, however, was "Cantleman's Spring-Mate," which began reappearing in the second edition of *Blasting & Bombardiering* released by the University of California Press in 1967 without any alterations save a minor substitution of em dashes (—) for Lewis's "=," an idiosyncratic punctuation mark characteristic of his prewar writings. While I am not interested in Lewis's motivations or intentions in neglecting to revise "Cantleman's Spring-Mate" along the lines of *Tarr* or the narrative cycle in *The Wild Body*, I do think that the story's uncastigated integrity through and beyond the postwar period tends to justify its juxtaposition with the strategies and concerns evinced in the final version of "Bestre." Perhaps most importantly, although these two pieces face each other across the putatively insurmountable partition set up by the Great War and the postwar, both narratives are structurally homologous insofar as they concern themselves principally with the representation and critique of failed (or otherwise fatally flawed) comportments toward hostile milieus.

As we have seen, the problem with Bestre's strategy has little to do with his spectacular antagonisms in and of themselves. If anything, Ker-Orr's story expresses bemused wonder at the subtle blows and pains one can deliver solely with the aid of one's own eyes as well as at the scrupulous dedication Bestre brings to his role in these mute quayside brawls: "The key principle of his strategy is provocation. The enemy must be exasperated to the point at which it is difficult for him to keep his hands off his aggressor. The desire to administer the blow is as painful as the blow received. That the blow should be taken back into the enemy's own bosom, and that he should be stifled by his own oath—*that* Bestre regards as so many blows, and so much abuse, of *his*, Bestre's, although he has never so much as taken his hands out of his pockets, or opened his mouth" ("B," 84). In their repetitiousness, their calculated coordination of stimuli and responses, and their reliance on nothing more than a balefully steady gaze, Bestre's campaigns resemble crude behaviorist experiments, with Bestre doing triple duty as observer, stimulus, *and* lab rat. What in turn makes Bestre's revisionary version of behaviorist experimentation so instructive for Ker-Orr and (presumably) Lewis is that it reduces the world not so much to behaving surfaces as to *badly* behaving surfaces. Bestre's eyes act to break up the socially scripted complacencies and roles of those they malign through the act of observation itself; they work by singling some*one* out from the herd and fixing him or her with a confrontational stare, thereby disrupting the mimetic lures to which this particular person's public life may be otherwise susceptible. Against the standardizing tendencies of Watson's behaviorist machine, Bestre operates by aggressively drawing out his opponents' singular identities over against those forces (advertising, cinema, books, etc.) that tend to dissolve such identities into one big undifferentiated mass. As argued previously, however, the signal failure of Bestre's approach occurs when he stops staring and starts to open his mouth to speak, for it is then that he gives in, along with his contingently encountered enemies, to the sorts of "common impulse[s]" governing all and against which he otherwise dog-gedly hurls the waste matter of his body, if only by way of his nauseating glances ("B," 87).

Cantleman, in this regard at least, would appear to turn himself to account better because he manages to remain silent. An occasional sidelong reference is made to conversations he has with Stella, but the story never gets around to report-ing his speech directly. Instead, the narrative emphasizes his stratagems in gaining the attention of the young woman, which looks an awful lot like what those of a novice Bestre might be: "At the village he met the girl, this time with a second girl. He stared at her 'in such a funny way' that she laughed. He once more laughed, the same sound as before, and bid her good evening. She immediately became civil" ("CS-M," 10). What of course sets Cantleman's funny stare apart from that of Bestre's, however, is that the former aims to seduce in order to covertly antagonize. That is to say, Cantleman's sacrifice to the animal and, correlatively, to nature has all the doubtful efficacy of a performative contradiction:

> In the factory town ten miles away to the right, whose smoke could be seen, life was just as dangerous for the poor, and as uncomfortable, as for the soldier in his trench. The hypocrisy of Nature and the hypocrisy of War were the same. The only safety in life was for the man with the soft job. But that fellow was not conforming to life's conditions. He was life's paid man, and had the mark of the sneak. He was making too much of life, and too much out of it. He, Cantelman [sic], did not want to owe anything to life, or enter into league or understanding with her! The thing was either to go out of existence: or, failing that, remain in it unreconciled, indifferent to Nature's threat, consorting openly with her enemies, making a war within her war upon her servants. In short, the spectacle of the handsome English spring produced nothing but ideas of defiance in Cantleman's mind. ("CS-M," 13)

Consequently, Cantleman's retreat into putatively lower life-forms is tactical; he gives in to the natural world around him in order to wage war against that world, just as he plays the part of suave soldier-suitor in order to take out his aggressions on Stella. Like the dangling feet of the bacillary Phasmidae, the excrement-smeared *Chrysomelid* larvae, and the magic rituals of primitive civilizations later described by Lewis's younger contemporary Roger Caillois in "Mimicry and Legendary Psychasthenia" (1935), Cantleman's mimetic self-assimilation into his immedi-ate surroundings acts to derange spatial perception and to achieve his apparent depersonalization.[52] Persisting illusions of velleity, however, are precisely what Cantleman continues to believe separate him from tribal magicians and insect larvae. Cantleman's wager is that the merest of intentions distinct from one's actions have the potential to transform utterly the significance of those actions by the bare force of will itself. In other words, to act *as if* one has depersonalized oneself by retreating into pigs, birds, and horses is understood by Cantleman to perform the function of a sort of modern-day moly that ensures that he remains consistently himself despite this drastic assimilation. Angling ultimately to play the part of a modern-day Odysseus, Cantleman casts himself as Circe *and* as Odysseus's metamorphosed shipmates in order to rail at both. Yet, what Cantleman cannot see without becoming Lewis, Bestre, or the narrator of "Cantleman's Spring-Mate" is the degree to which there is no way to distinguish *as if* from *as* in nature or life: "And when [Cantleman] beat a German's brains out, it was with the same impartial malignity that he had displayed in the English night with his Spring-mate. Only he considered there too that he was in some way outwitting Nature; he had no adequate realization of the extent to which, evidently, the death of a Hun was to the advantage of the animal world" ("CS-M," 14).

V

Upon hearing of the U.S. Post Office's decision to confiscate the October 1917 issue of *The Little Review*, Margaret Anderson quickly took out a motion to restrain the postmaster of New York, and at trial the inimitable modernist art collector, patron, and lawyer John Quinn "brilliantly and . . . humorously" defended *The Little Review*, much as he would do four years later when the journal again faced charges of obscenity for publishing the "Nausikaa" episode of *Ulysses*.[53] As would happen in these later legal ordeals surrounding the serialization of Joyce's novel, however, Quinn's defense did not prevent the little magazine from being found "obscene, lewd, or lascivious" under Section 211 of the U.S. Criminal Code.

Manifestly ambivalent about affirming the postmaster's decision, Judge Augustus Hand remarks at some length in his opinion as to the uneven merits of "Cantleman's Spring-Mate" considered both as a piece of art and as a moral tale. After briefly describing the circumstances surrounding the case as well as quoting the relevant portions of the statute at issue, Hand's brief opinion begins by offering a pretty astute summary of the story's plot in which he emphasizes both its deterministic milieu and the rebellious reactions that this milieu occasions in young Cantleman:

> The publication which is particularly objected to by the Postal Authorities is a short story about a soldier in the British Army who reflects upon the topsy-turvy condition of the world and feels that gigantic forces, which he is pleased to call those of nature, are arrayed against the individual—forces that in most cases will overpower him. He regards his own destruction in the

present European conflict as more than likely, and under all these conditions feels at war with the world. With satirical satisfaction he seduces a young girl and disregards her appeals when she becomes a mother. In his revolt at the confusion and injustice of the war he feels justification at having wreaked his will and obtained his satisfaction—thus, as he says, outwitting nature.[54]

Hand admits that a number of reassuring morals can be glimpsed in all of this, whether these be understood as the demonstration either of "the wickedness of selfishness and indulgence" or of "the degradation of camp life and the demoralizing character of war."[55] In particular, he readily concedes that Lewis's narrative "naturally causes a reflecting mind to balance the heroism and self abnegation that always shines forth in war with the demoralization that also inevitably accompanies it. The very old question suggests itself as to the ultimate values of war."[56]

Hand's qualms about ultimately acceding to the putatively conventional morality of "Cantleman's Spring-Mate," however, have to do with what he regards to be the untenable assumption that the story is aimed at those with reflecting minds like his own. After all, what is perhaps most objectionable about "Cantleman's Spring-Mate," he argues, is the relish with which it addresses itself to readers in ways that cannot be contained or mastered through contemplation: "But no outline of the story conveys its full import. The young girl and the relations of the man with her are described with a degree of detail that does not appear necessary to teach the desired lesson, whatever it may be, or to tell a story which would possess artistic merit or arouse any worthy emotion. On the contrary it is at least reasonably arguable, I think, that the details of the sex relations are set forth to attract readers to the story because of their salacious character."[57] The first thing to note here is the degree to which Hand's comments in the first *Little Review* trial anticipate the holistic test for obscenity most famously articulated sixteen years later in John Woolsey's favorable opinion in *United States v. One Book Called "Ulysses."* In that case, it will be remembered, Woolsey held that "reading 'Ulysses' in its entirety, as a book must be read on such a test as this, did not tend to excite sexual impulses or lustful thoughts but that its net effect on them was only that of a somewhat tragic and very powerful commentary on the inner lives of men and women."[58] For many interpreters of this test, aesthetic judgments on the model of something like form-content relations could hereafter be used to mediate the application of obscenity statutes to works with literary or artistic pretensions. Understandably, liberalizing jurists and literary critics have tended to present Woolsey's holistic test as an unequivocal victory in the fight of artistic expression against its suppression. Within the terms such a test sets out, after all, it seems possible in theory to see any and all troubling content in a book as passing, negligible moments of an integral and nonobjectionable whole.[59] In this view, *United States v. One Book Called "Ulysses"* was understood to have set an important and incontrovertible precedent for the deproscription of book obscenity, and to cite and make use of its test from here on out was to be as good as deproscribing book obscenity through piecemeal judicial effort.

This is all well and good, save for the fact that it shuts its eyes both to history and to Woolsey's holistic test itself. For one thing, judges in the 1940s who scrupled giving "literary" books a free pass when it came to obscenity proved more than adept at regrounding their proscriptions in aesthetic terms and concepts. To insist that art required more of judges than the technocratic application of statutory and precedential standards alien to art itself did not in turn require courts to cede the field of obscenity altogether to aesthetic autonomy. This proved especially true in those cases where the charged book, when judged as a whole, arguably *did* tend or aim to excite sexual impulses or stir up lustful thoughts. At the very least, to deny that such aims and tendencies in fact predominate in works such as William Burroughs's *Naked Lunch* (1959) or John Cleland's *Memoirs of a Woman of Pleasure* (1748–49) is to risk inadvertently admitting that one has read neither text. Moreover, in its explicit separation of the one from the other, the *Ulysses* holistic test would disqualify sexual excitation and lust from artistic production altogether, resulting in what one critic has charitably described as Woolsey's "well-intentioned lies" regarding the immanent differences separating art from obscenity or pornography.[60] Such a distinction seems illegitimate, however, if we consider at all closely the mutually interdependent development of aesthetic taste and the pornographic book trade since the eighteenth century.[61] Burroughs, for his part, impishly forces the issue by putting a protracted graphic description of a snuff film at the center of his novel.

Rereading Hand's opinion on Lewis's story in light of the *Ulysses* case thus reveals the merely formal nature of Woolsey's test, which now appears as the value-neutral device it always was. Hand has no problem admitting that a compelling argument can be made for the conventionality of "Cantleman's Spring-Mate," for taken as a whole it is indeed an artfully written narrative pointing out the timely return of a "very old question" pertaining "to the ultimate *values* of war." What keeps him from giving Lewis's text a pass, however, is the pointed attention it pays to salaciously developed details. Hand's own holistic test for obscenity is therefore more forthright in confronting the discomfiting possibility that there might now exist artistic practices that give the lie to hoary old assumptions regarding form-content relations. What, after all, is one to do with those texts whose parts not only evade being assimilated into a totalizing whole but also address themselves to the body more explicitly than does that same text taken as a whole? How does one adjudicate the potential for obscenity of a work whose net effect fails to stimulate the lustful thoughts and sexual impulses of its readers but whose parts may be quite efficacious in doing precisely that? In short, what defense can aesthetics offer to art if it cannot guarantee the separability of art from pornography or obscenity?[62]

81

Because he is willing to face up to the possibility that these questions and the problems they partly circumscribe cannot be thought away with the reverent incantation of the words "aesthetics" and "art," Hand's opinion seems the more insightful piece of literary criticism than does Woolsey's celebrated affirmation of a masterwork of literary modernism. At the very least, Hand entertains the possibility that something was happening to and within art. While this "something" may have not been specified at the time (for an educated lay audience at any rate), it nevertheless did appear to "reflecting minds" that clichés and commonplace notions about the integral relations of form and content could no longer adequately grasp these "new" developments in art. Hence Hand's reluctance to countermand the decision of the postmaster of New York and his judgment that the October 1917 issue of *The Little Review* could not be mailed. Because he was unable to articulate what Lewis's preoccupation with sordid details had to do with his story considered as either literature or moral pedagogy, Hand had to concede that the postmaster had not abused his administrative duties: "While it has been urged with unusual ingenuity and ability that nothing under consideration can have the tendency denounced by the Statute, I do not think the complainant has made out a case for interfering with the discretion lodged in the Postmaster General, whose 'decision must be regarded as conclusive by the courts, unless it appears that it was clearly wrong.'"[63] In 1917 something may have been changing in art, but artists had not as yet gotten around to explaining themselves with sufficient persuasiveness as to be heard in official quarters.

In her article in *The Little Review* responding to the suppression of "Cantleman's Spring-Mate," Margaret Anderson is quick to grant that something indeed was happening to art, but she was by no means going to be the broadcaster of its secrets. Lewis, she argues in that essay, is incontrovertibly a writer of prose, by which she means "that he is master of the mysterious laws by which words are made into patterns or rhythms, so that you read them for the spirit contained in the rhythm,— which is the only way of getting at the context; which in fact is a thing of distinct and separate entity, existing above and beyond the context. Many fairly good writers and critics do not understand these laws. It is not surprising that the Postoffice [*sic*] department does not understand them."[64] Distinct from the law of obscenity are the "mysterious laws" of prose, which Anderson says lift all such writing from its transient milieu and hence beyond the reach of postmasters and Societies for the Suppression of Vice. Anderson avoids explaining of what exactly these laws of prose may be understood to consist, beyond a fleeting glance toward the spiritual metamorphosis of mere words "into patterns or rhythms." Her willfully mystifying commentary is calculated to advance a much more ambitious agenda to change public policy, to have art's claims of autonomy registered by courts of law, a goal that would eventually be given (as we have seen) its most memorable expression in the form of Woolsey's "well-intentioned lies."

Courts after Woolsey's *Ulysses* decision were even more firmly persuaded that they must directly confront the challenges and problems that art posed to their attention, with the result that respecting art's autonomy increasingly meant integrating its principles into the more pressing matter of how to correctly apply the statutory and precedential standards regulating book obscenity. One conspicuous effect of this developing receptivity to art's difference as the century progressed was a growing willingness in many courts to accede to the testimony of experts, particularly in the field of literature. Woolsey himself had set an informal precedent for just such a procedure in the *Ulysses* case when he confessed to having two friends—"literary assessors" he calls them—separately read Joyce's novel and then casually compare their impressions with the present-day legal definitions of obscenity.[65] It must be stressed, however, that the mere fact that a Norman Mailer or an Allen Ginsberg was later allowed to defend the literary or social merits of an "obscene text" in a court of law did not entail that their opinions would thereafter be dispositive. Famously, the Ninth Circuit Court of Appeals in *Besig v. United States* (1953) had little difficulty in affirming a judgment of obscenity despite granting the literary merits of Henry Miller's *Tropic of Cancer* (1934) and *Tropic of Capricorn* (1939) based on the "voluminous affidavits and exhibits" filed on the behalf of various literary experts in that case.[66] Ultimately, to admit that a book was "literary" or "artistic" did not thereby make it any less obscene in the decades separating Woolsey's decision from the U.S. Supreme Court obscenity cases between 1957 and 1973.

Nevertheless, the year following *United States v. One Book Called "Ulysses,"* the Second Circuit Court of Appeals ended up affirming Woolsey's decision. Though doubtful of the claims made by "Joyce's laudators" as to the lasting value of the novel in literary history, the presiding circuit judge insisted that art should be given a chance to develop new techniques out of itself without the infringement of court supervision in matters such as obscenity:[67] "Art certainly cannot advance under compulsion to traditional forms, and nothing in such a field is more stifling to progress than limitation of the right to experiment with a new technique. . . . We think that Ulysses [*sic*] is a book of originality and sincerity of treatment and that it has not the effect of promoting lust. Accordingly it does not fall within the statute, even though it justly may offend many."[68] With seventeen years of modernist art production and criticism separating this case from the first *Little Review* trial, the inability of a judge to account for the unsettling quality of an experimentally "obscene" text no longer seemed to matter much—for the time being, at least. Something may have happened to art, and judges may never be given the training needed to grasp quite what that "something" was in time to have this competence guide their decisions; nevertheless, by 1934 they could most likely trust in artists to pursue "originality and sincerity of treatment" without intruding upon the grounds of obscenity for the sake of obscenity. Contemporary art worthy of the name had

83

proven itself to be a disciplined and disciplining project, meaning that offenses occasioned by it were "just" and should be allowed to pass without proscription. According to the Second Circuit Court of Appeals, such art could be trusted to treat "obscenity" as a technique like any other, as a means to ends greater than the mere promotion of lust. Lies such as these were not only well intentioned but also exigent. The circuit judge who ensured that Woolsey's decision and holistic test would stand as landmark precedents in U.S. obscenity case law? None other than Augustus Hand.

VI

If I have exhumed and reviewed the relationships between Hand's reluctant suppression of "Cantleman's Spring-Mate" and his subsequent affirmation of *Ulysses*'s nonobscenity, then it has been to resituate the temporal and public dimensions of modernism in terms of broader applicability than the idiosyncratic periodizations (prewar, postwar, post-postwar) Lewis develops in *Blasting & Bombardiering*. For one thing, the organs of Anglo-American modernist publicity (particularly its little magazines) had made their mark on popular consumer culture to such an astonishing degree in the 1920s that by 1933 (the year of the Woolsey decision) Gertrude Stein had moved from the pages of *transition* (1927–38) to the best seller list with *The Autobiography of Alice B. Toklas*. The following year, one could read about the "fad" of Gertrude Stein in *Vanity Fair*; see productions of her opera, *Four Saints in Three Acts* (written 1927–28), in either Hartford or New York; hear Stein herself lecture in numerous cities across the country; and buy *The Making of Americans* (written 1902–11; first published 1925) in a mass-market edition.[69] Moreover, by the end of the 1920s, modernism and its public forums appeared to young struggling writers such as Erskine Caldwell to be vitally important to their professionalization, even if the work these writers produced had little overt relationship to the projects, forms, and devices usually ascribed to literary modernism as such. No longer regarded as desirable venues of publication in and of themselves, significant little magazines such as *transition*, *New Masses*, *Blues*, and *Pagany* instead appeared to writers such as Caldwell to encompass so many way stations along the road to bigger and better things, such as *Scribner's Monthly*, *Esquire*, and (eventually) the lucrative mass-market paperback boom of the 1940s. Hereafter, modernism could be treated as an artifact of one's aesthetic self-formation.

Consequently, the Woolsey decision must be understood first and foremost as indexing the absorption of modernism into commercial mass culture. For one thing, by accentuating the artistic merits of *Ulysses*, Woolsey gave credence to those who sought to defend modernist literature as a legitimate form of aesthetic expression, howsoever strange or disturbing it may have once appeared to contemporary

84

minds and sensoria. In turn, by maintaining that art in and of itself was not at all reducible to obscenity, Woolsey exempted from proscription any claims "new" art made on the body. Such works were to be excepted from obscenity on grounds similar to those used in defending the "classics," so long as one could reliably discount the possibility of their unreflective reception, which seemed a reasonable assumption provided these texts made a point of compositionally sublimating their pleasures—even if, as in *Ulysses*, these pleasures were scatological, masturbatory, or sadomasochistic. Crucially, Anderson's essay on Augustus Hand's ruling against the October 1917 issue of *The Little Review* also calls into question the claims modernist writing makes on bodies. For her, to read literature—or rather "prose"—involves our gaining access to spiritualizing laws superior to those of our temporal institutions. Ideally, then, reading provides both the means of contemplative escape from the vulgarity of prevailing conditions as well as the occasion for consorting with that select group of contemporary readers and writers who share our tastes, biases, and experiences regarding art and its superiority to life as it is now lived. The emphasis in Anderson's account is not only on subordinating life to art but also on building a select community constituted by refusing access to the many (e.g., the masses, the public). Indicative of both these points are Anderson's concluding remarks in her response to Hand's opinion: "Any life that is capable of being destroyed, in the popular sense of the term, *should be destroyed*. It might then take on that tragic significance which would make it material for Art. That these arguments may still be regarded as childish or immoral by the majority of the world is the supreme human joke. That I could be called an 'iconoclast' for making them is a measure of contemporary fatuity."[70] In the end, it is on grounds such as these that Anderson "can see nothing brutal in 'Cantleman's Spring-Mate.' [She] can see no warning or lesson in it."[71] Lewis's story can neither be reduced to a function nor proscribed for its loose moral economy. To judge it in terms other than those called for by the self-reflexive and ineffable standards of art is simply to mark one out as the fatuous Other against whom journals such as *The Little Review* and their readers partly constituted their social identities.

Despite Anderson's protests, however, it takes an awful lot of mental acrobatics to deny that Lewis's story is brutal or that its brutality derives in no small part from its willingness, unlike Anderson, to depict reading as a potentially hazardous activity. On the third page of the narrative—but diegetically *before* Cantleman's salacious experience in the field—Lewis reveals an unlikely motivating force for Cantleman's prewar all-out assault on nature: Thomas Hardy. Contrary to one's likely expectations, however, the specific model for Cantleman's carnal and carnivorous rampage is revealed not to be *Jude the Obscure* (1895), Hardy's "obscene" novel; instead, the relatively minor (and most certainly unwarlike) historical novel, *The Trumpet-Major*, instigates the soldier's premature martial pursuits. At those

85

regrettable times when he finds himself stuck in camp, Cantleman avoids all social intercourse with his roommates (whom the narrator gives letters—A., B., C., and D.—rather than names) by voraciously digging into a copy of Hardy's novel that he has stolen from one of these very same roommates:

> [Cantleman] had even seemed to snatch Hardy away from B. as though B. had no business to possess such books. Then [Cantleman's roommates] avoided his eye as though an animal disguised as an officer and gentleman like themselves had got into their room, for whom, therein, the *Trumpet-Major* and nothing else exercised fascination. He came among them suddenly, and not appearing to see them, settled down into a morbid intercourse with a romantic abstraction. The Trumpet-Major, it is true, was a soldier, that is why he was there. But he was an imaginary one, and imbedded in the passionate affairs of the village of a mock-county, and distant time. Cantleman bit the flesh at the side of his thumbs, as he surveyed the Yeomanry Cavalry reveling in the absent farmer's house, and the infantile Farnese Hercules, with the boastfulness of the Red, explaining to his military companions the condescensions of his infatuation. Anne Garland stood in the moonlight, and Loveday hesitated to reveal his rival, weighing a rough chivalry against self-interest. ("CS-M," 11–12)

On its face, Cantleman's encounter with Hardy's text here would seem to hew closely to Anderson's argument, at least so long as his responses confine themselves to reflective and contemplative reactions that protectively lift him up from and beyond the reach of his degraded camp surroundings. Lewis's "imaginary" soldier likewise more happily consorts with Hardy's "imaginary" soldier, who is unsuccessfully courting an "imaginary" woman in "the village of a mock-county" existing in a "distant time." The characters of Hardy's Wessex at the time of the Napoleonic wars, thus, appear to provide Cantleman with a more consequential set of companions, interlocutors, and models for approaching his own time's great war than do the persons with whom he must have daily, but meaningless, contact.

Yet the passage quoted just now also intimates a relationship between reader and text excluded entirely from Anderson's account, for in reading of John Loveday's quaint dilemma when faced with the opportunity of revealing the drunken state of his rival to their mutual object of affection, Cantleman bites (satirically? amorously? jadedly?) the fleshy sides of his thumbs. Later, Lewis describes in even greater detail Cantleman's boisterous reactions to Hardy's novel: "[Cantleman] chuckled somewhere where Hardy was funny. At this human noise [his roommates] fixed their eyes on him in sour alarm. He gave another, this time gratuitous, chuckle. They returned with disgust at his habits, his peculiarity, to what he considered their maid-servant's fiction and correspondence. Oh Christ, what abysms! Oh Christ, what abysms! Cantelman [*sic*] shook noisily in the wicker chair like a dog or a fly-blown old gentleman" ("CS-M," 12). In part, Cantleman's superfluous chuckles reproduce Anne's own hilarity at Festus's advances as well as the "fly-blown" state of old Benjamin Derriman, the elderly property owner whose role in *The Trumpet-Major* depends principally upon his paranoiac and comically lame attempts to keep his final will and testament out of the hands of his good-for-nothing nephew, Festus.[72] Yet mimetic parallels such as these between the behaviors of "imaginary" characters and those of one of their "imaginary" readers are negligible when compared to the spectacular effects Hardy's text seems to have on Cantleman's body more generally. Reading for Cantleman, as it turns out, is a thoroughly corporeal activity and performance: he reads with his whole body (letting loose a chuckle when Hardy earns it) for the benefit of others ("He gave another, this time gratuitous, chuckle"). An adequate account of his reception of *The Trumpet-Major* thus has to address the effects of that text on his body, be it in the form of gnawed fingertips, palsied fits of chortling, and, as it happens, even more violent modes of physical expression.

As much as he may enjoy reading, Cantleman's "morbid intercourse" with Anne, Festus, and the Loveday brothers ultimately demands more than immediately achieved gratification with Hardy's words and their ticklish aftereffects on his diaphragm. What simply reading Hardy's text leaves wanting, in fact, is a wider scope for action in the here and now: "In [Cantleman's] present rustic encounter, then, he was influenced by his feelings towards his first shepherdess [i.e., Stella] by memories of Wessex heroines, and the something more that being the daughter of a landscape-painter would give. Anne, imbued with the delicacy of the Mill, filled his mind to the injury of this crude marsh-plant. But he had his programme. Since he was forced back, by his logic and body, among the madness of natural things, he would live up to his part" ("CS-M," 12). What catches Cantleman's eye and guides his plan for action is neither the plot of Hardy's historical novel nor the ironic defense of decorum and chivalry it nostalgically proffers but rather the arousing figure that Anne Garland cuts. If Augustus Hand suppressed the October 1917 issue of *The Little Review* because he was reluctant to ignore the vividly descriptive parts that do not quite make a whole out of "Cantleman's Spring-Mate," then that reluctance finds its indirect confirmation in Cantleman's habits as a reader of Victorian historical novels. In particular, the attraction of reading for one such as Cantleman appears to be the attention one can devote to desirable parts without concerning oneself at all with the compositional functions and forms of the whole, and this is true even if such parts do not in and of themselves seem all that libidinally suggestive. Compare, in this instance, Cantleman's aggressive sexual desire for Anne (desire that makes her the physical superior in every way to the "real" body of Stella, that "crude marsh-plant") and the sorts of descriptions of her in *The*

Trumpet-Major that occasion it. Hardy's narrator observes that "Anne was fair, very fair, in a poetic sense; but in complexion she was of that particular tint between blonde and brunette which is inconveniently left without a name. Her eyes were honest and inquiring, her mouth cleanly cut and yet not classical, the middle point of her upper lip scarcely descending so far as it should have done by rights, so that at the merest pleasant thought, not to mention a smile, portions of two or three white teeth were uncovered whether she would or not. Some people said that this was very attractive."[73] Except for the detail regarding her faulty upper lip, Hardy's description of Anne is pointedly nondescript, and upon cursory reflection, it appears in keeping with the overdeveloped irony of Hardy's novel taken as a whole. Even if one were to consider this passage in all of its specificity (with modes and claims of address of its own), this initial descriptive account of Anne's person would still continue to operate so as to take the wind out of any presumptive claims to beauty a reader might come to expect of the heroine in a novel such as this: "Some people [not the narrator, surely] said that this was very attractive." Yet walking home with Stella after his transformative experience with the horses, birds, and pigs in the field, Cantleman refers directly to this passage from *The Trumpet-Major*: "He wished that [Stella] had been some Anne Garland, the lady whose lips were always flying open like a door with a defective latch" ("CS-M," 10). Anne Garland's "defective latch" lips are not a blemish to ignore; instead, they are a feature to seek out and lament the absence of in those rustic mates who happen to be around and very much game for a roll in the hay. Amazingly, Cantleman is able to muster and then sustain his lust for the composite Anne/Stella not despite but *because of* the ironic and critical narration of Hardy's text. Notwithstanding Augustus Hand's certainties about such things, Cantleman's implacably reflecting mind makes Anne all the more arousing.

VII

"Cantleman's Spring-Mate" thus presents obscenity to us as a violation of the rules of use, whereby reading—and *not* writing—more appositely forms the crux of the problem obscenity names. In this view, Lewis's story does not demonstrate that Hardy pulled a fast one on the Victorian authorities but instead discloses that he who finds Anne Garland not merely attractive but literally fuckable is potentially a very, very dangerous sort of reader. In this respect, "Cantleman's Spring-Mate" can be seen to take its rightful place alongside Joyce's "An Encounter" (1905) as one of the great early twentieth-century short stories in which the onus of obscenity shifts conspicuously from production to reception. In Joyce's story, it will be remembered, though the narrator and his boyhood schoolmates get rebuked by their instructor for reading "chronicles of disorder" such as westerns and American detective fiction, it turns out that the "classics" upheld as exemplary by Father Butler end up corrupting readers even more completely than do the dregs of contemporary popular commercial publishing.[74] While playing hooky from school, the narrator and a friend (Mahony) meet an old bookworm who tries to draw them out on the subject of their reading habits as well as their interactions with girls before he moves away from them to engage in a bit of public masturbation while viewing—and in full view of—them. The man is physically grotesque, and from his twitching forehead down to his gapped yellow teeth and his generally shabby attire, he provides the narrator with a living image of the sort of fellow Father Butler describes when referring slightingly to the hypothetical writer of detective and cowboy narratives as "some wretched scribbler that writes these things for a drink."[75] Yet in his conversation with the boys, the old bookworm reveals himself to be well versed not in penny dreadfuls but in the "classics," by which he would have the boys understand him to mean the works of authors such as Sir Thomas More, Sir Walter Scott, and Edward Bulwer-Lytton. In fact, it is on these figures that Joyce's narrator dwells in order to make the point that no matter how lofty Father Butler's standards may appear to his terrorized pupils, "An Encounter" places them on the same level as the old bookworm's overworked genitalia.

If we take obscenity law and its enforcement as comprising an important context for these two narratives, then both Cantleman and the old bookworm emerge as oblique—if nevertheless tendentious—responses to what is arguably the most infamous decision in Anglo-American obscenity case law, *Regina v. Hicklin*. As we saw earlier, Lord Chief Justice Alexander Cockburn had held that the proper test for obscenity simply involved the determination of "whether the tendency of the matter charged as obscenity is to deprave and corrupt those whose minds are open to such immoral influences, and into whose hands a publication of this sort may fall."[76] Though subject to numerous criticisms in the decades to come, Cockburn's test proves upon closer inspection to offer a more nuanced approach to obscenity than many of the liberalizing judges and jurists were willing to admit in the first half of the twentieth century.[77] For one thing, in drawing attention to the uneven demographics of the state's literate population, Cockburn does not comfort himself with illusions of such a thing as a universalized (aesthetic) subject. Unlike Woolsey's *l'homme moyen sensuel* or the converging opinions of his "literary assessors," the depravable, corruptible minds in *Hicklin* are not presented as absolutes.[78] Cockburn is careful instead to mark these minds and their corruptive reception of a given "obscene" work as thoroughly exceptional, though in doing so he further attests as to why they pose such a problem for state management and regulation. Therefore, anticipating developments in obscenity case law that would not occur in the United States until the 1960s, the *Hicklin* test presents obscenity as exceedingly variable: it is not so much a quality of a text or object but rather of the shifting relations between channels of distribution and targeted audiences.[79] As some critics have described

89

it, Cockburn's nascent formulation of variable obscenity "was [not] a sign of middle-class hypocrisy. It simply meant—as literary theory is now claiming to have discovered—that a book is not the same across different contexts of consumption and use."[80] The problem with the *Hicklin* ruling, however, of course remained that while Cockburn was able to conceptualize the relativity of textual reception, he was far too comfortable with constructing a test for the total proscription of obscene books based on this differential distribution and formation of cultural capacities. Whereas his premises refreshingly avoid absolutes, his conclusions nevertheless insist on them.

"An Encounter" comprises a noteworthy intervention into the field of obscenity as delimited by nineteenth-century legal discourses such as *Hicklin*. For one thing, as we have seen, it puts the "classics" and ephemeral cultural matter such as *The Apache Chief* on a level playing field: neither the artistic qualities of the former nor the supposedly gauche artlessness of the latter guarantees their socially normative reception once they are out in the world. As a result, despite the tacit hierarchies underwriting Woolsey's holistic test, high/low distinctions in literary production appear to be of no use when it comes to dealing with obscenity, and it is in this regard that the elliptical lapses in Joyce's story's narration start to accrue an added significance. Somewhat notoriously, the narrator proves to be so squirrelly about revealing what exactly happens in "An Encounter" that Grant Richards, the eventual publisher of *Dubliners* (1914), did not realize what the old bookworm was doing in the story until Joyce made the unwise decision of telling him. Thereafter, six years of struggle between Joyce and Richards ensued before Richards finally agreed to publish the story collection with "An Encounter" included.[81] The reasons for this initial oversight by Joyce's publisher are not incidental failings on his part, however, because the narrator treats the story he tells as if it were in fact an "elaborate mystery."[82] While the old bookworm publicly masturbates, the narrator ensures that his retrospectively presented boyhood self keeps his eyes looking elsewhere so that all he can report of it are Mahony's elliptical exclamations:

> After a silence of a few minutes I heard Mahony exclaim:
> —I say! Look what he's doing!
> As I neither answered nor raised my eyes Mahony exclaimed again:
> —I say . . . He's a queer old josser![83]

What Joyce's story presents is a narrator who would make a piece of detective fiction out of public masturbation and the threat of pederasty, thereby reducing the threats both acts pose to a simple matter of epistemological nonrecognition.[84] Despite Richards's worries, in other words, "An Encounter" came before its public already precensored, insofar as the story's narrator uses popular genre forms to depict his boyhood self as the product of outdated ways of organizing subjectivity, whereby obscenity appeared to be a pathological matter in need of juridico-medical policing.[85]

If Joyce's story looks backward with a great deal of criticism, then Lewis's Cantleman shows the budding head of the behavioristically constituted subject, replete with hideous zoomorphic pedigrees, finding happiness in its states of absorption in sexual activity and raising merry hell on its way into a hideously blank and violent future. Rather than take stock of inherited forms of subjectivity, Lewis has Cantleman read the work of an influential late Victorian in order to reveal a historical mutation in the field of cultural reception. For in the end what Cantleman constitutes a prelude to is the imminent extirpation of subjectivity as such by a variety of convergent social forces. In his exhaustively developed cultural critiques of the 1920s and 1930s, Lewis seeks to reveal to the lay European's sight the multiform and impending threats undermining the stability of subjective identity in the early decades of the twentieth century. Because it often seems that these threats assail the resisting subject equally from everywhere at once, even Lewis's best works in this vein of cultural criticism can strike one as the insights of an exceptionally gifted paranoiac for whom every popular trend and every cultural figure plays a malignant part in a totalizing conspiracy whose object is the erasure of the para-noiac's very self.[86] After all, to see Henri Bergson, Albert Einstein, and Anita Loos as interchangeable agents in an all-encompassing cultural project aiming to rub out the stable self root and stock does indeed strain the present-day reader's credulity.[87] Yet precisely because Lewis is so insistent on detecting a consistent ideological undertow in widely divergent cultural phenomena, his essays and fiction can be understood as ultimately comprising so many complementary reinscriptions of the classic naturalist problematic. His fictional and satirical works depict, estrange us from, and beset lifeworlds in which one's actions prove to be hopelessly more determined than determining. As a result, this evocation of a faintly registered but nevertheless omnipresent sense of control by outer forces makes his work natural-ist*ic* if not strictly naturalist.

Given the invidious short- and long-term effects ascribed to forces such as rel-ativistic physics, behaviorist advertising, and childishly stammering literature, such naturalistic depictions could no longer trust that the descriptive monographs of nineteenth-century naturalism were at all equal to the representational challenges this spectacular and cyclopean modernity posed. It seems reasonable, therefore, to view Lewis's uncommon facility with a host of modernist styles—which he discards almost as soon as he evinces a passing mastery of them—as the symptomatic reflux of his critical projects as social diagnostician and surgeon. If the threats to the integral self were in fact as variable and parlous as Lewis believed them to be, then there was no hope in approaching them with a single ready-made mode of writing, least of all one left over from the last century. On the one hand, the cultural field had developed so expansively that it now contained and made use of hitherto separate spheres of human activity to such a degree that likely would not have been conceivable to the likes of a Zola. On the other hand, the category of the new, whether deriving from avant-garde or modernist practices, had been so successfully assimilated by the broader culture that any attempt to embody social critiques like Lewis's in fictional forms had to keep up with what happened to be in fashion, whether intellectually, artistically, or popularly. Making manifest the psychic pressures then being exerted by the vulgarization of Bergson's flux-philosophy, for instance, may have demanded *Finnegans Wake* (1939) parodies and Steinian stream-of-consciousness stutters in *The Childermass* (1928) but not necessarily the gestural puppet show machinations of *The Apes of God*, which attacks instead the increasingly indiscernible boundaries porously separating artist from public and patron.

Keeping this in mind, we can finally approach "Cantleman's Spring-Mate" as a first take in Lewis's representation of the sociocultural assault on individuality and the self. In particular, this suppressed story confronts the behaviorist functions of just such an assault, meaning that the relationship between writing and reading has as much thematic weight as the relationship between humans and animals in the text. After all, as Lewis would later contend in a characteristically ironic passage included in both *The Art of Being Ruled* and *Time and Western Man*, words comprise the major obstacle to the smooth functioning of Watson's projected behaviorist utopia:

> We live largely, then, in an indirect world of *symbols*. "Thought" having been substituted for action, the word for the deed, we live in an unreal word-world, a sort of voluminous maze or stronghold built against *behaviour*, out of which we only occasionally issue into *action* when the cruder necessities of life compel us to. Some of us live in this world more than others, of course. Some of us actually *like* it. And (a democratic note) *what* sort of person do you suppose enjoys living in this word-world? Words are symbols of ideas, as the old psychology would put it—some people "have ideas," are "theorists," "highbrows," and so forth: and SOME (like YOU and ME) are just plain people who prefer *deeds* to *words*! (that's US—that's our way!) What's the use of a word-world to *us*? We're not brilliant conversationalists, or anything of that sort! Speech is of silver, silence is of gold. And this is the age of *iron*, the age of *action*. We may not have much to *say* for ourselves, but we can hit a ball or turn a screw with the best. To hell with mere words! Up behavior![88]

This lengthy, duplicated passage foregrounds the performative contradictions required of Lewis in his fictional and satirical depictions of behaviorism, from

"Cantleman's Spring-Mate" onward. No matter how faithful Cantleman-the-behaviorist-reader may appear to be in his aggressive responses to literary stimuli, Lewis's logorrhea continues to stand in the way so long as words in and of themselves resist reliably eliciting behaviorist responses from their readers. Yet this assumes of course that the technocratic aims and goals of behaviorist projects and educational theories have not yet produced a fully operational mechanistic world, crass and raw in the extreme, in which words function just as well as any other stimuli to move the ganglionic action masses that were threatening to replace people.

That such theories and projects remained a preoccupation of Lewis's well into the 1930s attests to their enduringly menacing influence, however. In lighter moments, he remains capable of comically reducing the problem of behaviorism and obscenity to ridiculously literalized expressions. For instance, in his libelous and suppressed 1936 novel, *The Roaring Queen*, Lewis refers many times to the failed attempts of the young Honorable Baby Bucktrout to bed a member of her family estate's staff, despite her reliance on the estimable models provided a woman of her class in *Lady Chatterley's Lover*.[89] Such easy levity, however, all but disappears in the behaviorist defense of murder cunningly and disturbingly unfolded in *Snooty Baronet*, Lewis's "fictionist essay in Behavior."[90] That text cycles through a proliferating set of literary stimuli to get at the conditioning functions novels perform for the social personae assumed to be increasingly replacing individual selves in the face of new historical pressures on modern subjectivity. It is as if Lewis sought in *Snooty Baronet* to demonstrate that Watson was right and that in general men are in fact what the situation calls for—a Samuel Butler over dinner with their lover, a D. H. Lawrence in the bedroom, a white whale in a world of Ahabs, a dangerously maladroit Ernest Hemingway in the bullring, and an expert assassin patterned after Eastern adventure stories when presented with the distant form of their superfluously chinny literary agent.

What *The Roaring Queen* and *Snooty Baronet* cumulatively describe, therefore, is a world overrun with readers who behave like Cantleman and not at all like the consumers once found in the pages of *The Little Review*'s "Reader Critic" section. As a result, we err considerably if we take the animality depicted early on in "Cantleman's Spring-Mate" to be little more than the degradation of the human as such. In the end, the experience of animality in that story serves the more consequential function of clearing the ground for new forms of social identity and sociability patterned after acculturated behaviorist theories and methods, whereby the masses were to be reduced to a well-oiled stimulus-response mechanism. So long as behaviorism continued to comprise a substantial social force, therefore, the problem of obscenity would persist because for Lewis the problem of the obscene reader and the cultural dissemination of behaviorism were increasingly coterminous.

This is to read obscenity in Lewis as the representation of something like ironic embodiment, and what keeps it from swinging uncontrollably over into embodiment as such is repetition. Cantleman's second rip-roaring chuckle while reading Hardy for the benefit of his fellow officers, Kell-Imrie's second shot at Humph in *Snooty Baronet*, and even the second iteration of the lengthy passage on behaviorism from *The Art of Being Ruled* in *Time and Western Man*—all of these second takes exist to assert a barely subsisting will independent of one's reflexes or habituated actions.[91] They are meant to ensure that the words one reads are held at a distance and not treated as so many coordinated stimuli demanding proximate action. Obscenity for Lewis is merely a content like any other; it does not have to get embodied like laughter does in his satirical and fictional works.

Nevertheless, it would be a mistake to let the matter rest there and present a Lewis for whom the paired representations of obscenity and behaviorism might appear as satisfactory responses to a world less and less livable with each passing year in the run-up to World War II. Nor, for that matter, does irony provide an easy escape hatch, for as we have demonstrated throughout this chapter, irony tends to take the form of performative contradictions in Lewis's work, both critical and fictional. That is to say, it is far from certain that Lewis (like Cantleman before him) can play a role without losing part or all of himself. To revise ourselves a bit, it appears that what Lewis cannot see without becoming the narrator of "Cantleman's Spring-Mate" is the degree to which there is no way to distinguish *as if* from *as* in nature or life: "And when [Cantleman] beat a German's brains out, it was with the same impartial malignity that he had displayed in the English night with his Spring-mate. Only he considered there too that he was in some way outwitting Nature; he had no adequate realization of the extent to which, evidently, the death of a Hun was to the advantage of the animal world" ("CS-M," 14). "Cantleman's Spring-Mate" comes down to us and should be read as an early posted warning, marking off the types of pitfalls and traps in modern life that Lewis's subsequent fiction and critical writing would assay in ever more daredevil fashion: "Beware: whoever pretends to be a ghost will eventually turn into one."[92]

94

3. Erskine Caldwell, Smut, and the Paperbacking
   of Obscenity

[Erskine Caldwell] shows surprisingly naïve delight in all the possible ram-ifications of the thought that girls may be without panties, and he seems to have searched the length and breadth of the country for new situations whereby some significant part or parts can be exposed to us.

—KENNETH BURKE, "CALDWELL: MAKER OF GROTESQUES," 1935

Women are frequently a hindrance to sexual gratification, but as such are erotically exploitable.

—KARL KRAUS, *SPRÜCHE UND WIDERSPRÜCHE*, 1909

I didn't say that.

—CARRIE MEEBER, AUGUST 1889

I

Let's begin *in medias res*! In the early 1950s, having just completed his self-styled "cyclorama" of novels depicting the contemporary South, Erskine Caldwell took time from his abidingly prolific production of fiction to draft and publish *Call It Experience* (1951), the first of two autobiographies he would compose in his lifetime.[1] Described by Caldwell as "an informal recollection of authorship," *Call It Experience* details his apprenticeship, early travails, and hard-won successes as a storyteller whose stories eventually came to pay his way in life.[2] Somewhat surprisingly, however, Caldwell does not celebrate his incredible popularity as a writer in this work so much as defend his celebrity in the face of mounting criticisms of his writing and its stature in contemporary U.S. fiction. His remarkable book sales were increasingly becoming the occasions for both his isolation from other writers (with whom, to be sure, Caldwell never had much meaningful or sustained intercourse anyhow) and his exclusion from both academic criticism and the nascent canons of Anglo-American literary modernism as well.[3] Emblematic here is Edward Wagenknecht's gruff assessment of Caldwell's work in *Cavalcade of the American Novel* (1952): "At the moment, indeed, Caldwell seems destined for survival only in the mansions of subliterature. His sales continue enormous—largely in twenty-five cent, paper-covered editions, decorated with crude pictures of half-naked women—but his critical stock is now so low that it is difficult to believe he ever enjoyed the acclaim which was given to him only a few years ago."[4] For the most part, Wagenknecht's eviction notice has proven normative in the critical reception of Caldwell's fiction.[5] In turn, Caldwell's animus toward critics and his reluctance to join a community of writerly peers can be detected in his choice to end *Call It Experience* with his chilly reception at a writers conference at the University of Kansas, the description of which immediately follows a lengthy account of a successful publicity stunt in Kansas City involving Caldwell, the mayor, a motorcade, and the key to the city.[6] The authors attending the conference, which notably featured Katherine Anne Porter and Allen Tate, were evidently "displeased" with Caldwell because they felt he had "brought disrepute to the profession of authorship—and to the cause of higher education, as well—by participating in such an undignified publicity scheme in Kansas City, and by autographing twenty-five-cent books in a drugstore" (*CIE*, 227).

With the exception of the epilogue, in which he snappily responds to fan mail and pan mail, these are the final words of *Call It Experience*, and their strangely neutral presentation helps bring into focus his motivations in drafting such a work at this time in his life. Though Caldwell does not directly respond to the charges of his peers at the end of the text, the entirety of *Call It Experience* acts to preempt the criticisms of those who would scruple his reasons for participating in the advertising of the paperback reprints of his works. Rather than bringing disrepute upon the profession of authorship, Caldwell would have us understand his work as an attempt to disenchant the writing of fiction for a mass public. Asked by a woman at one point in the book about what it is he sells for a living, Caldwell laconically responds: "Paper—with words on it" (*CIE*, 94). Characteristically, then, many of the unattributed questions fielded by Caldwell in the epilogue to *Call It Experience* have to do with advice concerning the pursuit of fiction writing as a profession:

> I have written several short stories in my spare time. How can I get them published? (*CIE*, 234)

> I have submitted short stories to all the leading magazines but I still haven't been able to get one published. I'm beginning to get discouraged. What should I do? (*CIE*, 236)

> Will I be able to learn how to write short stories and novels by taking a course in a school or university? (*CIE*, 236)

> I want to be a short-story writer. Will working as a reporter on a newspaper be helpful or harmful? (*CIE*, 237)

> What do you consider the most important steps in learning to write? (*CIE*, 239)

These questions have a rhetorical force in context that controverts their apparently tangential relationship to *Call It Experience*'s downer of an ending. In the face of an increasingly institutionalized modernist myth predicating value on aesthetic autonomy, Caldwell's first autobiography refutes such claims by reminding authors and readers that writing was simply a means of pushing paper, something to make a living by, if one could.

Consequently, in one of the opening chapters of *Call It Experience*, Caldwell offhandedly tells the story of how he came to be an "authentic kind of writer"—that is to say, "a writer who sees his stories in print" (*CIE*, 47). In the summer of 1929, heartened by the first acceptance letter of his career as a short-story writer, Caldwell packed a suitcase full of manuscripts (including short stories, novellas, chapters from incomplete novels, poetry, essays, and jokes) and took a bus from Maine to New York City. "I had twelve dollars, a round-trip bus ticket, and a copy of the first edition of *Sister Carrie* [1900], by Theodore Dreiser, when I left Portland," Caldwell writes. "I had hopefully saved the book, for which I had paid thirty-five cents in a secondhand bookshop in Atlanta and which was said to have a value several times its original published price, for just such an occasion, and I planned to sell it to help pay my expenses in New York" (*CIE*, 72).

New York proved to be more expensive than Caldwell had anticipated, however, and after only one day and night in the city, he decided to take his copy of Dreiser's first novel to an East 59th Street bookdealer specializing in first editions. After equivocating as to its value, the dealer was able to convince Caldwell to leave his copy of *Sister Carrie* with him overnight so as to have time to show it to a prospective buyer on Long Island. When Caldwell, "optimistically hopeful of receiving ten or twelve dollars for the book," returned the next day, the dealer pretended not to recognize him:

> As soon as I spoke to him, he disclaimed any knowledge of me or of what I was talking about. Furthermore, the dealer said that he had never seen me before in his life. I reminded him of the conversation we had had the day before, I described the book I had left with him, and I even remembered well enough the tie he had been wearing to describe that, too. He angrily claimed that I was trying to make trouble of some sort and threatened to call the police if I did not leave immediately. I had no way of proving my story, and there was nothing I could do but go. I remained slightly hungry the remainder of the time in New York. (*CIE*, 73–74)

The tacit homology between text and life here almost strains credulity: the act of selling *Sister Carrie* provides an occasion for living out a scene comprising a vivid inversion of the opening pages of that book. As opposed to the magnetic desires of Carrie Meeber for frilly luxury goods beyond her means during the Chicago passages of Dreiser's first novel, Caldwell appears here as the victim of the more timely pangs and impulsions of hunger, which he ultimately does not satisfy because he is unable to sell the one luxury item he has been able to acquire despite his subsistence-level existence in Portland. The initial indifference of high-quality consumer goods to Carrie's desire for them becomes, in Caldwell's autobiography, the criminally dispossessive interests of one bookseller regarding the property rights of another. The systematicity and structural concerns of Dreiser's text—deriving from a mélange of discourses running from chemistry to sociology and (more broadly still) on to Spencerian evolutionary theories—contract to the anecdotal dimensions of a particularized case of petty theft in Caldwell's.

Notwithstanding these facets of his rather allusive experience involving the sale of *Sister Carrie*, Caldwell's encounter with the duplicitous bookseller primarily underscores his lifelong disenchantment of the literary by way of economic and vocational concerns. For a bookshop owner from Maine, which Caldwell had recently become, a first edition of *Sister Carrie* was simply a special type of commodity whose relative scarcity and perceived cultural worth accrued to it a value that could be realized in exchange with a savvy buyer.[7] Accordingly, the fact that the dealer involved in this particular exchange cheated Caldwell does not change the material status of Dreiser's novel as a commodity circulating, as Lawrence Rainey has concisely described it, "in that intangible yet perceptible social space where aesthetic value became confused with speculation, collecting, investment, and dealing."[8] Simply put, *Sister Carrie* was a rare, durable commodity that had appreciated over time; whether it was a book one actually read remains an unanswered—because unposed—question in *Call It Experience*. In any case, beyond suggestively identifying an unfortunate experience in his life with the underclass experiences in Dreiser's fiction, Caldwell does little to indicate whether he has in fact read *Sister Carrie*. What this passage makes abundantly clear, however, is that Caldwell does not risk confusing the market value of Dreiser's book with its aesthetic value, because aesthetics simply never enters into the matter.

Nor did Caldwell fail throughout his life to make a similar distinction with regard to his own work as a writer of fiction, for as his autobiographical writings emphasize over and over again, the only thing worth writing is work that is capable of realizing a socially recognized value.[9] Unable to secure a meeting with an editor anywhere in the city during his trip to New York, Caldwell randomly selected a literary agent from the phone book and made an appointment: "When I got there with my suitcase of manuscripts, the agent, whose name I have forgotten, took a long hard look at the contents and told me that I would have to leave everything for him to read at a later date. The later date was so indefinite that I decided that it was not something I wished to do" (*CIE*, 73). Curiously, Caldwell inserts this encounter *before* the description of his return to the unscrupulous bookdealer, suggesting that his wariness here is not at all the behavioral by-product of a painfully learned lesson in the rare books trade. In fact, it is independent of any such lessons, for it does not qualify Caldwell's self-presentation of naïveté so much as point out the difference between texts one buys and those one writes to sell. The former are a matter of speculation, so getting cheated out of a rare book altogether is simply a risk one runs. The latter, however, are subject to a more straightforward calculation that Caldwell emphasizes here. Though perhaps willfully a waif among forces in the rare book trade, Caldwell retrospectively presents a firm enough grasp of intellectual property here.

Cash poor and hungry, Caldwell ultimately did manage to turn his 1929 trip to New York to account. After two meetings in taxicabs (presumably because he had no office), Erich Posselt agreed to bring out an edition of one of Caldwell's novellas through a small publishing concern of his called The Heron Press. "When the contract was signed for the novelette," Caldwell writes, "it was then that Erich let it be known that he was going to publish the book under the title of *The Bastard* [1929]. It seemed to me to be an unusual title for a book of fiction, but I assumed that Erich knew the business of publishing far better than I" (*CIE*, 74–75). At the beginning of November, *The Bastard* appeared in a pricey edition. The Heron Press published eleven hundred numbered copies of the novella in Caslon Old Face font. The first two hundred copies were printed on American Handicraft and bound in balloon cloth. These copies were also signed by Caldwell and Ty Mahon, the artist who contributed six full-page illustrations to the volume. The remaining copies were printed on Mellow Book and bound in Holliston Cloth.[10]

In its first published version, *The Bastard* appeared in a material form we have come to recognize as distinctly modernist: the limited edition.[11] Along with the little magazines, limited editions constituted a tenuous institutional compromise throughout the 1920s as Anglo-American modernist writers and their patrons tried to cope with the incursions of commodity relations into areas of culture and art long held to be autonomous. By making the modernist text a means of drawing distinctions *within* commodity cultures between consumer commodities and unique investment opportunities, costly limited editions both gave in to and obliquely resisted the commodification of modernist writing. A canonical example: by arbitrarily choking off the number of available copies of the first edition of James Joyce's *Ulysses*, Sylvia Beach's Shakespeare and Company submitted to capitalist exchange even as it sought to manufacture an artificially achieved inapproachability for the published form of Joyce's text. In essence, what the modernist practice of publishing limited editions sought to do was to make rare, auratic commodities *despite* the age of mechanical reproducibility. Consequently, though both were commodities, the first edition of *Ulysses* was ultimately different in kind from the modes of publication and distribution of something like the first trade edition of Dreiser's *An American Tragedy*. Whereas the latter, published by Boni and Liveright, was priced so as to circulate among booksellers and those who presumably bought books for consumption's sake— that is to say, for reading—the former was an object of speculation primarily for bookdealers and export agents, who purchased it with the hopes of realizing considerable profits sometime in the future.[12] The limited edition both presupposed that the text would endure beyond immediate consumption and utilized its relative scarcity to extort an economic value subsequently understood to confirm that same text's aesthetic value. At first glance, then, it would appear that The Heron Press published Caldwell's first long work in the institutional space carved out by Anglo-American modernist publishing practices earlier in the decade. Like Shakespeare and Company's *Ulysses* or the 1923 Hogarth Press edition of T. S. Eliot's *The Waste Land* (1922), *The Bastard* was an object one tended to invest in rather than read, meaning it was more likely to be found on the shelves of Caldwell's cozening East 59th Street bookdealer than in the hands of, say, either a New York City subway passenger or a schoolteacher from Portland, Maine.[13]

However, by the end of November 1929, Black Tuesday had followed Black Thursday, and the modernist publishing practice of releasing texts through limited editions more or less came to an abrupt end.[14] Whether *The Bastard* managed to sell well despite the onset of the Great Depression remains unclear because, as he often complained in letters and interviews in later years, Caldwell received no money from the sale of his first major publication; Posselt, it seems, had run off with whatever proceeds there might have been.[15] *Call It Experience*, however, makes no mention either of the stock market crash that month or of how *The Bastard* went the way of Caldwell's first edition of *Sister Carrie*, perhaps indicating a pair of occasions for his subsequent embrace of mass-market trade paperbacks over residually modernist avenues of publication and distribution. In any case, the ending Caldwell chooses instead to give to this episode in his first autobiography remains suggestive. Rather than describe how he was cheated out of the money from his first book-length publication, Caldwell alludes in passing to a problem that would in many ways come to define him as an immensely popular figure of mass culture in the decades to come: "A few weeks [after the publication of *The Bastard*] in Portland I received word from a county official that, although he made no claim to being a literary critic, he did know what he saw when he looked at pictures, and consequently considered it his duty to declare that the book should not be offered for sale in Portland" (*CIE*, 75). Caldwell could not sell his first novella in his own bookshop because the county attorney had deemed it obscene without trial before either a judge or jury. Furthermore, he came to his decision without even reading Caldwell's words because the obscenity of Ty Mahon's illustrations was self-evident enough.

101

II

Although his reference to the official suppression of *The Bastard* in Maine acts almost as an epigrammatic flourish to what is otherwise a self-deprecating account of his literary wanderings around New York City in the late 1920s, the immediate effects of the obscenity charges on Caldwell were in fact a good deal more violent than he lets on in *Call It Experience*. In addition to drafting a short, vitriolic (and still unpublished) *Künstlerroman* depicting the struggles of Fritz Mann, a young writer who confronts the hypocrisies of a repressed, but sex-obsessed, Maine community, Caldwell quickly published a one-page broadside, "In Defense of Myself," in which he justified both *The Bastard* and his intentions in writing it.[16] Denied due process, Caldwell nevertheless sought to get *The Bastard* a public hearing in Portland and Cumberland County:

> Not having the opportunity to defend myself or my novel, [*sic*] means that with the consent only of County Attorney Ingalls himself *The Bastard* contains

an impure word, or words. No attempt was made to isolate these words in my hearing by the county attorney and neither was the offer made to permit my defense of them as being thought necessary in the construction of the story. With this comedy of justice bowing from the stage, the novel was blanketed with this brand of obscenity and hustled out of town. In the City of Portland and in the County of Cumberland, one superimposed upon the other in the State of Maine, *The Bastard* is obscene, lewd and immoral; likewise the author, by command of County Attorney Ingalls, is obscene, lewd and immoral in the City of Portland and in the County of Cumberland, all imposed upon the State of Maine. Therefore, it is a crime in this county to sell the novel, give it to my friends and, tomorrow perhaps, read it.

All of which gives me an involuntary urge to vomit profusely.[17]

Pointing out repressive features of legal obscenity beyond proscription, Caldwell describes how the effects of obscenity charges tend to move well beyond the proscribed texts themselves into all sorts of interpersonal relationships presupposed in a text's production and sale, if not necessarily in its reception. Perhaps alluding to the treatment of Hester Prynne, the "brand of obscenity" initially applies to *The Bastard* as textual artifact in the broadside. The book itself allegedly contains "an impure word, or words," making the work as a whole "obscene, lewd and immoral." Notably, all of these terms ("impure," "obscene," "lewd," "immoral") comprised synonymous parts in the hazy and often tautological definitions of obscenity found throughout the early twentieth century in U.S. statutory and case law.

With seemingly negligible concern for the broader discursive shifts in the strategies for legalizing obscene books, however, Caldwell does not question the equating of obscenity with impurity, lewdness, or immorality in his broadside. In fact, he seems willing to ascribe these properties to particular words; obscene texts apparently *are* classifiable as such because they in fact use these "impure" words. Caldwell thus accepts the legitimacy of obscenity and its prosecution. What he strenuously objects to, however, is having this opprobrious "brand" affixed to his own words and himself without an opportunity for a writerly defense. If Caldwell is willing to grant such a thing as obscenity, he nevertheless would have the Portland community and government recognize a distinction between obscenity as such and compositionally necessary obscenity. Consequently, the concerns of "In Defense of Myself" have not so much to do with the legitimacy of obscenity as law but rather with the artistic and technical grounds for producing a text that potentially makes use of obscenity, if not as an end in itself, then as a means. To be sure, such an attempt to subordinate a practice proscribed by case and statutory law to nominally aesthetic ends would have likely had little effect in a court of law in 1929 or 1930. Under Lord Chief Justice Cockburn's test in *Regina v. Hicklin*, which continued to comprise the obscenity standard at this time, distinctions based on authorial intent had no legal standing in the adjudication of obscenity. Compositional necessity was simply no defense against obscenity.

Because his fiction had a great impact on the young Georgian writer, the work of D. H. Lawrence on censorship bears brief consideration in connection with Caldwell's first brush with obscenity. The target of a variety of purity-movement protests and obscenity prosecutions both in the United States and Great Britain, Lawrence was himself a vehement supporter of the censorship of pornography, if not obscenity. Terminological issues are a matter of no small importance here because Lawrence was careful, particularly in "Pornography and Obscenity" (1929), to distinguish the one from the other. He understood obscenity to come down to particular offensive words ("shit" and "arse" are his two implied examples in that essay) and their socially determinate, if endlessly fungible, meanings. In particular, Lawrence proposed that all words principally evoke a mob meaning and an individual meaning. Subject to all sorts of demagogic uses, mob meanings were to Lawrence's eyes suspect elements in the interpretation of words and texts. Under their influence, he argues, the masses became considerably easier to control, manipulate, and dispossess than those few individuals able to distinguish between their own idiosyncratic responses and the stereotypical responses instilled in them by mob meanings. Effectively, mob meanings evoked a concern about the power of words to manipulate people through their bodily reactions that we have already seen at work in the critical writing of Wyndham Lewis, John B. Watson, and I. A. Richards. For Lawrence in particular, however, "the public, which is feeble-minded like an idiot, will never be able to preserve its individual reactions from the tricks of the exploiter. The public is always exploited and always will be exploited. . . . The mass is for ever vulgar, because it can't distinguish between its own original feelings and feelings which are diddled into existence by the exploiter. The public is always profane, because it is controlled from the outside, by the trickster, and never from the inside, by its own sincerity. The mob is always obscene, because it is always second-hand."[18] Despite the concluding imprecation aimed at the obscenity of the mob, obscene words in Lawrence's view are no bad thing in and of themselves "if the use of a few so-called obscene words will startle man or woman out of a mob-habit into an individual state."[19] In conspicuous contrast to Lewis's assumptions about the behaviorist undertone of obscene reading practices, obscenity potentially serves the function of ideological awakening for Lawrence by way of its violent capacity to interrupt stubbornly persisting thoughts and habits. Conversely, pornography is said to pose a real threat to life and health because it "is the attempt to insult sex, to do dirt on it."[20] Moreover, pornographers and their clientele "have a disgusting attitude towards sex, a disgusting contempt of it, a disgusting desire to insult it."[21] More particularly, pornography for Lawrence results from the willful—if often

103

unexamined—confusion of sexual and scatological functions in pornographers themselves, and in order to impede the contagious appeal and spread of this confusion to the masses, he "would censor genuine pornography, rigorously."[22]

Critical responses to Lawrence's defense of censorship have been notably dismissive. In the course of discussing *Lady Chatterley's Lover* in his book-length celebration of Lawrence, Henry Miller is even forced to concede: "It is a pity, however, that Lawrence ever wrote anything *about* obscenity, because in doing so he temporarily nullified everything he had created."[23] Somewhat more strikingly, in her exemplary attempt to approach the study of European and U.S. obscenity comparatively, Elisabeth Ladenson remarks: "Lawrence provides an exceptionally ripe example of an author who does himself (if not the profession as a whole) harm with virtually every word he writes about censorship. Lawrence the essayist is remarkable especially in the extent to which he is willing to assume seemingly self-annihilating positions."[24] Nothing less than an act of outright literary suicide, Lawrence's writing on censorship would seem to pose the problems of obscenity and pornography in terms radically incommensurate with his own creative practices and work.

As a counterpoint to this dismissive view of Lawrence's support of censorship, we should turn briefly to Caldwell's own reworking of the Lawrentian obscenity/pornography distinction.[25] In *Writing in America* (1967), a brief quasi-ethnographic collection of essays on the craft of writing published late in his career, Caldwell distinguishes obscenity from pornography in terms roughly congruent with Lawrence's own. In the course of arguing that institutional forms of censorship increasingly appear to be outmoded in the United States, Caldwell expresses a timely rejoinder to those who would construe such a relaxing of pressures as a public danger:

> People themselves are the qualified judges of what is right by tradition and what is wrong by custom. Obscenity and vulgarity are matters of bad taste and are not welcomed where decorum and propriety exist. Pornography is something else. It is a condition of psychic malady that can be alleviated by prescribed doses of erotic laxative. The pornographic has the curative properties of a prescribed drug, when taken as directed, and serves a moral purpose when it purges the mind of latent aberrations. The purification of the mind serves this moral purpose by eliminating harmful reactions. It is for this same reason that static electricity is grounded and discharged at periodic intervals to prevent dangerous explosions.[26]

Obscenity, for both Caldwell and Lawrence, only appears as such against the screen of custom and tradition. However, whereas Lawrence is willing to ascribe potentially revolutionary capacities to obscene words, Caldwell sees in them only "bad taste," indecorum, and impropriety. Obscenity, he argues, seems hardly capable of startling men and women out of their habitual modes of thought or patterns of behavior because at most it betokens underdeveloped cultural capacities or poor manners. Furthermore, and in pointed contradistinction to Lawrence, Caldwell presents pornography not at all as a disgusting travesty of sexuality but rather as a way of homeopathically tamping down otherwise explosive impulsions. Part prescription laxative and part electrical ground, pornography acts on the mechanomorphically conceived mind by discharging it of its "latent aberrations." Caldwell effectively depicts pornography as the opposite of Lawrentian obscenity. Rather than rousing one from ideological slumber, Caldwell's pornography ensures that one continues to sleep without interruption. In effect, from his perspective at the height of the worldwide student, sexual, and political movements of the late 1960s, Caldwell soberly recasts Lawrentian sexual liberation into a model that implicitly recognizes the insidious possibility of something like repressive desublimation.[27]

Such distinctions notwithstanding, however, it was the Lawrentian conception, and not its Caldwellian revision, that impacted a variety of reformulations of legal obscenity in the United States. Though seemingly unconnected to properly juristic defenses of his own works, Lawrence's remarks on pornography and obscenity eventually proved probative in subsequent case law involving obscenity. For instance, in *Kingsley v. Regents* (1959) the United States Supreme Court reversed the decision of the Regents of the University of the State of New York to deny a license for exhibition to the distributors of a French film adaptation of *Lady Chatterley's Lover* (1955, dir. Marc Allégret). While the court opinion by Justice Potter Stewart overturned this decision on the grounds that the New York Education Law unconstitutionally prevented the advocacy of an idea (not only did the Regents object to those scenes in the film that could be construed as promoting adultery, but also they did so precisely *because* those scenes promoted adultery), Justice Felix Frankfurter drafted an opinion that both concurred in the result and objected to the scope of Stewart's opinion. Citing "Pornography and Obscenity" with approval, Frankfurter reminded the court that "even the author of 'Lady Chatterley's Lover' did not altogether rule out censorship, nor was his passionate zeal on behalf of society's profound interest in the endeavors of true artists so doctrinaire as to be unmindful of the facts of life regarding the sordid exploitation of man's nature and impulses. He knew there was such a thing as pornography, dirt for dirt's sake, or, to be more accurate, dirt for money's sake."[28] By the late 1950s and early 1960s, therefore, Lawrence had gone from comprising a target of obscenity trials to being yet another source one could marshal in the service of justifying the continuing applicability of obscenity statutes to media such as film. Consequently, while authorial intention and compositional necessity counted for little at the time of *The Bastard*'s suppression in Portland and Cumberland County, such concerns would come to play a significant part in the increasingly contentious field of obscenity jurisprudence across the next four decades.

In addition to *The Bastard* and Erskine Caldwell himself, however, "In Defense of Myself" alleges that the county attorney branded one other party with obscenity by proscribing the sale of Caldwell's novella in Portland and Cumberland County. After describing the novella as an attempt to write about "an important and untouched phase of American *mores*," Caldwell offers an impassioned defense of the people and identities represented in *The Bastard*:

> But I have not finished what I have to say about the people in this novel that has been suppressed: I have an intense sympathy for these people. I know them and I like them. I have slept with them in jails, I have eaten with them in freight cars, I have sung with them in convict camps, I have helped the women give birth to the living, I have helped the men cover up the dead—but I have said enough. I have said that I know these people, that I love them. That is why I could not stand silent while the story of their lives was branded obscene, lewd and immoral; because this story belongs to them even more than it does to me. It is of no concern to me that I, too, have had this same brand placed upon me by Cumberland County. But these friends of mine—I shall defend them until the last word is choked from me.[29]

The branding of *The Bastard* with obscenity is said to mark its characters as well, and in this passage Caldwell comes tactlessly close to identifying these characters directly with their real-life models. In fact, his Whitmanesque embrace of entire swaths of the American underclasses is said to be so expansive that disciplinary divisions between fiction and the social sciences seem no longer to hold. In this view, *The Bastard*'s obscenity brands not so much the text or its author but rather the social types the text ventures to represent. Caldwell appears to defend his novella—and himself, ultimately—on anthropological and sociological grounds in an attempt to deflect the stigmatizing effects of legal discourses surrounding obscenity by relinking his own obscene text back to contemporary U.S. society. In this view, the brand of obscenity finally comes to mark the milieu in which obscenity is to be found. Obscenity, Caldwell finally argues, was very much the case in U.S. popular life of the late 1920s.

III

Yet it is hard to deny that *The Bastard* makes for sordid reading. Implicitly on the trail of his harlot mother, Gene Morgan (the titular bastard) meets a stranger who has a photograph of a scarred prostitute with a nipple-less left breast who may or may not be Gene's mother. This stranger goes on to tell Gene some stories involving a stunted pony, twenty-seven men, and a woman who also may or may not have been Gene's mother. We learn that Gene remembers having seen his mother only twice before in his life, and that during the first such encounter he picked her up "in a burlesque theatre in Philadelphia: in a hotel on Twelfth Street he spent the night with her, but she did not know he was her son, or if she did know she didn't care."[30] After arbitrarily murdering the stranger and disposing of his body in a nearby river, Gene goes on a binge in an undisclosed city. Subsequent chapters follow his return to Lewisville, the not-so-sleepy Southern cotton town of his birth, where Gene gets work at the cottonseed oil mill, sleeps with or rapes a number of local women (black and white), befriends and moves in with the sheriff's son, aids and abets the sheriff's son in the murder of a black worker at a local sawmill, murders the night watchman at the cottonseed oil mill while in the midst of bedding that night watchman's wife, and falls in love with a young woman loitering outside the Lewisville high school. This woman, Myra, shares a last name with Gene, and throughout the novella the narrative refers in passing to the possibility that they are in fact half siblings. Soon after their first meeting, the two leave Lewisville and strike out for the North. In Philadelphia, Gene settles down and finds work as a truck driver to support his new family. They eventually have a son who is physically deformed and developmentally challenged to a monstrous degree: "Little Leon was now nearly two years old, and, while his body had lengthened, his skin was still loose and dry and, most important of all, he could not coordinate the movements of his body. Still he required the same attention from his mother as he did when he was a week old. He was horrible to look upon, even through the eyes of his mother and father" (*TB*, 169–70). Gene and Myra subsist fitfully for a time before *The Bastard* concludes with Gene drowning their son (although this scene is not directly represented) and abandoning his wife.

In its awkward fascination with gruesome acts of violence and coerced sex pursued by the socially dispossessed, as well as in its feigned neutrality in presenting characters with an apparently innate predisposition for brutality and rapine, *The Bastard* evinces nothing so much as atavistic naturalism. What differentiates Caldwell's novella from earlier novels by Frank Norris or Jack London, however, is its studious subtraction of those two hoary old coordinates of literary naturalism, milieu and familial history, from the composition of Gene Morgan's story. *The Bastard* instead presents Gene as a hereditary case through the accumulation of increasingly sordid incidents and actions rather than through details pertaining to family background or setting. The frequent violence of Gene's actions indicates a compulsive predisposition in his character, yet the novella's narrator obstinately refuses to "explain" Gene through either environmental conditions or hereditary pressures. In fact, so little effort is made to account for Gene and his behavior that the barest intimations of a lurid family history given in the book's first chapter start to accrue an unlikely explanatory weight by the middle of the narrative. In short, Caldwell dramatizes adverse hereditary forces by evading direct statements as to their determinate powers as such. *The Bastard* self-reflexively invites natural-ist explanations for atavistic behaviors even as it reduces them to rumor, hearsay, and intimation. In the course of presenting his readers with a series of character reactions utterly incommensurate with their accompanying stimuli, Caldwell thus composes a naturalist world shorn free of the discourses and theories that would seek to motivate it causally.

The Bastard offers a striking version of this in a brief interlude at the Lewisville cottonseed oil mill. Fairly early in the novella, a carnival comes to town, and the men working the night shift at the mill engage a performance by a "hooch dancer" for their midnight lunch hour. When the break whistle blows, Gene hurries along with the other men to a shed on the mill property:

> Already a dozen men were perching themselves on the seed oval, already impa-tient at the delay. Down in the mouth of the crater, where the cotton seed had been scraped from the floor, stood the woman who was to furnish the body for the dance and the body for the men. Standing there in the centre of the circle of men she was the target for handfuls of cotton seed and the vulturous words from their mouths. Over her body she wore a thin cloth of orange silk. Under the garment rose swelling thighs and unstillable breasts. She was talking to one of the several men beside her, her words broken under the pelting shower of flying cotton seed. (*TB*, 52)

After collecting a dollar from each of the gathered men, the woman begins her hip dance on the floor of the cottonseed crater: "Even before she was nude the shed was in an uproar, and by the time she had thrown the garment beside her pocketbook the din was headsplitting. She smiled forcedly around the circle and began her hip dance. The motions and effect were purely sensual, studiously calculated to inflame the lust of the men. The woman was an accomplished dancer it was quite evident, and placed amidst finer surroundings she would no doubt have achieved with the motions of her hips and breasts an effect not quite as crude and obscene" (*TB*, 53). Following the dance, which climaxes with small photographs of her child falling from an unclasped locket hanging from her necklace, the woman retires to the shed where the men line up to pay her another dollar to sleep with her, and the chapter ends as this "line closed up" (*TB*, 55).

Despite the surprise and disgust feigned by Caldwell in his broadside, the hooch dancer episode in *The Bastard* already offers a pointed elucidation of her potential for obscenity and the novella's as well. Characteristically, little effort is made in the passage to represent the woman's dance beyond direct statements as to its abstract coordination of cause and effect. "The motions and effect [of the hip dance] were purely sensual" because the one is assumed to be capable of fully (i.e., sensually) determining the other; the art of inflaming "the lust of men" is subject to studious calculations that can be embodied in imagined performance, if not by the novella's text itself. At the very least, *The Bastard* attempts neither to imitate the hip dance nor to strive for its effects in the meaning or form of its words. Instead, in keeping with the novella's critical instantiation of naturalist methods and premises, the dance itself is merely the occasion for asserting a fairly crude determinism (*these* motions lead to *these* effects) without the exhaustive presentation of the causal networks that presumably make the operations of that determinism possible in the first place.

Moreover, the narrator complicates this assertion as to the strong determinism of obscenity by insisting that it is subject to its audience. The same dance "placed amidst finer surroundings" than that of a cottonseed pit supporting twenty-five to thirty riotous men "would no doubt have achieved . . . an effect not quite as crude and obscene." There is no such thing as obscenity in and of itself, it would appear. Instead, there is only potential obscenity, which depends upon situation and class because obscene effects are not something that can be readily achieved "amidst finer surroundings" than those afforded by a cottonseed oil mill pit.[31] Contexts of production as well as those of reception are thus vital for recognizing obscenity, a term the narrator of *The Bastard* defines as the creation "of beauty or rhythm . . . by the actual indulgence of artificially generated lust" (*TB*, 53).

The hooch dancer comprises more than just a verbally represented emblem of *The Bastard* as a text that was proscribed on grounds of obscenity. In The Heron Press edition of the novella, Ty Mahon's illustration of her hip dance at the cottonseed oil mill appears on the leaf facing the title page (see fig. 1), highlighting the significance of the scene for those apt to read *The Bastard* for its obscene potentials. Lazily angling bare calves, torso, arms, and head, the hooch dancer in Mahon's visualization of the episode appears at first glance to be more luridly posed than artfully arrested in "purely sensual" motion. Unlike the men whose split-pea eyes leer from the circle around her, she is free of excessive shading. Whereas the cartoonish features of these men gathered about her seem to be seen indistinctly through a curtain of hasty vertical and diagonal marks (perhaps an attempt to visualize Caldwell's spermatic "shower of flying cotton seed"), the predominant feature of her illustrated version is arguably the virtual absence of features: musculature, jaw, chin, belly button, and digits appear indistinctly on the page. Mahon also excludes not only the dancer's pubic hair but also her locket, a detail that preoccupies Caldwell enough for him to momentarily violate the novella's point of view, which until this point has been third person limited to Gene.[32] Within the white space expelling the murky torrential shadings of the millhands, the hooch dancer emerges as if from the nub end of an eraser, and the ultimate effect of Mahon's illustration is arguably less qualified than the ones pursued by Caldwell's text. The surroundings of the hooch dancer do not seem as open to variability in this visual representation of the hip dance as they do in Caldwell's verbal account, because the halo of white space draping her nude body demarcates not so much a zone of inapproachability as a covering to be punctured, either by the grasping paw of the millhand reaching toward her hips from her right or by the keenly staring man to her left, whose right arm and hand dip suggestively toward his own crotch. Poised literally between rape and the voyeuristically achieved self-pleasures of ogling men on the leaf facing *The Bastard*'s title page, the illustrated hooch dancer appears to promise unmixed pleasures that the text itself either estranges us from or evades altogether. If Caldwell cannot make it through the scene without including digressions as to the mere potential of female bodies, given the right circumstances, to promote "the actual indulgence of artificially created lust" in men, Mahon's illustration seeks instead to interpose no such impediments beyond the depiction of a female body and what that body is to be used for by men (i.e., coerced sex or masturbation). The body for the dance can be nothing other than the body for the men in Mahon's drawing, and it would seem that viewing this and other illustrations in the novella in this way caused the Cumberland County Attorney to declare the book obscene. Anticipating the infamous pronouncement of Potter Stewart in *Jacobellis v. Ohio*, he quite simply knew obscenity when he saw it.

Yet Mahon's illustration is arguably as estranging as the coordinated causes and effects described by Caldwell's narrator in the hooch dancer episode. Though momentarily warding off the imminent threat of a millworker's hand, the halo of whiteness surrounding the dancer's nude body also indicates the potential transposability of that body. More than just a tenuous protective covering to her body when surrounded by a crowd of aroused night laborers, the negative space encircling the woman also implicitly facilitates the provisional cutting and pasting of her body into entirely different scenes and surroundings altogether. Consequently, the illustration of the hooch dancer also represents the reduction of her body to an occasion for "the actual indulgence of artificially created lust" in *this* particular case; despite the fact that the drawing arrests the scene just before the moment this will no longer be the case—another second or two, and the hand of the millworker will seize the body of the woman—setting, dance, and dancer do not necessarily reinforce each other in Mahon's drawing. That is to say, the depicted uses of the hooch dancer's body are contingent and subject to self-reflexive (and possibly self-canceling) gestures that complement similar representations in Caldwell's text.

The mere placement of this particular illustration on the leaf facing the title page, however, is still another turn of the screw regarding the obscene potentials of *The Bastard*. Though plausibly supporting more complex interpretations than those given or presumed by the Cumberland County Attorney, Mahon's visual emblem

1. Ty Mahon, illustration from *The Bastard*, 1929

for Caldwell's novella indicates a different genealogy for its mode of publication than the ones that most studies on modernist publishing practices have tended to offer. In fact, Rachel Potter's recent work on modernism and the trade in salacious books productively ambiguates the significance of modernist limited editions and subscription lists for readers and state authorities in the 1920s and 1930s by asking us to reconsider what these authorities and readers actually saw when presented with works like Shakespeare and Company's *Ulysses*. Rather than follow the influential arguments in Lawrence Rainey's *Institutions of Modernism* (1998) regarding the myriad uneven processes of commodification that modernist texts and publishing practices underwent in this period, she stresses instead legal and social features mentioned only in passing in his account. In addition to providing the means by which publishers in the 1920s could present Anglo-American modernist works to wealthy patrons as opportunities for speculative investment, subscription lists and limited editions were also publishing practices long associated with pornography. Since at least the nineteenth century, the use of limited editions and subscription lists had been a common practice in the publishing of pornographic texts that vexed legal distinctions between public and private. By pricing texts beyond the reach of those with low-to-average incomes and making such works available solely to those on a mailing list, publishers intended to remove potentially suppressible texts from public spaces and resituate them in presumably more private realms, helping to ensure that these texts would be safe from purity groups and nosy customs officials.[33] According to Potter, "if Rainey sees Beach's use of subscription lists as part of an attempt to create *Ulysses* as a special, luxury commodity, he downplays the fact that such means of dissemination had a long and complex history. It is only in retrospect that the distinctions between *Ulysses* and pornographic texts, and the literary market and the pornography trade, are straightforward. It did not look so clear-cut to some lawyers, judges, vice crusaders, publishers, customs officials, or others at the time."[34]

Consequently, *The Bastard* must have seemed a strange object indeed to patrons of Caldwell's Longfellow Square Bookshop in Portland. Though priced and published in a way potential buyers would have associated with the pornographic book trade, Caldwell's novella nevertheless appeared for public sale in a bookstore, and not for a more confidential exchange via the supposed privacy of a subscription list. Furthermore, though Caldwell defended the naturalist pretenses of its words, *The Bastard* incurred the censorious attentions of the Cumberland County Attorney because of Ty Mahon's illustrations of women in various stages of undress and arousal. It is these illustrations that confirmed the pornographic implications of the edition's scarcity and price, neither of which were sufficient in themselves to connote modernist publication practices of the sort commonly associated with either Shakespeare and Company's *Ulysses* or the Hogarth Press's *The Waste Land*. In short, Caldwell's public sale of *The Bastard* frustrated both the modernist *and* the pornographic implications of its mode of publication.

IV

The hooch dancer scene in *The Bastard* also prompts questions that are worth asking of Caldwell's writing more generally. What do we in fact get to *see* when his anecdotal narratives appear to stall and groups of people stare at a couple in flagrante delicto or at the figure of a young woman said to be so attractive that she makes "you just ache to get down and lick something"?[35] To what extent is "the reader . . . inscribed into sexualized scenes in the form of another character who watches the erotic action unfold" in Caldwell's fiction?[36] More plainly, just how consequential are representations of voyeurism to Caldwell's potential obscenity? I would like to make a start at providing some answers to these questions by offering readings of two texts. The first is a passage from the last of Caldwell's novels in the 1930s, and the second is one of the most famous illustrated book covers in U.S. paperback publishing history. Articulating the interrelationships between these two texts should help to give us a better sense of the complex and variable functions performed by visuality in Caldwell's work as it lucratively underwent paperback republication throughout the latter half of the 1940s.

The most remarkable instance of voyeurism in all of Caldwell's published fiction occurs about halfway through *Journeyman* (1935), which tells the story of the mysteriously charismatic influence of a sinful traveling lay preacher (given the provocative name of Semon Dye) on both a family and a small community in the Depression-era South. After cuckolding Clay Horey as well as conning him out of his car, a watch, and one hundred dollars, Semon takes a trip with Clay to view the schoolhouse in which he will be delivering a sermon to the residents of the dirt-poor agrarian town of Rocky Comfort on the following day. Along the way, they stop at a neighbor's property to drink some corn whiskey and pass the time before driving on to the schoolhouse. They find the neighbor, Tom Rhodes, alone in a cowshed, in which he sits "perched on a stool, looking through a crack in the wall of the shed. He had not seen them."[37] Semon and Clay startle Tom and begin to interrogate him: "'What in thunder are you doing peeping through that crack, Tom?' Clay said, stepping inside and stopping to look closely at Tom" (*J*, 169). Tom ineffectually tries to hide his embarrassment by laughing off their questions, but Semon and Clay press him further. The crack in the cowshed wall has piqued their interest.

> Semon went across the shed and bent over at the crack. He peered through it for a few minutes, shutting one eye and squinting the other.
>
> "I don't see a thing but the woods over there," Semon said, standing erect and looking at Tom. But he was still wondering what it was that could be seen through the crack.
>
> Tom did not try to explain.
>
> "What in thunderation's going on over across there, Tom?" Clay asked. He bent over and looked through the crack in the wall. He shut one eye, squinted the other one, but he could still see nothing except the pine trees. (*J*, 169)

Semon asks Tom about his corn whiskey, and the men start to take long drafts from it in turn. Once the whiskey passes to Clay and Tom, Semon takes a stool over to the cowshed wall and bends his head to the crack there.

> He sat there, looking through it with his eye squinted for several minutes. After that he raised his head and looked at the others rather sheepishly.

> "See anything?" Clay said.
>
> "Not much."
>
> "Move over, then, and let me take a look through it."
>
> Clay sat down and looked through the crack. There was nothing much to be seen except the trees on the other side of the pasture. The fence over there that bordered that side of the pasture was barbed wire, and the posts were split pine. He saw all that in a glance, and there was nothing else to see, but he continued to look through the crack as though he saw something that he had never seen before in his life. (*J*, 171)

Tom and Semon talk for a spell about the Rocky Comfort schoolhouse before Tom starts to get anxious and demands his turn at the crack in the cowshed wall.

> [Tom] pushed Clay away from the stool and sat down to press his face against the wall where the crack was. He moved his head slightly to the left, then lowered it a fraction of an inch. After that he sat motionless.
>
> "See anything, coz?" Semon said.
>
> Tom said nothing. (*J*, 172)

Semon drinks deeply from the corn whiskey jug and admits to Clay there is not much sense in their seeing the schoolhouse before his revival the next day after all.

> Semon walked nervously around the cow shed. He came to a stop behind Tom.
>
> "Don't hog it all the time, coz," he said, pushing him. "Let a white man take a look once in a while."
>
> Tom got up and looked for the jug.
>
> "I can't seem to remember when I liked to look at a thing so much as I do now," Semon said, adjusting his eye to the crack. (*J*, 172–73)

Clay cleans his harmonica of the tobacco flakes embedded in it and starts to play a tune ("I've Got a Gal") while Semon, an eye still pressed to the crack in the cowshed wall, "began keeping time with his feet on the bare earth" (*J*, 173).

At this point, Tom starts to soliloquize about the unaccountable attractions of the crack in the cowshed wall:

> "That's the God-damnedest little slit in the whole world," Tom said. "I come down here and sit on the stool and look through it all morning sometimes. There's not a doggone thing to see but the trees over there, and maybe the fence

posts, but I can't keep from looking to save my soul. It's the doggonest thing I ever saw in all my life."

Semon settled himself more comfortably on the stool.

"There's not a single thing to see," Tom said, "and then again there's the whole world to look at. Looking through the side of the shed aint like nothing else I can think of. You sit there a while, and the first thing you know, you can't get away from it. It gets a hold on a man like nothing else does. You sit there, screwing up your eye and looking at the tree or something, and you might start to thinking what a fool thing you're doing, but you don't give a cuss about that. All you care for is staying there and looking." (J, 173–74)

Clay's harmonica-playing and Semon's bare-feet timekeeping are now joined by Tom's intermittent singing and humming: "*She wore a little yellow dress—* ... *— those eyes were made for me to see. . . . In the night-time is the right time—*" (J, 174). An eye still pressed to the crack in the cowshed wall, Semon starts to reach for the corn whiskey: "His hand was searching in a circle for it, but it was beyond his reach. He would not stop looking through the crack for even a second to see where the jug really was" (J, 174). Tom tells Semon to get up and away from the crack in the cowshed wall if he wants any more corn whiskey. Semon lingers, and Tom pushes him away from the crack in the cowshed wall.

Semon sat down on the other stool, rubbing the strain from his left eye. He blinked several times, resuming the tapping of his feet.

He took a long drink and put the jug down at Clay's side.

"That's the God-damndest slit I ever saw in all my life," Semon said. "You can look through there all day and never get tired. And come back the next day, and I'll bet it would look just as good. There's something about looking through a crack that nothing else in the whole wide world will give you." (J, 175)

After Clay has problems making himself quit his harmonica-playing, the song somehow manages to climax finally, and he takes a break. Semon offers Clay two turns instead of one at the crack in the cowshed wall if he starts playing "I've Got a Gal" again. He also manages to convince Clay to give up his next turn at the crack in the cowshed wall. Clay resumes the song.

With his head pressed tightly against the shed wall, Tom started humming again. He patted his feet on the ground, swinging into rhythm with the tune Clay was playing.

"There's never been but one gal like that in all the world," Semon said. The tears welled in his eyes and dripped against the backs of his hands. "If I could just look through the crack and see her, I wouldn't ask to live no longer. That crack is the God-damnedest thing I ever looked through. I sit there and look, and think about that gal, thinking maybe I'll see her with the next bat of my eye, and all the time I'm looking clear to the back side of heaven."

He strode to the wall and pushed Tom away. Without waiting to sit down first, he pressed his eye to the slit in the wall. After that he slowly sat down on the stool. (*J*, 176)

Tom takes his turn at the corn whiskey and puts the jug at Clay's feet, but Clay is too involved in playing the song to stop.

"*When I'm loving you, I'm telling you—*"

Semon put his hand to his face and wiped the tears from his cheeks.

"I don't know what I'd do without that crack in the wall," Tom said. "I reckon I'd just dry up and die away, I'd be that sad about it. I come down here and sit and look, and I don't see nothing you can't see better from the outside, but that don't make a bit of difference. It's sitting there looking through the crack at the trees all day long that sort of gets me. I don't know what it is, and it might not be nothing at all when you figure it out. But it's not the knowing about it, anyway—it's just the sitting there and looking through it that sort of makes me feel like heaven can't be so doggone far away." (*J*, 177)

With this, the chapter comes to an end, and the narrative shifts jarringly on the next page to midafternoon the next day at the Rocky Comfort schoolhouse, where Semon's revival is about to get under way.

At least two things are notable about the scene at the crack in Tom Rhodes's cowshed wall. First, there is the almost compulsive deployment of repetition at the levels of action, character, and narrative voice. Dialogue and behavior seem to be comprised of a few simple units of action that the narrative voice establishes within a page or two (Tom starts to soliloquize about "the God-damndest little slit," Semon closes one eye and squints the other, Tom pushes Clay away from the crack in the cowshed wall, etc.). The text then successively recombines them with a changing cast of subjects (*Semon* starts to soliloquize about "the God-damndest slit," *Clay* closes one eye and squints the other, *Semon* pushes *Tom* away from the crack in the cowshed wall, etc.) until Tom's monologue about feeling closer to heaven somehow comes to constitute an end to the chapter, if not to the men's experience at the crack in the cowshed wall that day.

Though its functions in Caldwell's fiction are variable and complex, in this particular passage repetition does seem to capture something of the development of ideologies of modernization in the early twentieth-century United States.[38] As

116

represented by way of repetition here, individual autonomy dissolves in the behaviors and speeches shifting and misfiring between Caldwell's characters, whom it is often quite difficult to distinguish from one another without the punctual insertion of their proper names to designate who speaks a particular group of words or performs a given set of acts. Just as Lewis's cultural criticism of the 1920s and 1930s warned, one's deeds and very speech here become drastically alienable, and it is this alienability as mediated by repetition in Caldwell's fiction that potentially bears the marks of a radically transformed social existence in the early decades of the last century in the United States. Rather than marking out a space for ironic embodiment and the bare possibility of agency, as it does in the creative work of Lewis, repetition in Caldwell merely confirms that characters are all of a piece, adopting each other's words as well as taking up each other's gestures and actions. To the extent that it is at all proper to speak of subjectivity in Caldwell's fiction, then, the terms in which one does so should be collective or communal rather than individual.

What paradoxically holds together this collectively conceived subject in Caldwell's work, however, is the radical *de*linking effected by its compulsion to repeat itself. In the course of exploring binding and unbinding tendencies in psychic structures, Sigmund Freud's *Beyond the Pleasure Principle* (1920) introduced the possibility that those very structures could come undone, as is famously said to happen in the chaotic disorder of the death drive and its potential to actualize itself in the compulsion to repeat.[39] Although such a repetition can possibly invest libidinal energy in painful affects, in doing so it also prevents those affects from becoming part of an integral ego. Impeding the interconnections of inner life, repetition compulsions therefore ensure that these affects and their associated behaviors remain fragmentary, iterative, stagnant.[40] In this view, then, what binds Clay, Tom, and Semon in the scene at the crack in the cowshed wall (their repetitious actions and speech) would appear to foreclose any future for their shared behaviors. Caldwell thus abruptly cuts off the chapter because the scene in principle has no end in sight. Unlike Gertrude Stein's *The Making of Americans* and its interminably ramifying examples of the differential intensities of repetition (e.g., the vital repetition of repeating vs. the repetition without difference that Stein designates as mere copying), the *Journeyman* passage instead repurposes repetition as a mode of free indirect discourse.[41] That is to say, Caldwell's text enacts the bafflement that is occurring inaudibly at a visual level by mimicking it within the undertones of its banally repetitive narration, which regressively circles around an unintelligible "seen" figure.[42]

Closely related to this use of repetition, the hole itself clearly suggests that the object of compulsive looking in Caldwell's fiction is absence itself. As represented in his work, gaps and laterally viewed blurs in the voyeur's field of vision precipitate both an overmastering compulsion to look again and a spreading confusion about how to rationalize this seemingly unmotivated behavior. Voyeurism here is hence defined by disruptions of its conventions of use. There certainly is *Schaulust* in his fiction, but we as readers are not invited to partake of it; instead, we are merely invited to oversee or overhear the distorted traces of its enactment and the strange effects it has on Caldwell's characters, if not on us as well. His prose does not attempt to visualize erotic scenes of looking but uses such scenes instead to help depict characters' desires and fantasies of presence by means of something that remains unseen or is but poorly glimpsed within the illegible tableau on display.[43]

Journeyman's scene at the crack in the cowshed wall can thus be said to anticipate the response of some major twentieth-century visual artists to the self-reflexive, formalist "opticality" famously espoused by Clement Greenberg, who stressed the purity not only of artistic mediums but also of visual experience itself. In contrast to Greenberg, Caldwell's hick voyeurs embody both visuality and its effects in conspicuously prosaic discourse, all while calling into question the separability of naturally occurring perceptual elements such as visuality and tactility, or eyes and the mobile body in space.[44] Not unlike minimalist critiques of Greenbergian modernism such as Robert Smithson's *Enantiomorphic Chambers* (1964) or Marcel Duchamp's invitation/frustration of voyeurism in *Étant donnés* (1946–66), the scene at the crack in the cowshed wall objectifies pure "opticality" through the frustration of sight.[45] Caldwell does little to make appear before his readers' eyes the objects of his characters' fantasies or even the gap-filled visions onto which these fantasies are projected. In general, this is what makes matters of sight and visuality structural— but not representational or interpellative—in his work. Strictly speaking, there is very little content that can be or in fact is shared in the erotics of Caldwell's looking. His supernumerary voyeuristic scenes do not function as invitations to pleasure so much as demonstrations *that there is* voyeuristic looking in these imagined life-worlds and that such looking is itself marked by a field of vision dotted with blurs, sties, and blind spots. In short, the obscene potentials of Caldwell's texts depend upon entirely different circuits than those provided by the problems of representational space or visuality alone.

V

Here is a second text with which we can further assess the obscene potentials of Caldwell's work (see fig. 2). In the mid-1940s, Caldwell's agent (Max Lieber) and hardback publisher (Duell, Sloan and Pearce) sold North American paperback reprint rights to all of his fiction to the U.S. branch of Penguin Books, and these rights were subsequently transferred to the New American Library of World Literature (NAL) and its Signet imprint after Victor Weybright and Kurt Enoch

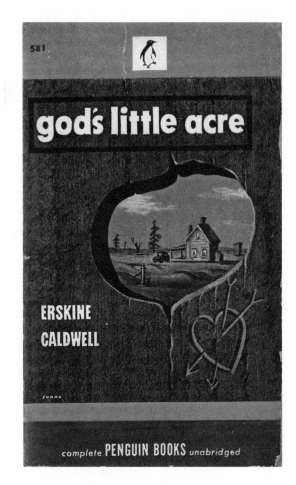

2. Robert Jonas, cover illustration for the first Penguin edition of *God's Little Acre*, 1946

left Penguin to start their own paperback company later in the 1940s.[46] Notably, the midcentury rise of paperback publishing, distribution, and advertising was instrumental in driving Caldwell's book sales to unprecedented heights even as the quality of his later cyclorama fiction was said by most critics to be diminishing markedly with each new novel.[47] U.S. sales of the Penguin *God's Little Acre* reached three million copies within two years of the first paperback edition, and those of *Tobacco Road* reached one million copies within nine months of the first Penguin edition.[48] In addition to the aggressive use of advertising, which included Caldwell's personal involvement in the promotion of the Penguin/Signet reprints of his work at drugstores across the country, the remarkable success of the first Penguin edition of *God's Little Acre* has traditionally been attributed to Robert Jonas's pop-Magritte peephole cover for that book. As Robert L. Bonn notes in his historical overview of the American mass-market paperback industry, *God's Little Acre* "became a runaway bestseller, and the knothole cover that promised forbidden insights into Southern comforts was credited with stimulating much of the sales. The peephole device, placed within the rather rigid front-cover frame design, gave birth to literally hundreds of paperbound keyholes, wall chinks, and assorted spyholes. For many readers the Jonas knothole has become a symbol of paperback publishing."[49]

While Jonas's illustration appears to be covering the wrong Caldwell novel—its peephole looking out onto a rural landscape free of people recalls the scene at the crack in the cowshed wall in *Journeyman* more than it does any voyeuristic encounter in *God's Little Acre*—the cover to the first Penguin edition *God's Little Acre* is nevertheless consistent with the structural functions ascribed to Caldwellian voyeurism earlier. As in *Journeyman*, the object of sight here is an absence waiting to be filled with libidinal projections that the "object" itself (in this case, the hole-dotted field and rural house) does not offer beyond the barest hints provided by the frame: the arrows piercing the heart carved below the vaguely heart-shaped knothole. On its own, then, the Jonas cover to *God's Little Acre* seems a fit emblem for the representation of visuality in Caldwell, withholding as it does the referents (women in various stages of undress and/or arousal) stereotypically ascribed to such peephole devices. Yet Bonn's account of the influence of Jonas's illustration on subsequent paperback covers claims that this influence was predicated on the "forbidden insights into Southern comforts" that the cover was understood to be promising with regard to the contents of *God's Little Acre* itself. Given Caldwell's typical frustration of clearly visible representations of voyeuristic peeping, however, the illustration itself appears to be subject to the sorts of projections and fantasies alluded to in *Journeyman*. Therefore, the Jonas peephole cover should not be interpreted without taking into account subsequent Penguin and Signet editions of Caldwell's work to see the kinds of visions and projections to which it did in fact give rise.

Looking at a chronological sampling of covers to the paperback reprints of Caldwell's work from the late 1940s, we find the following (see figs. 3–7). That these illustrated covers comprise so many repetitious revisions of Jonas's peephole cover to *God's Little Acre* goes without saying. If Jonas's first Caldwell illustration managed to get at how vision and voyeurism appear to function in Caldwell's novels by evacuating the object in sight of anything remotely arousing in and of itself, then the following Signet editions of Caldwell's fiction acted to project onto the screen of Jonas's famous peephole cover the fantasies of sexual difference and desire that that illustration pointedly avoided depicting. In fact, it is these later paperback covers—and not the words they enclosed—that increasingly support the view that Caldwell's fiction and potential for obscenity depend upon fairly simplistic representations of *Schaulust* in which the reader/viewer gets himself "inscribed" into or otherwise hailed by the desiring men and desirable women on display.

The strategies for this interpellation and inscription are mixed: in some cases, a foregrounded male voyeur is shown to be watching the suggestively clothed and posed body of a woman through a frame, as in the *Journeyman* cover (fig. 3) and the cover to *The Sure Hand of God* (fig. 7). In others, such as the cover to *Tragic Ground* (fig. 4), foreground and background relations are reversed, with the proffered libidinal object of view moved to the near side of the peephole device.[50] Jonas's cover to the Signet edition of *A House in the Uplands* (fig. 5) plays on a number of features in his illustration for *God's Little Acre* (the columns of a Southern mansion replace the clapboard structure in the earlier cover, the lush hillocks substitute for the pockmarked fields on the Waldens's property, etc.) even as it inserts the sort of object for sight that that cover had famously withheld. The sleeve of her form-fitting dress sliding down her left shoulder, a woman leans against the frame of a door functioning as the peephole in the illustration. She both obscures the putative object of view (the Southern mansion and its surrounding property) and reveals the dormant libidinal potentials inhering in that object when seen focalized through the opening provided by the doorframe. Save for her hair color and some details of dress, she bears a remarkable resemblance to the woman in the *Journeyman* cover. In particular, the cover to *A House in the Uplands* studiously copies the form-fitting red dress, the sliding left cap sleeve, and the pose of the woman used in the earlier illustration. By the time of the Signet publication of *A Woman in the House* (fig. 6) in February 1949, the variability of the earlier covers in their deployment of bodies, apertures, objects, and male viewers had seemingly resolved itself into the facile singularity of a literal keyhole through which a young woman can be seen (un)dressing. While certainly less than generous, it would not be entirely unfair to understand this particular cover as expressing the truth of Jonas's *God's Little Acre* illustration for the paperback industry, revealing as it does the sorts of objectifications and asymmetrical relationships to which the peephole device readily lends itself. Over and over again, the paperback illustrations covering Caldwell's work in the 1940s attempted to fill in the absences in the field of vision upon which he bases his voyeurism. At the very least, it is here, if anywhere, that the aggressively crude male gaze is to be more properly located in Caldwell's work.[51]

Yet we miss something about how these covers converge with Caldwell's own optical apparatuses if we insist on simply reading them as so many attempts to neutralize the disruptive indeterminacies in the Caldwellian field of vision. If we bracket for the moment the screen-without-depth quality of Jonas's *God's Little Acre* cover, that illustration can be seen to offer us a vantage point of one interior out onto an exterior (the clapboard structure) containing yet another interior into which we are not yet close enough to see. If we frame the relationship of this illustration to the one covering *A Woman in the House* as one marked by a transit *into* that distant interior sketched by Jonas, then it is as if we have somehow made it through Jonas's

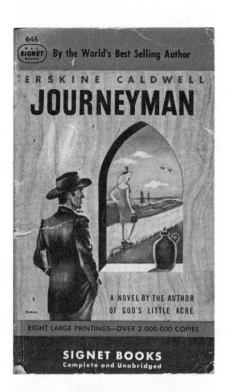

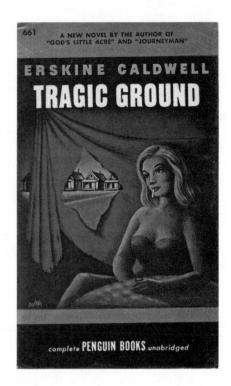

3. (above left) Robert Jonas, cover illustration for the first Penguin/Signet edition of *Journeyman*, 1947

4. (above right) Robert Jonas, cover illustration for the first Penguin/Signet edition of *Tragic Ground*, 1948

5. (left) Robert Jonas, cover illustration for the first Signet edition of *A House in the Uplands*, 1948

6. (opposite left) Unknown illustrator, cover illustration for the first Signet edition of *A Woman in the House*, 1949

7. (opposite right) James Avati, cover illustration for the first Signet edition of *The Sure Hand of God*, 1949

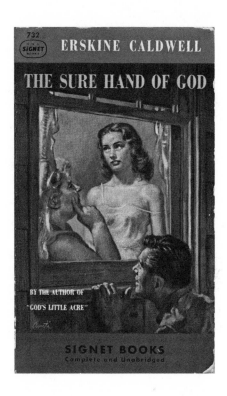

knothole, crossed the hole-dotted field, and gotten up close enough to the house to take a peek through the keyhole only to find . . . another covered hole.[52] In this view, we end up not so much with a totalizing male gaze but rather with an infinite regress of interiors that frustratingly appears to shift the obscene potentials of the paperback book cover onto the words it encloses.

The paperback branding of Caldwell's novels as a popular literary commodity bringing forbidden sights into view also helps a great deal in our understanding why the historical record of the attempts to proscribe his work on grounds of obscenity is so uneven and sporadic. After the unsuccessful prosecution of *God's Little Acre* on charges of obscenity levied by the New York Society for the Suppression of Vice in 1933, thirteen years passed before purity groups, cities, and nations started prosecuting or banning the book in earnest. For instance, only in 1946 did the city of St. Paul start to enforce a municipal ban of *God's Little Acre*. The following year, the Penguin twenty-five-cent edition of Caldwell's novel was banned in Denver because of a concern in that city about the potentially adverse effects of the book on teenagers. Boston seized and tried *God's Little Acre* in 1950, and in 1953 the National Organization of Decent Literature in Chicago included the novel among its list of disapproved works. Also in 1953, the *National Newsagent, Bookseller, Stationer* in England put *God's Little Acre* on a list of published books that local magistrates had singled out for destruction. That same year, Ireland banned both *Tobacco Road* and *God's Little Acre*.[53] It would seem that the strange delay in the prosecution and proscription of Caldwell's 1930s novels (and of *God's Little Acre* in particular) depended upon contemporary developments in the paperback industry. At the very least, without our first taking into account paperback publishing practices and their reception in the 1940s and 1950s, the lag time in the proscription of Caldwell's novels on grounds of obscenity otherwise appears to be arbitrary.

The signal innovations of American paperback publishing in the 1940s were not only the considerable reductions in the price of books that publishers managed to implement and then sustain but also the opening of new markets that they achieved by altering substantively what were then the standard models of distribution in the book publishing industry.[54] Rather than distribute their products in traditional trade bookstores, paperback publishers followed the example set by Robert DeGraff's Pocket Books and shifted their products to unconventional outlets such as newsstands, drugstores, and grocery stores by way of independent wholesale distributors.[55] Due in part to conditions arising from this change in distribution and reduction in price, the incredible sales and popularity of paperbacks at this time tended to hinge principally upon the successful targeting of demographics (e.g., various youth markets) and classes (especially the lower socioeconomic strata) hitherto not expressly catered to by bookstores or hardcover book publishers in the United States. When coupled with the physical appearance of these volumes, which often seemed intent on outdoing each other in terms of sensationalized covers depicting salaciously posed and often barely clothed female bodies, the nature of the threats posed by paperbacks in the 1940s called forth a coordinated system of public concern in which categories of youth, class, and sex found their place.

It is in this changed and charged world of mass-market paperback readership that Caldwell's reputed obscenity finally became visible to a large number of his contemporaries. In hardcover, *God's Little Acre* had occasioned a single obscenity trial upon its release in 1933.[56] It was only following its immensely successful paperback reprinting in 1946 that the novel came to be commonly viewed as posing the sorts of obscene threats to which courts, cities, and even nations needed to react proscriptively. Determining whether Caldwell's work itself or mass-market paperbacks in general were the problem, then, is no small matter in discussing the obscene potentials of his fiction, for it complicates the very time and site of what literary critics have taken to calling "obscene modernism" or "modernist obscenity." To take but one striking example in this respect, I would note that the prosecution of William Faulkner's *Sanctuary* and *The Wild Palms* on grounds of obscenity did not begin until 1948, respectively seventeen and nine years *after* their initial dates of publication, but roughly contemporaneous with the initial release of their paperback reprint versions. Accordingly, mass-market paperback publishing would seem to be worthy of study alongside limited-edition modes of distribution as well.

As a mode of book publishing, marketing, and distribution, paperbacks comprised such a distinctive public threat at the time that they were subjected to intense federal scrutiny. In 1952 a Select Committee on Current Pornographic Materials (dubbed the Gathings Committee in the press) began holding hearings in the United States House of Representatives in order to assess the editorial and marketing procedures of the paperback publishing industry. The chairman of the committee, Representative Ezekiel Gathings (Democrat-Arkansas), initiated the investigative hearings because he was deeply troubled by the paperbacks, magazines, and comic books he saw displayed in plain view on newsstands and in drugstores on his daily walks to the House of Representatives. With the authorization of House Resolution 596, the Gathings Committee undertook "a full and complete investigation and study (1) to determine the extent to which current literature—books, magazines, and comic books—containing immoral, obscene, or otherwise offensive matter, or placing improper emphasis on crime, violence, and corruption, are being made available to the people of the United States through the United States mails and otherwise; and (2) to determine the adequacy of existing law to prevent the publication and distribution of books containing immoral, offensive, and other undesirable matter."[57] In the report issued on December 31, 1952, a majority of the Gathings Committee acknowledged that the scope of obscenity in the paperback industry was indeed cause for considerable alarm, even though "obscene" paperbacks themselves comprised only a small proportion of the overall output of any given paperback publisher. To combat the effects and influence of obscene paperbacks, the committee offered three recommendations to the House based on the results of their investigation:

(1) Congress should enact legislation making it "a Federal offense to knowingly transport in interstate or foreign commerce for sale or distribution certain specified articles and matters, including books and pamphlets of an obscene, lewd, lascivious, or filthy character."[58]

(2) Congress should enact legislation permitting the Postmaster General "to impound mail pendente lite which is addressed to a person or concern which is obtaining or attempting to obtain remittances of money through the mails in exchange for any obscene, lewd, lascivious, indecent, filthy, or vile article, matter, thing, device or substance." The committee also recommended that Congress should exempt "the Post Office Department from the provision of the Administrative Procedure Act," which included a number of routinized steps that apparently gave the putative pornographer both time

125

and opportunity in which to continue to profit from the dissemination of obscene materials while the bureaucratic wheels slowly turned.[59]

(3) The paperback industry should "recognize the growing public opposition to that proportion of its output which may be classified as 'border line' or 'objectionable,' and take the steps necessary to its elimination on its own initiative, rather than to allow this opposition to increase to the point where the public will demand governmental action."[60]

An accompanying minority report strenuously objected to the first two recommendations by noting that obscenity was already a heavily legislated problem at the federal and state levels—only New Mexico did not have an obscenity statute on the books in 1952—and that the abrogation of the Administrative Procedure Act on behalf of the U.S. Post Office was not within the powers of the committee itself to recommend.[61]

Suggestively, the split in the committee between the authors of the *Report* and those of its highly critical minority report hinged upon which parts of the increasingly contentious body of U.S. case law on obscenity each group felt possessed precedential force in the current discussion and investigation of paperbacks. In its opening pages, the official *Report* of the Gathings Committee positions itself against those recent lower and appellate court cases (e.g., *United States v. One Book Called "Ulysses"* and *Commonwealth v. Gordon et al.*) that had attempted to nullify the provisions of the Cockburn test by arguing instead for holistic readings of those texts charged with obscenity:

> [The Woolsey test] held with reference to alleged obscene books that in determining whether or not a particular book is obscene, the yardstick is that the pertinent theme is controlling and that if the obscene contents are only for the purpose of delineating character, it will not necessarily cause the book to be held obscene, particularly if otherwise the literary character is such as to place it in an acceptable category. It is as elastic as rubber in its interpretive susceptibility and supplies the purveyors of obscenity with an excuse regardless of what is the degree of obscenity involved and requires each and every book to be judged separately, an almost impossible task.

The Woolsey test is subsequently described as a "revolutionary" overturning of "a long-existing principle of law [i.e., the Cockburn test] dealing directly with obscenity in literature," and the *Report* goes on to contend (ungrammatically) that because of it, "the judicial viewpoint on the subject of obscenity in literature today, establishing [sic] a new legal philosophy in that field but one so elastic that it serves as the basis for excuse to print and circulate the filthiest most obscene literature without concurrent literary value to support it, ever known in history. Referred to constantly by every publisher of obscene literature whenever approached on the subject, a layman finds it difficult to successfully counter the argument of the publishers citing the Ulysses [*sic*] case."

As for Judge Curtis Bok's attempts to deproscribe and altogether unsettle legal formulations of obscenity in *Commonwealth v. Gordon et al.*, the Gathings Committee spends most of its discussion of that case looking at circumstantial evidence in order to suggest that Bok's views on the matter of obscenity and books were unavoidably biased (*Report*, 6). Rather than read and analyze the opinion in *Commonwealth v. Gordon et al.*, the *Report* simply notes that Bok is the grandson of the founder of the Curtis Publishing Company, the acting vice president and director of which at that time was Bok's brother. Moreover, Bok's mother sat on its board of directors, and the company owned 42.5 percent of the stock of Bantam Books, Inc., "one of the largest producers of pocket-size books of the type of those referred to in the committee hearings." Immediately after offering this information, the committee hastens to disavow any intention of calling Bok's "honesty or integrity as a judge" into question in any way. The *Report*, however, does go on to assert that it is "reasonably possible that having been associated so closely with the publishing business that [Bok] became inherently imbued with a liberal conception of the tradition founded upon the constitutional provision guaranteeing the freedom of the press" (*Report*, 7). Against the unduly influenced views of Judge Bok in *Commonwealth v. Gordon et al.*, the Gathings Committee devotes the next six pages of the *Report* to the extensive quotation from and interpretation of an opposing precedential body of case law on obscenity, namely one in which the proscriptive force and applicability of contemporary obscenity laws to books had been consistently reaffirmed despite the corrosive effects ascribed to the Woolsey and Bok opinions (*Report*, 7–13). Not surprisingly, the attached minority report simply reverses the *Report*'s evaluations as to which legal precedents ought to be followed within the terms set by the House for the committee's investigative hearings (*Report*, 122–23). Against the authors of the *Report*, the minority report prizes and defends the Woolsey and Bok opinions as estimable and authoritative attempts "to separate the realm of obscenity from what amounts to legitimate written expression" (*Report*, 122).

VI

Not simply because it comprises a landmark of sorts in the efforts of liberalizing lower court and appellate judges in the twentieth century to deproscribe the obscenity of books in this country, Judge Bok's opinion in *Commonwealth v. Gordon et al.* will occupy us for the remainder of the chapter, as will *God's Little Acre*, one of the books charged with obscenity in that case. In 1948, following a Fundamentalist minister's complaint, the chief inspector of the Philadelphia Vice Squad had a patrolman purchase and read a number of books sold in the area. This patrolman focused initially on twenty-five books, in which he marked passages containing obscene or otherwise objectionable descriptions and words. Based on these findings, a raid—for which no warrant was secured—took place on the premises of fifty-four Philadelphia booksellers, during which the police seized about two thousand putatively obscene texts. Officers subsequently got warrants for the arrest of five of these booksellers, who were charged for the possession and intent to sell nine allegedly obscene books: William Faulkner's *Sanctuary* and *Wild Palms*, James T. Farrell's *Studs Lonigan* trilogy and *A World I Never Made*, Calder Willingham's *End as a Man*, Harold Robbins's *Never Love a Stranger*, and Erskine Caldwell's *God's Little Acre*.[62] While there is no mention made in accounts of the raids or in the trial opinion itself as to the format in which the seized and charged books were found (hardcover or paperback), all of these texts either had recently appeared as paperbacks (*God's Little Acre* [Penguin/Signet 581, March 1946], *Sanctuary* [Penguin/Signet 632, April 1947], *Young Lonigan* [Penguin/Signet 643, September 1947], and *The Wild Palms* [Penguin/Signet 659, January 1948]) or were soon to be republished in that form (*End as a Man* [Avon 240, January 1950], *The Young Manhood of Studs Lonigan* [Signet 810, September 1950], *Never Love a Stranger* [Bantam A814, 1950], *Judgment Day* [Signet S875, January 1951], and *A World I Never Made* [Signet D926, January 1952]).

A trial without jury began in the Common Pleas Court of Philadelphia County later that year, and on March 18, 1949, Judge Curtis Bok delivered a lengthy opinion in which he held that the books at issue in the case of *Commonwealth v. Gordon et al.* were not obscene as alleged by the district attorney. In the course of reaching this decision, Bok's opinion extensively reviewed the precedential histories of legal obscenity in England and America; relativized concepts of decency, censorship standards, and moral codes; argued that obscene books can only be proscribed provided they have a dominant effect of erotic allurement that poses a clear and present danger to the community; and suggested that the marketplace, and not the courts, was "the best crucible in which to distil an instinctive morality" (*Gordon*, 66 Pa. D.&C., at 127). According to Bok, neither did the books in this case possess "a calculated and effective incitement to sexual desire" as an end nor could the reading of them be said to lead to the commission or to the imminence of the commission of criminal behavior (*Gordon*, at 151 and 155). Subsequently, both the Superior and Supreme Courts of Pennsylvania upheld Bok's decision. *Sanctuary*, *The Wild Palms*, the *Studs Lonigan* trilogy, *God's Little Acre*, and the other allegedly obscene books were hereafter free to circulate in Pennsylvania bookshops and drugstores.

The question guiding Bok in *Commonwealth v. Gordon et al.* may be posed simply as "What is obscenity?" To which Bok gives the categorical answer, "Not books." After reviewing the Pennsylvania statute at issue in the prosecution of these particular booksellers, Bok refuses to grant any immediately apparent or transhistorical significance to the term "obscenity": "I assume that 'obscenity' is expected to have a familiar and inherent meaning, both as to what it is and as to what it does. It is my purpose to show that it has no such inherent meaning; that different meanings given to it at different times are not constant, either historically or legally; that it is not constitutionally indictable unless it takes the form of sexual impurity, i.e. 'dirt for dirt's sake' and can be traced to actual criminal behavior, either actual [*sic*] or demonstrably imminent" (*Gordon*, at 104). There are two prongs to Bok's test for obscenity here: to be indictable as obscenity, the putatively obscene object itself must be sexually impure and demonstrably linked to manifestly criminal acts. That is to say, one must be able to translate the sexual impurity of the text itself to the indictable—and apparently sexually impure—behaviors of those who have encountered that text in the world. This would appear to assume that "sexual impurity" is any more definable than "obscenity," though Bok soon enough ventures a definition: "Sexual impurity in literature (pornography, as some of the cases call it) I define as any writing whose dominant purpose is erotic allurement—that is to say, a calculated and effective incitement to sexual desire. It is the effect that counts, more than the purpose, and no indictment can stand unless it can be shown" (*Gordon*, at 151). For Bok, "sexual impurity" is synonymous with a successful seduction that would lead to a sexual act proscribable under criminal law. The tautology of the test is quite obvious: "sexual impurity" names an effective cause just as the criminal behavior linked to it must reveal itself to be the caused effect of that effective cause.

Furthermore, Bok's test seems on its face to be as useful for those seeking to strengthen and expand the scope of the proscriptive powers of obscenity laws as it would be for liberalizing judges and jurists. That is to say, there seems to be a considerable haze of uncertainty concerning how one is supposed to apply the cause-and-effect machinery of this test to indicted books in obscenity proceedings. Bok spends the remainder of his opinion attempting to foreclose any indefinite interpretation of his test by arguing that books cannot be obscene, because they do not fall within the purview of "sexual impurity" as defined by him and consequently cannot lead to criminal behavior (*Gordon*, at 117). A book "cannot be a present danger unless its reader closes it, lays it aside, and transmutes its erotic allurement into overt action. That such action must inevitably follow as a direct consequence of reading the book does not bear analysis, nor is it borne out by general human experience; too much can intervene and too many diversions take place." Against the diversions and indeterminacies involved in regulating how books relate to or bear upon physical acts, Bok counterposes laws proscribing public lewdness, understood by him to be far less dubious, since a person "who is publicly lewd is in himself an open and immediate invitation to morally criminal behavior" (*Gordon*, at 153). By refusing to specify the mediations involved in transmuting printed textual matter into bodily responses, Bok expresses a radical doubt as to their possibility in the first place. The mediations that may take place between book texts and corporeal acts cannot be regulated like public lewdness, the clear and present danger of which Bok does not question but rather directly opposes to the weak, perhaps illusory, threats said to be posed by books. In *Commonwealth v. Gordon et al.*, the danger of lewdness is its immediacy, while representations of lewdness, such as those appearing time and time again in *God's Little Acre*, are so mediated that they pose little direct harm. As Lewis's critiques of Watsonian behaviorism pointed out earlier, words would continue to gum up the functioning of stimuli-response reactions so long as the world failed to be governed by behaviorist principles. *Commonwealth v. Gordon et al.* thus reveals that Lewis was far too quick to take the eventual victory of behaviorism for granted because by the 1940s people were becoming less, not more, responsive to the sensory content of words on the page. He had greatly overestimated how many potential Cantlemans were out there incubating among the literate masses.

Resistant to theorization and regulation though they may be, the claims books make on bodies nevertheless remain what is at issue in obscenity case law from this period. Accordingly, it is a signal failure of Bok's opinion that it renders unproblematic a set of arrangements and encounters in the world that continued to be problems. More particularly, however, his opinion does not simply miss something about the effects books can have on their readers; it also completely disregards the reflexive staging of the specific effects for which Caldwell's novel strives.

A brief detour through Sigmund Freud's *Jokes and Their Relation to the Unconscious* is needed if we are to form a clearer sense of how this reflexive staging takes place. In that work, Freud argues that smutty exchanges generally occur among the relatively uninhibited and thus do not arise to the level of jokes proper. Smut (*Zote*) appears as a marginal case in Freud's book, as do the people from among the lower social strata who pursue such exchanges. Unlike that of the joke proper, the typical smutty encounter requires the presence of three people: a speaker—always a man in Freud's account—who uses his sexually explicit words as a way of seducing a woman—and it is always a woman—in front of another man. The function of the other man is crucial because his presence helps ensure the graphic wooing speech attains the condition of smut: if the woman were to yield too quickly to the speaker's words, then we would not have smut but rather a successful seduction.[63] According to Freud, the presence of the other man means that "an immediate surrender by the woman is as good as out of the question," thereby guaranteeing her (temporary) intransigence, which is the first condition of smut.[64] Without this intransigence, the sexually exciting speech would not come to be an aim in itself and thereby become smut. This is a crucial point: smut becomes a pleasurable end as such in the face of

130

the hindrances thrown in its way by the woman. This woman is now taken to be the object of sexual aggression as the speaker turns to the other man, originally an impediment to his wooing speech, now his ally. In fact, one of the possible results of the smutty encounter is the satisfaction of the other man's libido by exposing to his imagined sight the woman's nudity.[65] It must also be kept in mind, however, that the intransigence of the woman in the face of smut is not understood by Freud to be implacable; instead, "it seems merely to imply a postponement and does not indicate that further efforts will be in vain."[66] When smutty words do not lead to sexual actions, they can become an autonomous pleasure, albeit one thereafter primed to rouse one into sexual action with a change in circumstances.[67]

Many of these features of Freudian smut are relevant to understanding the formal structures of God's Little Acre, the events of which often depend on the susceptibility of male characters to the multiple attempted verbal exposures of women. More than the Waldens's fruitless search for gold on their land or the ineffective seizure of the mill in Scottsville by Will and his proletarian cohort, smutty encounters in God's Little Acre offer continuity between episodes and the means for accounting for that continuity. The book's narration does little beyond describe actions and physiological reactions. Save for striking moments of free indirect discourse, such as Will's vivid reverie of the ivy-covered mills run by women and the bloody-lipped men spitting their lungs out on the street (GLA, 68–75), the novel's attention to how objects and people look is mediated by what its characters say. For example, it is because Darling Jill says so that we know that Pluto Swint's eyes look like watermelon seeds (GLA, 29). Likewise, it is because of Ty Ty Walden's repeated verbal exposures of her before other men that we get a sense that his daughter-in-law, Griselda, has creamy skin, gold in her hair, pale blueness in her eyes, and "the finest pair of rising beauties a man can ever hope to see" (GLA, 30–31).

This last example perhaps registers the degree to which dialogue in Caldwell's novel has ends independent of interpersonal communication or neutral description. In fact, the typical smutty encounter in God's Little Acre consists of the exposure of Griselda by Ty Ty to other men: first to Pluto Swint (GLA, 29–31); then to Will, the millworker husband of Ty Ty's daughter, Rosamond (GLA, 88–90); and finally to Jim Leslie, Ty Ty's estranged son (GLA, 117–20, 125–27). The result of Griselda's exposure in front of Pluto Swint is relatively benign. When Ty Ty's smutty description of her reaches a peak—"The first time I saw you, when Buck brought you here from wherever it was you came from, I felt like getting right down there and then and licking something" (GLA, 30)—Pluto finds himself putting his hand on Griselda's legs and leaning against her. Griselda slaps him, and the Walden family laughs heartily at Pluto. We should note here that the roles in Freud's normative account of the smutty triad prove transitive in Caldwell's novel: the first man's speech, meant to incite the woman to sexual action, ends up goading the other man

131

to cop a feel. Subsequent smutty exposures bear this transitive quality out, insofar as Ty Ty's verbal exposures of her do not end up seducing Griselda so much as they do other men. In the case of Will—to whom Ty Ty again repetitively presents Griselda as having a pair of breasts so "pretty it makes me feel sometimes like getting right down on my hands and knees like these old hound dogs you see chasing after a flowing bitch. You just ache to get down and lick something" (*GLA*, 88)—the verbal exposure proves *too* effective, since Will goes on to sleep with Griselda before his death at the mill (*GLA*, 155–57). In the final case, Ty Ty's smutty speech concerning Griselda leads indirectly to Jim Leslie's murder at the hands of Buck, his brother and Griselda's husband, as he tries to take her away from the Walden farm for good. Whereas verbally exposing Griselda before other men is a pleasure in and of itself for Ty Ty, it does not satisfy his male listeners, for whom hearing and seeing in imagined sight are ultimately no substitutes for touching. They are aroused but not satisfied with mere arousal or with releasing that arousal through laughter, and it is conspicuously Ty Ty who arouses the men around him and gives the novel's readers a suggestively gap-filled and hard-to-visualize object for that arousal. Without Ty Ty's exposing speech, at least, Griselda would be as undifferentiated in the Walden family as Rosamond because there is little in the narration itself to set either woman apart.

What we thus find in *God's Little Acre* is a tissue of smutty encounters in which the functions of the Freudian smutty triad stay put, but the people and genders to whom those functions were originally attached do not. Ty Ty verbally exposes Griselda for the pleasure verbal exposure itself, and not the hope of sex with her, gives him. Hence his repetition of phrases in whole or in part ("finest pair of rising beauties," "makes you want to get down and lick something") to describe Griselda every time he strips her bare in words before other men. These phrases are saturated with the imagined nudity and sexual activities of Griselda; for him these particular words have all the affective force of Griselda's nude body itself, much like the repeated phrases used in the scene at the crack in the cowshed wall in *Journeyman*. They are the charged formula of an elusive pleasure that can be expressed and repeated, giving a pointed intensity to the novel's vast and belabored repetitious extension.

The transitive quality of the smutty encounter in Caldwell's novel is perhaps better illustrated, however, by looking at how women and the narration itself come to fill and fluctuate between these roles. There are at least two times in the novel when Darling Jill verbally exposes *a man* in front of Griselda. In the first instance, that man is Pluto Swint (*GLA*, 40–43), while in the second it is her father, Ty Ty (*GLA*, 109–13), and in both cases the exposure does not lead to sexual advances but to explosive laughter. Pluto is the one man with whom Darling Jill will not sleep, Ty Ty a man she presumably cannot, and Griselda's relative passivity in these scenes is of a piece with her role as the slightly intransigent object of verbal exposure elsewhere. Women in the novel thus appear to engage in smut with no other seductive ends in view; they use and respond to smut like a Ty Ty Walden.

However, this is not as straightforward as it might sound at first. Compare, for instance, the degree to which women's use of smut in *God's Little Acre* resonates with the most notable scene of verbal exposure in all of Southern literature: Janie Crawford's smutty unveiling of her husband, Joe Starks, before the residents of Eatonville in Zora Neale Hurston's *Their Eyes Were Watching God* (1937). Though Joe has constantly depicted his wife in a smutty way up to this point so that "it was like somebody snatched off part of a woman's clothes while she wasn't looking and streets were crowded," in unveiling her husband Janie is said by the narrator to have "done worse, she had cast down his empty armor before men and they had laughed, would keep on laughing. When he paraded his possessions hereafter, they would not consider the two together. They'd look with envy at the things and pity the man that owned them."[68] What this brings out in the use made of smutty language by women and Ty Ty Walden in *God's Little Acre* is its aggressivity. Of the three men to whom Ty Ty smuttily exposes Griselda, two are murdered by the end of the narrative, while the third (Pluto) is a constant object of ridicule for all of the other characters in *God's Little Acre*. In using smut the way Ty Ty does, then, the women in Caldwell's novel effectively—that is to say, violently—respond to a world in which their capacities for action and expression are attenuated, but not entirely foreclosed.

After Will and Griselda have coupled, but before his fatal march on the Scottsville mill, the hitherto relatively neutral reporting of the narration begins to get inflected with Will's free indirect discourse: "[Griselda] put two spoonfuls [of sugar] into the coffee cup. She knew. It wasn't every woman who would know how much sugar to put into his cup. She's got the finest pair of rising beauties a man ever laid his eyes on, and when you once see them, you're going to get right down on your hands and knees and lick something" (*GLA*, 163). This passage betrays a doubled consciousness of sorts in Caldwell's book. On the one hand, the text seeks to manifest the degree to which these particular phrases have become as affectively soaked with Griselda for Will as they manifestly are for Ty Ty; on the other hand, they implicate the narration, potentially the book itself, in the smutty triads presented throughout the text. The narration starts to verbally expose Griselda before the reader, not with Ty Ty's speech but mediated by a discourse loosely imitative of Will's interiority. Yet this narrative arrangement raises questions of address, since it seems to call forth the reader and "his" body (Caldwell's masculine norm seems in line with Freud's in this respect) into the smutty encounter. Words cartoonishly adumbrating images of and responses to a female body here would seem to arrogate to themselves the capacity to evoke bodily actions—riotous laughter or more directly genitalized pleasures—but only when coupled with an intransigent object,

8. Robert Jonas, cover illustration for the first Penguin edition of *Trouble in July*, 1945

134

be it in the form of an attractive daughter-in-law or a paperback book. Accordingly, Caldwell's use of Freudian smut is not simply a veridical or ethnographic reflection of lower-class mores and comportments but is also an active attempt to construct and reorganize experience along those very lines. As *God's Little Acre* demonstrates—and despite Bok's conclusions in *Commonwealth*—sensual immediacy is potentially the goal of all sorts of frustrating mediations, especially those we give the name of smut.

We can see how far Caldwell's obscene potentials are from the immediate lewd threats Bok discerned in mid-twentieth-century visual culture by glancing briefly at his extraordinary 1940 cyclorama novel, *Trouble in July*. Instead of just giving the libidinal and affective features of this novel a smutty form, Caldwell generalizes Freudian smut in such a way that the frustration of an experience ends up making that experience all the more violently possible. Caldwell's novel is a lynching novel, albeit one in which no one seems able to do what is expected of him or her in such a text: Sonny, the African American man erroneously charged with the rape of a white woman, cannot quite manage to make good his escape, even though he is given ample opportunities and time to do so; Katy Barlow, the alleged victim of this rape, cannot quite muster the willpower needed to admit Sonny's innocence to her family or community, though she feels a good deal of compunction about the prospect of the gruesome public death he faces; the white male rabblement in turn cannot quite work up enough focalized animus to put together an effectively functioning lynching party because they spend most of the novel pursuing old enmities and bickering among themselves instead; and Jeff McCurtain, the morbidly obese sheriff of the town of Andrewjones, cannot quite figure out what—much less *how*—to do what is needed of him in time to do it. *Trouble in July*, therefore, is a lynching novel that acts at each step of the way to avoid having to depict a lynching, even though these repeated instances of frustration ultimately do give rise in the last chapter to the brutal murder of Sonny and the confession of Katy, whom the lynch mob promptly stones to death.

Republished in October 1945, five months *before* the famous paperback reprint of *God's Little Acre*, *Trouble in July* was the first Caldwell paperback to be released by Penguin, and its cover suggests a more troubling genealogy with which to assess the "obscene" functions of the peephole structures we explored previously in the first run of Caldwell paperback reissues (see fig. 8). Posed next to a pictographic representation of a courthouse and partly framed by angled strands of rope, a darkened man-shaped aperture looks out on to a brown wasteland over which a noose hangs from a bare tree backlit by a fiery horizon. If reading from the *God's Little Acre* paperback forward to *A Woman in the House* led us through an endlessly receding series of covered holes, then starting from Penguin's *Trouble in July* leaves us with a different absence to be filled, for looming over those later illustrations is not simply the ever-deferred promise of nude white women but also the threatened torture and murder of African American men. Caldwellian smut and frustration thus disclose the uncomfortable proximity of obscenity to Jim Crow, the obsessive focus of a fellow Georgian writer, Lillian Smith.

4. Sin, Sex, and Segregation in Lillian Smith's Silent South

So now she knew I knew she knew I knew, and I wondered how we would play out the Proust bit.

—SAMUEL R. DELANY, "AYE, AND GOMORRAH . . . ," 1967

Over the last twenty-five years, the life's work of the writer and civil rights activist Lillian Smith has proven to be a generative object of study for scholars of twentieth-century Southern literature and culture, particularly as these fields relate to ideology, liberalism, racial conversion narratives, temporality, the grotesque, and same-sex desire.[1] For the most part, this critical interest has tended to focus on Smith's two major works of the 1940s, her first novel, *Strange Fruit*, and her first memoir, *Killers of the Dream* (1949). Even in those cases where her later texts—composed in a variety of genres, ranging from occasional essays, fiction, and lyrical memoirs to documentary writing and new journalism—come into consideration, these works have often been treated in isolation from, or in pointed contrast to, her earlier writings. Part of my aim here is to use *Strange Fruit*'s legal troubles with obscenity in the 1940s as an occasion for suggesting how Smith's writerly output might be reconceived as a unified whole that is variously stimulated, provoked, disgusted, and haunted by the unmanageable appeals that words can conceivably make on bodies—appeals that seemingly thwarted the efforts of reformers such as herself to persuade others that their modes of organizing life and their very lives themselves must change. Segregation is thus obscene in Smith's work insofar as rituals, customs, and habits are able to be followed, adopted, and embodied by means of the obscene speech acts that characterize so much segregationist discourse. It is precisely in this way that obscenity becomes understood in Smith's writing early on as a way of representing and living race bodily. As they developed between the 1930s and 1960s, Smith's responses to the power of certain "obscene" words to do rather than to merely mean came not only to influence her later shift in attention from region to cosmos (and from racialist race to the human race) but also to highlight her specific contributions as a significant transitional figure in the history of twentieth-century Southern liberalism.

Yet this relationship between obscenity and segregation never goes away in Smith's writing, even as her thinking underwent a momentous recasting in the 1950s and 1960s, when she attempted to overcome its challenges by using the writings of Pierre Teilhard de Chardin to develop an optimistic philosophy of man's evolutionary history that would prove capable of neutralizing the obscene words (and thus bodily appeals) of segregation. Whereas the power of words to leave Southerners more done to than doing confronted Smith in the 1940s either with an overdetermined loss of agency or with idle speculation regarding alternate regional histories, her later reception of Teilhard's *The Phenomenon of Man* (1955) caused her instead to broaden her conception of history to units of measurement larger than region, country, or race. I thus end the chapter first by briefly situating Smith's preoccupation with alternate histories in terms of developments in midcentury liberalism and then by detailing how her attempt to overcome the obscenity of segregation in a new philosophy of history nevertheless reproduced some of the signal harms she had initially sought to circumvent. If the conclusion I draw from this does not let Smith off the hook, then that is not so much a criticism of her as it is an acknowledgment of just how deeply the harm of obscene words informed her way of seeing not just the South but eventually all that was, is, and shall be, and it is likewise a harm that received a complementary formulation from perhaps the most attentive, if unlikely, critics of her entire career as a writer: the Massachusetts Supreme Judicial Court.

I

During the first month of its release in 1944, a copy of *Strange Fruit* was purchased by a Boston-area resident as a birthday present for a daughter who was away at college. Before sending his gift, however, he decided to read the novel and was outraged to discover repeated instances of the word "fuckin."[2] The father notified the authorities of what he viewed to be the book's indecency, and after reviewing the text themselves, the police notified local booksellers that *Strange Fruit* was in fact obscene and could no longer be offered for sale in Boston, an order that most bookshop owners obeyed in the following months. Upset by the suppression of Smith's novel, popular historian and local resident Bernard DeVoto managed to convince a Cambridge bookshop owner, Abraham Isenstadt, to put the police chief's decision to the test by selling him a copy of the novel, even though this meant that Isenstadt would likely face arrest and criminal prosecution, which he indeed subsequently did. At trial Smith's publishers, Reynal & Hitchcock, helped provide counsel for Isenstadt's defense, and during the pretrial proceedings Smith herself was asked if she would be willing to obviate the need for prosecution by deleting parts of the novel, including objectionable words and in some instances entire passages and scenes. She refused, and the trial went forward in the Middlesex Superior Court, where Isenstadt received a judge's verdict of guilty for selling and having in his possession for the purpose of sale Smith's *Strange Fruit*.[3]

In 1945 Isenstadt appealed his conviction to the Massachusetts Supreme Judicial Court. At the time of both his trial and his appeal, the statute under which he was prosecuted (Massachusetts General Laws, Ter. Ed., chapter 272, §28, as amended in 1934 and 1943) read as follows:

> Whoever imports, prints, publishes, sells or distributes a book, pamphlet, ballad, printed paper, phonographic record or other thing which is obscene, indecent or impure, or manifestly tends to corrupt the morals of youth, or an obscene, indecent or impure print, picture, figure, image or description, manifestly tending to corrupt the morals of youth, or introduces into a family, school or place of education, or buys, procures, receives or has in his possession any such book, pamphlet, ballad, printed paper, phonographic record, obscene, indecent or impure print, figure, image or other thing, either for the purpose of sale, exhibition, loan or circulation or with the intent to introduce the same into a family, school or place of education, shall . . . be punished.[4]

Isenstadt's lawyers sought to undermine obscenity understood either as a legal definition or as an operational norm by taking an anatomist's knife to the statute in question. Both in the Middlesex Superior Court and on appeal in the Supreme Judicial Court, their defense consisted of a nineteen-point attack on Massachusetts obscenity law, arguing that *Strange Fruit* was not obscene (point three), nor indecent (point four), nor impure (point five); that the statute was in violation of the Fourteenth Amendment because it was too imprecisely worded (point eleven); and that the only relevant test for a book's obscenity required the court to take into account both the whole work's dominant effect *and* the opinion of literary experts as to the relationship of the work's objectionable parts to this holistically defined dominant effect (point nineteen). The Middlesex Superior Court judge ended up rejecting all of the defense's claims except the thirteenth (that the book should be judged as a whole) and seventeenth (that the court should take into account contemporary community standards in interpreting what is obscene, indecent, impure, or manifestly corruptive of the morals of the young) points, with which the judge agreed at trial, though he nevertheless found *Strange Fruit* to be guilty of obscenity.

The Massachusetts Supreme Judicial Court upheld Isenstadt's conviction on appeal because, when judged as a whole, *Strange Fruit* could be said in the court's "best judgment as trier of facts" to possess "the qualities of obscenity, indecency, or impurity" as described in the Commonwealth's statute.[5] The *Isenstadt* opinion begins by confronting Massachusetts's notoriety as the nation's region for unduly repressive censorship standards, especially those applied to books.[6] Citing recent law review articles highly critical of obscenity prosecutions in the Commonwealth, the court reminds its detractors and critics that as a part of the judicial branch it is not in the business of making public policy:

> With this background in mind it may not be out of place to recall that it is not our function to assume a "liberal" attitude or a "conservative" attitude. As in other cases of statutory construction and application, it is our plain but not necessarily easy duty to read the words of the statute in the sense in which they were intended, to accept and enforce the public policy of the Commonwealth as disclosed by its policymaking body, whatever our own personal opinions may be, and to avoid judicial legislation in the guise of new constructions to meet real or supposed new popular viewpoints, preserving always to the Legislature alone its proper prerogative of adjusting the statutes to changed conditions.[7]

Whatever legitimation problems obscenity law may have been undergoing in other state and appellate courts throughout the United States in the past decade, the Massachusetts Supreme Judicial Court argues that the Commonwealth's courtrooms were not the proper venue for taking sides in the matter. The polemical thrust of the court's opinion is thus made clear: other courts ought to be following, rather than disavowing, Massachusetts's example in literary censorship by sedulously administering obscenity law instead of drastically revising it.

As if to ratify its disinterested stance, the court in *Isenstadt* moves on to assert that the governmental separation of powers continues to function smoothly in the Commonwealth. Unlike the state of New York, for instance, Massachusetts had been able to amend its obscenity statute through the state legislature so that works charged with obscenity now had to be judged as a whole. Therefore, if Woolsey's test was in force throughout the Commonwealth by the mid-1940s, then that was because its lawmakers—rather than its renegade judges—had made it so. The Massachusetts Supreme Judicial Court can thus agree with the defense's claims that *Strange Fruit* should be evaluated as a whole in any obscenity proceedings. In a sharp rejoinder to those too quick to interpret Woolsey's test as necessitating the end of book obscenity once and for all, however, the court's opinion insists that a novel can still pose obscene threats even when judged as a whole, provided it "contains prohibited matter in such quantity or of such nature as to flavor the whole and impart to the whole any of the qualities mentioned in the statute."[8]

A matter of both quantity and quality, holistic obscenity requires that judges and juries have sense enough to follow Woolsey's lead in classifying with some precision the bodily reactions called forth by the matter charged with obscenity. As Woolsey himself admits in the *Ulysses* opinion, "I am quite aware that owing to some of its scenes 'Ulysses' is a rather strong draught to ask some sensitive, though normal, persons to take. But my considered opinion, after long reflection, is that, whilst in many places the effect of 'Ulysses' on the reader undoubtedly is somewhat emetic, nowhere does it tend to be an aphrodisiac."[9] Consequently, the Massachusetts Supreme Judicial Court reads Woolsey *along* the grain in claiming that "a book might be found to come within the prohibition of the statute although only a comparatively few passages contained matter objectionable according to the principles herein explained if that matter were such as to offer a strong salacious appeal and to cause the book to be bought and read on account of it." A text may very well make historical, social, literary, emetic, or otherwise innocent appeals to its presumed readership in addition to salacious ones, but that does not also mean that these latter proscribable appeals would be any less capable of predominating nonetheless. In the court's faithful construction of Woolsey, then, a work that is obscene on the whole need not be a wholly obscene work.

Of course, to speak of a text's salacious appeals raises a number of questions, not least those pertaining to address: to whom exactly are such appeals being made? The court in *Isenstadt* grants that obscenity's appeals do not subsist in a vacuum but rather are a matter of determinate effects on probable consumers, meaning they do not involve "any classification of [a book's] subject matter or of its words as being in themselves innocent or obscene" (*Isenstadt*, 318 Mass., at 549). There is no such thing as obscenity in itself; there is only obscenity for others, the proscribable effects of which include the incitement of "lascivious thoughts," the arousal of "lustful desire," and "the corruption of morals" among the community's youth. First of all, this quasi-pragmatist insistence on approaching obscenity in terms of its effects on the world should be understood as the court's attempt to demote the dispositive force of aesthetic criteria in making determinations as to a work's obscenity. No mere idiosyncrasy of the *Isenstadt* court, the aversion to taking taste into account here should be viewed in the context of the broader crises of legitimacy that legal obscenity was experiencing in the United States at the time. If the Massachusetts Supreme Judicial Court were to admit that it was relevant to evaluate "refinement, propriety and good taste" in reaching its judgments here, then obscenity—already

141

elusive enough in the court's present construction—would risk evaporating into the shapeless flux of ever more rapidly changing social conventions, taboos, and fashions: "A penal statute requiring conformity to some current standard of propriety defined only by the statutory words quoted above would make the standard an uncertain one, shifting with every new judge or jury."

By making effects rather than aesthetic taste the test for obscenity, the *Isenstadt* opinion seeks instead to offer some conceptual stability to the increasingly indistinct terrain of legal obscenity: "The statute does not forbid realistically coarse scenes or vulgar words merely because they are coarse or vulgar, although such scenes or words may be considered so far as they bear upon the test already stated of the effect of the book upon its readers" (*Isenstadt*, at 550). However, this nonaesthetic standard for obscenity remains consistent with a version of aesthetic autonomy, insofar as the court promises to leave purely aesthetic works outside the purview of Massachusetts's obscenity statute. Though the Massachusetts Supreme Judicial Court sees the danger in using aesthetic criteria to take the measure of obscenity, it cannot help suggesting at the same time that works whose qualities are simply aesthetic pose no obscene danger at all. A realist novel can be as vulgar or as coarse as it dares to be, so long as it does not coarsen or vulgarize those who come across it in the world to the point of moral corruption. Likewise, between realism and the real world there exists a gap that cannot be bridged through the bodies of readers because genuine realism, by virtue of its clearly fictional nature, avoids *embodying* its potential coarseness, vulgarity, or corruption despite its verisimilitude.

If the effect of a work on all or part of a community is the test for obscenity in 1940s Massachusetts, then texts charged with obscenity must "be judged in light of the customs and habits of thought of the time and place of the alleged offense" (*Isenstadt*, at 551). Notwithstanding the court's implicit antipathy toward the use of aesthetic standards in assessing what is so obscene about obscenity, it is not at all clear how judging obscenity's effects in terms of contemporary habits and customs avoids relativism any better than does the judging of obscene texts in terms of taste, convention, or taboo. In other words, the reformulation of the Massachusetts Supreme Judicial Court's aesthetic prejudices into quasi-sociological terms does not get rid of the problems posed by taste, remainders of which stubbornly persist in the *Isenstadt* opinion. For one thing, the echolaliac whirl of synonyms heard in the Massachusetts obscenity statute (obscene works are indecent, which means they are impure, which means they are obscene, which means they are indecent, which means they are impure, . . .) reproduces itself in the very distinction upon which the *Isenstadt* court hopes to find solid ground. After all, because the objected-to taboos, conventions, and tastes themselves all comprise so many customs and habits of thought, and vice versa, they suggest that obscenity in the Commonwealth is no less subject to the uncertainties plaguing courts and legislatures throughout the

United States at the time. Juries, "representing a cross section of the people, both old and young," may very well "commonly be a suitable arbiter" in obscenity trials (*Isenstadt*, at 558–60). Yet in the end it is not altogether clear how the manner in which juries arbitrate is necessarily different from the aesthetic procedures so forcefully objected to throughout the Massachusetts Supreme Judicial Court's opinion.

This confusion of community standards with community taste expresses itself again in the court's account of how juries should go about determining whether the charged work is "appreciably injurious to society" in the ways outlined by the Commonwealth's statute. "A book," the *Isenstadt* court writes, "that adversely affects a substantial proportion of its readers may well be found to lower appreciably the average moral tone of the mass in the respects hereinbefore described and to fall within the intended prohibition" (*Isenstadt*, at 552). That is to say, juries are to evaluate *both* obscene materials *and* their communities holistically: "the statute was designed for the protection of the public as a whole" (*Isenstad*t, at 551). Just as a text need not make salacious appeals on every or even in a majority of its pages to be judged obscene, the text does not have to be injurious to the entirety or even to a certain percentage of the local population before a jury can proscribe it as obscene. Instead, if the salacious appeals of the charged material predominate among a portion of the community to such a degree that those effects are of such a nature "as to flavor the whole [community] and impart to the whole [community] any of the qualities mentioned in the statute," then a determination of obscenity could be legitimately made (*Isenstadt*, at 549). The Commonwealth's juries at that time were thus instructed to read their local communities as they would an obscene book.

143

While it would be easy for one to interpret these slippages between art and obscenity as inadvertent and thereby undermine the reasoning used throughout *Isenstadt*, I take this somewhat fuzzily maintained distinction to offer us instead a more forthright account of the relationship between obscenity and art than any to be found in those obscenity cases of the period that acted to deproscribe book obscenity. After all, one of the key arguments used by liberalizing jurists in neutralizing contemporary perceptions of the threats posed by book obscenity was the contention that aesthetic quality necessarily trumped obscenity's unruly appeals. Typical of such an approach is the opinion of the Second Circuit Court of Appeals in *United States v. Levine* (1936), in which Circuit Court Judge Learned Hand (Augustus Hand's first cousin) observes that the standard for obscenity "must be the likelihood that the work will arouse the salacity of the reader to whom it is sent as to outweigh any literary, scientific or other merits it may have in that reader's hands."[10] Therefore, the underlying assumption in *Levine* is that a literary text maintains its identity as a literary text until its obscenity becomes too much, at which point it ceases to be literary and reveals itself instead to be simply an obscene text.

On its face, this argument is a good deal more facile than the *Isenstadt* court's convoluted formulation of the problem, in which aesthetic approaches to obscenity are demoted, though aesthetics as such does not disappear altogether. In other words, the Massachusetts Supreme Judicial Court refuses to settle for conceptualizing obscenity as a matter of either/or: "Sincerity and literary art are not the antitheses of obscenity, indecency, and impurity in such manner that one set of qualities can be set off against the other and judgment rendered according to an imaginary balance supposed to be left over on one side or the other. The same book may be characterized by all of these qualities. Indeed, obscenity may sometimes be made even more alluring and suggestive by the zeal which comes from sincerity and by the added force of artistic presentation" (*Isenstadt*, at 553). Unlike the obscenity case law that followed the deproscribing course marked out by Woolsey in *United States v. One Book Called "Ulysses,"* the *Isenstadt* opinion refuses to see the obscene and the literary as mutually exclusive. In part, this refusal is grounded in the court's already described commitment to the governmental separation of powers: "If it is thought that modern conditions require that [an aesthetic] exception be made, the Legislature and not this court should make it" (*Isenstadt*, at 553–54). More importantly, however, in declining to separate the aesthetic from the obscene once and for all, the *Isenstadt* court offers a nuanced account of what both categories are mutually capable of doing in the world. If the opinion's initial division of aesthetics from obscenity seemed to suggest that this autonomization of aesthetics implausibly requires that art be without effect (as in the hypothetical example of the genuinely realist novel), then in further developing its account of the art/obscenity split the *Isenstadt* opinion confronts the very real potential for there to be obscene artworks or literary obscenity or even a really salacious piece of realism.

With this fairly subtle account of the relationship between obscenity and art in place, the court's opinion summarizes (rather quickly) the plot of *Strange Fruit* and itemizes (at much greater length) the potentially obscene, indecent, or impure episodes and moments in Smith's novel. Such moments and episodes are said to include "four scenes of sexual intercourse, including one supposed to have been imagined," all of variable suggestiveness and lengths, "from a few lines to several pages"; a fifth scene involving "amatory attitudes, kissing, a loosened blouse, exposed breasts, and circumstances suggesting but perhaps not necessarily requiring an act of intercourse"; a sixth scene describing Tracy Deen's drunken and failed attempt to rape Nonnie Anderson, from which scene *Isenstadt* quotes extensively; and fifty instances containing a variety of suspect material, including, "indecent assaults upon little girls," accounts of masturbation involving boys, acts of excretion, bouncing breasts and rumps, and a boy exposing his genitalia to a group of laughing girls (*Isenstadt*, at 555). Though it argued earlier in the opinion that obscenity is more than a matter of counting pages, the *Isenstadt* court nevertheless made a

144

special point of dividing its 250-page copy of *Strange Fruit* by these fifty passages in order to agree with the Middlesex Superior Court's decision that the novel as a whole could be adjudged obscene (*Isenstadt*, at 549 and 555). Not the tragic emplotment briefly described by the court but rather the exhaustively itemized salacious scenes that punctually occur every five pages are said to comprise the connective tissue forming the novel into a whole.

The court goes on to take Smith's novel to task for "offer[ing] no remedy" for the problems it addresses (*Isenstadt*, at 556). Also, despite agreeing with Isenstadt's lawyers that illicit love outside of marriage is in itself a "permissible theme" for a novel, the opinion nevertheless faults *Strange Fruit* for its overreliance on obscene effects:

> Regarding the book as a whole, it is our opinion that a jury of honest and rea-
> sonable men could find beyond a reasonable doubt that it contains much that,
> even in this post-Victorian era, would tend to promote lascivious thoughts and
> to arouse lustful desire in the minds of substantial numbers of that public into
> whose hands this book, obviously intended for general sale, is likely to fall; that
> the matter which could be found objectionable is not necessary to convey any
> sincere message the book may contain and is of such character and so pervades
> the work as to give to the whole a sensual and licentious quality calculated to
> produce the harm which the statute was intended to prevent; and that that
> quality could be found to persist notwithstanding any literary or artistic merit
> (*Isenstadt*, at 556–57).

145

If the *Isenstadt* opinion goes out of its way to offer a more labile account of obscenity and art than that to be found in liberalizing obscenity cases of the period, then it does so in part to ensure that *Strange Fruit*'s artistry does not exempt it from obscenity law; rather, the Massachusetts Supreme Judicial Court finds Smith's novel to be an instance of the sort of literary obscenity that is not just possible but also proscribable in the Commonwealth. Simply put, *Strange Fruit*'s artistry intensifies its obscene passagework.[11]

In his dissenting opinion, Judge Lummus grants that the Massachusetts Supreme Judicial Court construes the statute correctly but has drawn the wrong conclusions from it. To be sure, *Strange Fruit* is "blemished by coarse words and scenes, some of which appear irrelevant to the plot," but ultimately this extraneous "coarseness is repellent," not attractive.[12] Alongside its disgusting qualities, Lummus sees the novel's tragic elements as *dampening* the force of such claims: "It is a grim tragedy, not relieved even by humor. Virtue is not derided, neither is vice made attractive. In the book, the wages of sin is literally death. The reader is left depressed, unable to solve a tragic problem."[13] Since *Strange Fruit* neither promotes lascivious thoughts nor arouses lustful desires, Lummus contends that if the novel now threatened to corrupt the morals of the Commonwealth's youth, then that was because it was being talked about in Massachusetts's courtrooms: "Such knowledge as I have leads me to believe that without such artificial stimulation novels of the class into which the book in question falls are read by few girls and by practically no boys."[14] Moreover, should a few of these hypothetical girls and boys actually get their hands on *Strange Fruit*, "they would find it dull reading. . . . And if by chance some should wade through it, I think it could not reasonably be found to have any erotic allurement, even for youth."[15] The unquestionably artful accomplishments of Smith's novel raises doubts in Lummus's dissenting opinion as to the potential for obscenity to be conveyed by means of those very same accomplishments. In fact, not even *Strange Fruit*'s foulmouthed words and scenes can enliven the deepening depression into which its overdetermined artistry puts its readers. Smith's novel repulses rather than salaciously attracts.

II

In a series of thirty chapters that alternate narrative focalization mostly through members of one white family (the Deens) and the college-educated siblings of one African American family (the Andersons) living in the small fictional Georgia town of Maxwell, *Strange Fruit* does seem on its face to tell a story in which "the wages of sin is literally death." Most conspicuously, two murders appear to be the direct consequences of Tracy Deen's illicit relationship with Nonnie Anderson. Tracy himself is gunned down by Nonnie's brother, Ed, who manages to escape Maxwell before the body is discovered by Henry, one of the African American servants in the Deen household and Tracy's best friend. Blame for Tracy's death falls on Henry, and even though members of the "decent" white community attempt to protect him by hiding him in the town jail, the poor white rabblement quickly descends upon Maxwell and eventually discovers him. The lynching of Henry comprises the novel's climax, and its varying effects on the town are described at length in the penultimate chapter as the narration starts to become serially focalized through different members of the community in a number of brief sketches that canvass the range of Maxwell's reactions to the spectacular brutalization of African American men. Along the way to this climax, Southern revival meetings come in for lengthy representations (the eighteenth chapter is narrated through the group consciousness constituted by the crowd gathered at one such meeting) and sustained criticism; the lack of an independent and openly critical Southern press gets punctually lamented; and by the end the black underclass, particularly its women, continue to serve the town's "decent" whites as they have always done: "'Time for working women to get up,' [Nonnie's sister, Bess] called briskly, and followed her words with a rough shake of

Nonnie's shoulder, a push of her foot in [the] side [of Henry's lover, Dessie]" (*SF*, 313). The lynching of Henry is not a rupture in time for these women but rather its cyclical renewal, because it is just a typical, albeit eventful, part of Maxwell's calendar to which Smith's novel apparently "offers no remedy," as the Massachusetts Supreme Judicial Court insisted.

More significantly, however, it would seem that *Strange Fruit* undermines the basis for such a remedy because words themselves overwhelm the prospect of ameliorative social change altogether. As the two rival views in *Isenstadt* contend, words in the novel do in fact have striking effects on people. For one thing, words in *Strange Fruit* are aprons with which to soothe troubled children. For instance, Tillie Anderson (the deceased mother of Bess, Ed, and Nonnie) is said to have once "use[d] words to take that look [of fear] off [her children's] faces as she would have used her apron to wipe their noses" (*SF*, 19). Words also manage to get so emptied of their meanings that their remaindered husks start to jangle hilariously: "That was the pattern. Prentiss Reid [Maxwell's 'liberal' newspaperman] said the tabooed, the terrible. Everybody laughed, making things all right, taking the meanings from words, leaving only their shells to rattle around in your memory" (*SF*, 40). Some words are also flammable when uttered aloud: "When Tracy said the word something happened to Nonnie's face and he was startled—as if he had lighted ten thousand candles with one small half-thought-out word" (*SF*, 49).

Alternatively, certain words devastate:

Negro. [Nonnie]'d said it. Now everything would be spoiled. Ruined as it always was [for Tracy]! (*SF*, 81)

Colored girl. Negro. Spoiling every good moment, like a hair that's got onto your food. Why under God's heaven did [Tracy] keep on thinking those damned words! Why couldn't he—Jesus! (*SF*, 121)

In addition to their fitfully ruinous, hirsute, and bioluminescent properties, words also appear to be magnetized: "Tracy and Henry, playing in the dark outside, drew near the words like bits of steel to a magnet" (*SF*, 96). They are also damnably cumbersome for Henry's father: "Words so heavy they seemed to fall back on his own chest as he said them" (*SF*, 96). Furthermore, words tend to cling to you irrevocably, as Ed Anderson well knows: "Those words and the white children's *chocolate drop* hurled at you on your way to school, which was their back way to school and the way they used most, you'd never forget. You'd pick up cow dung and throw it and *yan yan yan* back at them. It didn't help much. They could wash off cow dung, forget a yell that had no meaning. You could never forget *chocolate drop* long as you lived. It was smeared on you to the bone" (*SF*, 144). Yet even Ed can get nostalgic

147

for the days when older poor whites in the county would hurl words as if they were projectiles at African American laborers: "[Cap'n Rushton] looked petered out, slumped down in his chair. Not as he used to be, riding his white mare across fields, jacking up the choppers, throwing words around like a hailstorm, though most took them with a laugh, liking the boss" (*SF*, 146). When they are not being used to break shackles ("And for a second the words [of Preacher Dunwoodie] had snapped a chain in two" [*SF*, 160]), words themselves comprise so many rhythmic fetters ("The words attached themselves to a revival tune now and began coiling, uncoiling, coiling in [Nonnie's] mind" [*SF*, 193]) that may eventually start to detonate ("Words that, unspoken, seem so harmless would, once said aloud, become dangerous explosives containing hidden feelings that would flame into something [that Tracy's sister, Laura Deen,] dared not set free" [*SF*, 206]). Even on the novel's penultimate page, words still obstinately confront Nonnie, Bess, Dessie, and presumably Smith's readers as well with all the inexplicable violence of a natural disaster: "No, Nonnie wanted her [and Tracy's] baby, she had said, and with those few words great obstacles had been thrown across their future as casually as an earthquake or storm does its work" (*SF*, 313).

As this brief but by no means exhaustive survey suggests, words in *Strange Fruit* do not have meanings so much as they evoke erratic physical responses, ranging from arousal, attraction, and solace to sensations of involuntary confinement, disgust, and even destruction. In other words, Smith's novel approaches language itself in much the same spirit as does the Massachusetts Supreme Judicial Court. Words have significance for both only so long as they betray discernible effects in the world. A key difference, however, is that whereas *Isenstadt* is interested in the purely libidinal potentials the book's language has for likely readers, Smith's account of the good and the bad that words do seems more preoccupied with the identity-constituting functions they can perform as well, particularly along racialist lines. After all, besides Nonnie Anderson herself, what most noticeably links Tracy Deen to Ed Anderson (Tracy's murderer) are the derogatory effects that the language of blackness ("negro," "colored girl," "chocolate drop") is said to have had on both of them, despite their respective efforts to deny these words their unduly affecting force.

One notable strategy for attempting to carry through this denial in the novel is to emphasize the separability of signifier ("colored girl") from referent (Nonnie herself). For instance, as the second sentence of *Strange Fruit* highlights, and as the rest of the text averts to over and over again, Nonnie is so light-skinned that she could pass for white: "Tall and slim and white in the dusk, the girl stood there, hands on the picket gate" (*SF*, 1).[16] Given Nonnie's racially ambiguous appearance, Tracy is thus able to sustain the recurring fantasy that his relationship with her, which spans many years, is like any other same-race relationship in Maxwell, save for those moments in which other people mention or Nonnie herself alludes to her blackness in words, at which point their entire history together becomes "spoiled" for him. In short, Tracy's perception of the racial difference said to separate him from Nonnie increasingly becomes a function of the very language used to mark and maintain that difference, even as Tracy lamely tries to screen himself off from the effects that words like "colored girl" or "negro" manifestly have on him, if not on Nonnie herself: "But it wasn't ruined. Out there on the lime cliff, brown water swirling below you, sky paled out by the moon above you, great oaks with sagging moss draping your nakedness, hiding you from the world, you could think that word ["negro"] without getting sick at your stomach. You could say it, say Nonnie's name after it, and still believe in her and yourself. The world's wrong, you could say. Dead wrong" (*SF*, 81). Haltingly, Nonnie goes on to echo this reverie, albeit in terms that manage to be more self-aware than, though just as quixotic as, those of Tracy: "She'd turn then, as if she had read his thoughts. 'Race is something—made up, to me. Not real. I don't—have to believe in it. Social position—ambition—seem made up too. Games for folks to—forget their troubles with. Bess says I'm crazy, that I live in a dream world'" (*SF*, 81).

As this passage implies, Nonnie tends to read race like a good poststructuralist. After all it, like class, is said to be a discursive construct ("'something—made up'") that people use and are used by in order to get themselves distracted from the things that embroil their daily lives ("'games for folks to—forget their troubles with'"). Far from stabilizing the meanings of racial constructs, however, language makes not only a game of the Manichaean melodramas of racialist ideologies but also a game that Nonnie can refuse to play because she does not "'have to believe in it.'" That is to say, far from necessarily comprising the ever-present spoiler that they are for Tracy, "negro" and "colored girl" are simply words whose meanings and effects fail to fully actualize themselves because they never reliably refer to either objects or experiences in the real world; at the end of the day, race is "'not real.'" If they are really just another set of fictions within social experience, then "colored girl" and "negro" need not therefore stick to Nonnie as they obstinately do to her "chocolate drop"–smeared brother.

Though incapable of systematizing his views quite this cogently, the college dropout Tracy is still capable of sharing in Nonnie's refusal of race in epiphanic moments that prove to be as fleeting as they are routinized: "God! You could hear that damned word and not mind it. You didn't give a goddam what the world thought. She was yours, that's all! She's my girl. She's lovely and beautiful, and she's mine. He'd laughed, and pulled her to him again. Holding her there, he knew he loved her—as a man loves the woman for all his needs" (*SF*, 81). Tracy and Nonnie may be intermittently able to negate the significance that "negro" and "colored girl" have in the world, but they have nothing in their own world to affirm beyond a

149

relationship that is itself an effect of the power those words really do have and about which Tracy manifestly has more doubts than does Nonnie. "Colored girl" and "negro" may be unreal for Nonnie, but for Tracy they have a substance from which he cannot escape, despite his endless failed attempts to disavow or ignore them in his mind. Therefore, although Smith's novel almost marvels at them, Nonnie's postracial and proto-poststructuralist habits of thought are by no means efficacious or exemplary. No matter how susceptible blackness and the discourses sustaining it may prove to be to doubts and skepticism, in the theoretically obtuse everyday world they still retain their ability to hail, hierarchize, and—in at least two instances here—kill.

An important site for these functions as well as the efforts made to resist them is Nonnie's brother Ed, who from the very beginning appears before us as simultaneously blackened, quantified, *and* effaced: "[Ed] was a black digit marked out by white chalk. He wasn't there on the sidewalk. He never had been there . . . he just wasn't anywhere—where those eyes looked—where those damned eyes—" (*SF*, 7). As a quasi-Ellisonian invisible man, Ed's psychological ordeals in the novel understandably consist of so many struggles for recognition in his visit home to Maxwell, where his thoughts return continuously to how it is he came to be made this "black digit marked out by white chalk." His memories reveal that the carefully observed silences surrounding race have been just as effective in making him a dark spectral digit as its words have been. During a trip with Sam Perry, a friend from childhood who is now a doctor for the county's black population, Ed has an involuntary memory of when he was a teenager and boasted to Sam and a friend of theirs that he had already had sexual experiences with white women. Ed was forcibly silenced by them at that time: "'Boy,' Sam laid his hand on Ed's shoulder in his slow way, 'leave white girls out of your mouth. And your mind.' He added, 'Might as well pick up a rattler, Ed'" (*SF*, 149). The need for a black man to keep quiet about white women here is a product of the same sorts of forces that had traumatically smeared Ed with the words "chocolate drop" even earlier in his youth. Silence thus acts on people much as words do in *Strange Fruit* insofar as Ed's subjection to the distorting pressures exerted upon what he does and does not say follows from the feigned knowledgeableness with which he sought, and presumably still seeks, to cover up "the feel of his ignorance" (149). In short, pretending to "know white girls" is sure to get Ed deprived of the freedom to express or give name to his real sexual desires (149), whatever they may actually be.[17]

What this suggests is that, according to *Strange Fruit*, segregation has turned the mid-twentieth-century South into the nation's closet. It is a region in which knowledge refers us ultimately to sexual knowledge, and what this sexual knowledge might mean exists in all sorts of fraught relationships—collusive, oppositional, competitive, or instrumental—to ignorance.[18] Smith's text is thus invested in determining how and why race manages to get embodied in and confused with the silences, words, and assumptions connected to the forms that sexual desire happens to take.[19] Accordingly, *Strange Fruit* demonstrates how significant irregularities in a community's knowledge aid in the continuing enforcement of segregation in the Jim Crow South. The closet, in this view, comprises the messy ideological adhesive that effectively holds together that which it nevertheless keeps asunder. For example, Ed may not be able to do much about the knowledge other people claim to have regarding his blackness, but the insidious means by which he is made to self-identify as just another "chocolate drop" also require him to give up whatever discretion he might otherwise expect to have over the kinds of knowledge that others very well cannot have of him. As Smith confesses in *Killers of the Dream*, "regardless of statistics, this every one knows: Whenever, wherever, race relations are discussed in the United States, sex moves arm in arm with the concept of segregation."[20] The grounding of racial difference in the stratified zones of one's own body is therefore Smith's bedrock for what she elsewhere calls in *Killers of the Dream* the Southerner's intransigent "psychic fortifications" (*KD*, 65).[21]

Curiously, however, it is those bodies that happen to be covered with *white* skin that are said to reproduce in turn the subjugations and hierarchizations at work in the community at large, a point that gets even more comprehensively formulated elsewhere in *Killers of the Dream* when Smith verbalizes the monitory lessons every child is said to silently receive in the South: "'Now, parts of your body are segregated areas which you must stay away from and keep others away from. These areas you touch only when necessary. In other words, you cannot associate freely with them any more than you can associate freely with colored children'" (*KD*, 73). In short, segregation derives its implacable effectiveness from its capacity for mimetic embodiment. It operates in the Jim Crow South by reducing the *white* Southerner's body to a strange assimilative mechanism whose boundaries are hard to determine and whose figural and natural processes require a social hermeneutic like that of Smith's to decipher. As Patricia Yaeger describes it: "For Smith, to be a white southerner is to know and to be the grotesque—to overwrite, overread, and participate in an economy of cruelty, defensiveness, reaction formation, and overcompensation."[22] At the very least, Smith's work strives to unveil to her readers a "Colored Town" always already existing in the erogenous zones of the bodies of all white Southerners, thus privileging these bodies as the sites for simultaneously internalizing and externalizing segregation's relentless enforcement.[23] After all, looming over every such body in *Killers of the Dream* is a sign that reads, "'Simply remember that morality is based on this mysterious matter of entrances and exits, and Sin hovers over all doors. Also, the authorities are watching'" (*KD*, 74). According to Smith, what goes into and comes out of a white Southerner's body is necessarily a public and civic matter.

151

All of this starts to make segregation's closet look an awful lot like obscenity in the Commonwealth of Massachusetts. According to Smith, the Jim Crow South creates complicit subjects out of white Southerners by teaching them to parcel up their bodies just as they are acculturated to parcel up their communities and relationships into a proliferating series of inclusive and exclusive binaries: sanctified/sinful, skin/body, white/black, silence/words. This last binary is of particular interest because it suggests that perhaps segregation operates most effectively when it is least talked about. Just as there are parts of town and parts of the body that must be put in parentheses by white Southerners as they go about their day, the words attached to both of these somatic and topographical areas undergo coercive pressure to remain silent, since their mere expression risks upsetting the *whole* town and the *whole* body. As Jay Watson has pithily observed of *Killers of the Dream*: "Integration becomes the social equivalent of onanism; it boils down to playing with the wrong thing, the thing that must not be recognized as an integral and pleasurable part of you."[24] Segregation, like obscenity in *Isenstadt*, is thus a matter of parts potentially threatening to overwhelm wholes (whole texts, whole bodies, and whole communities), which in turn requires public interdictions and proscriptions against the unruly part in defense of the whole, against the word in favor of silence. The repression of sexuality accordingly facilitates the sexualization of segregation.

Quite literally, then, segregation is obscene for Smith:

Out of [the] confusion [created by white fathers who disinherited their mixed-race children] came that obscene word *mongrelization* and the phrase *enforced intimate relations*, both of which were mirrors of their own shabby past. Like all criminals, they felt compelled to confess their misdeeds and did so with the naïveté of a child by the use of these words. Now today's politicians deliberately reach for these worn-out phrases when they need them to stir up excitement and fear and fantasies. (*KD*, 108)

Now, suddenly, shoving out pleasures and games and stinging questions come the TERRORS: . . . the singsong voices of politicians who preached their demonic suggestions to us as if elected by Satan to do so: telling us lies about skin color and a culture they were callously ignorant of—lies made of their own fantasies, of their secret deviations—forcing decayed pieces of theirs and the region's obscenities into the minds of the young and leaving them there to fester. (*KD*, 2)

In the name of *sacred womanhood*, of *purity*, of *preserving the home*, lecherous old men and young ones, reeking with impurities, who had violated the home since they were sixteen years old, whipped up lynchings, organized Klans, burned crosses, aroused the poor and ignorant to wild excitement by

152

an obscene, perverse imagery describing the "menace" of Negro men hiding behind every cypress waiting to rape "our" women. (*KD*, 126)

Obscenity here is a matter of words enacting racial difference through the dangers said to be presented by particular forms of sexual desire: "*mongrelization*," "*enforced intimate relations*," and "the 'menace' of Negro men" to "'our' women" are all said to be the properly obscene means by which segregation changes from merely being a thought to becoming behavior. For Smith, the segregating harm done by obscene words derives from their unmanageable capacities for action.

Unlike more recent literary criticism investigating language's power to do things in the world, Smith believes that the obscene speech acts of segregation are fully intentional and do indeed function just as their speakers, writers, and users intend; in other words, she does not distinguish between the threats posed by segregation's obscene words and the actions by which those threats would actually be achieved in the world.[25] Segregation's obscene words thus cannot ever really fail in the speech act theory that Smith tacitly develops in *Strange Fruit* and *Killers of the Dream*. Consequently, the possibilities described by Judith Butler for the "performative" to overturn or derail threats posed in language remain unthinkable in Smith's work.[26] Instead, the obscenity of segregation in Smith's work functions as pornography does in the essays of Catharine A. MacKinnon because obscenity is not so much a matter of defamation (the obscenity of segregation is not what it *says*) as it is an instance of discrimination (segregation's obscenity is harmful because it always *does*).[27] Consequently, in Smith's texts the harm to be found in the obscenity of segregation appears to be located in the functions necessarily performed by—not in the contents of—obscene words.[28]

Of the various violent functions performed by these obscene words, perhaps the most troubling ones discussed in *Killers of the Dream* involve the ways in which such words create what women (black and white) *are* in the mid-twentieth-century South by framing them in terms of what *can and cannot be done to them*. For one thing, the only roles to which women can aspire are defined almost exclusively in terms of what kinds of service they can offer to the white men in their lives. As we have seen, the obscene words identified by Smith in her first memoir make a symbol of white women for white men, and this symbol simultaneously denies these women their desires (white women are not individuals with bodies so much as venerated abstractions like "*sacred womanhood*," "*purity*," or preservers of the home) while it elaborately and paradoxically forbids access to and knowledge of these putatively nonexistent desires (an interdiction mounted against "the 'menace' of Negro men"). As for African American women in Smith's silenced South, obscenity's words reduce them to mere objects for the contingent whims of white male desire and thus to monstrously productive wombs churning out "mongrels" by the millions.

153

Extrapolating from all of this, we are presented with the following situation: if, as a pamphleteer and little magazine publisher advocating civil rights in the early 1940s, Smith is able to advise white Southerners that they can do their part for desegregation by empathizing with, making friends with, or simply standing/sitting next to African Americans whenever possible,[29] then as a fiction writer and memoirist she seems to be saying that the problems that racially coded and sexually managed antagonisms raise in the Jim Crow South appear to be too ineluctably determined for human agents to ever confront and meaningfully alter. In *Strange Fruit*, this unduly hard determinism appears most clearly during the almost futile contemplation of paths not taken. Consider the following examples of characters contemplating the wrong turns made in their region's past and in their own:

> If [Laura Deen] could go back far enough . . . there'd be a place where she would find a Tracy and a Laura who had been, maybe, fond of each other. Surely if she could get back far enough, she'd find a time when maybe they'd played together as little children and enjoyed each other. And beginning there, she could take his path and travel it until she found out why it led—where it did. And yet she knew that she did not want to do it. If she began to see it, his way, she would travel his path again and again and again, all her life, trying to understand, assuming all he had felt, hurting with his pain. No, it was easier, easier to keep on feeling resentment—or nothing. As he must always have felt toward her. (272)

> [Sam Perry, who has just helped Ed escape Maxwell,] turned his car south. Started on the longest journey a man ever makes as he tried to go step by step back through his life and the lives of those nearest him, to find the place where things had taken a wrong turn. Seeking, as children seek in recapitulating play, to master a painful experience, repeating it until it can be summoned back and forth at will. And as he drove on and on from Macon to Maxwell, from fresh early dawn to blazing dead heat, trying to find a way into the past, he kept pushing back a feeling that stole through his body like a soft tune he'd never let himself listen to. It was as if he told himself, "You can't think that now . . . maybe later," though he told himself nothing. (283)

> Better let [the lynching] pass. Let the thing go! Do something [for the next day's newspaper] on the great need for a paved road through the county. Always safe to write about roads. God! [Prentiss Reid] laughed aloud, threw his cigarette into the spittoon.
>   Yeah . . . [writing an editorial criticizing the lynching would] make folks worse . . . do more harm than good—. . .

> That's the South's trouble. Ignorant. Doesn't know anything. Doesn't even know what's happening outside in the world! Shut itself up with its trouble and its ignorance until the two together have gnawed the sense out of it. Believes world was created in six days. Believes white man was created by God to rule the world. As soon believe a nigger was as good as a white man as to believe in evolution. All tied up together. Ignorance. Scared of everything about science, except its gadgets. Afraid not to believe in hell, even. Afraid to be free. (309–10)

Segregation and its obscene words may have repugnantly violent effects, but they are an overlapping pair of problems without any likely solution in the 1940s South. If social and race relations are as bad as these passages cumulatively suggest, if the ideological effectiveness of segregation is securely rooted in and enacted throughout a history no Southerner can hope to touch—after all, Prentiss Reid's thoughts seem to suggest that paving roads to let the world into the South will not efface the tobacco roads in Southerners' minds—then the only reasonable responses appear to be either hypocritical mutism or science fiction. Either Southerners ought to start acting like their "liberal" press and respond to segregation and lynching with a disapproving silence (just as Prentiss Reid does in *Strange Fruit*) or they should get busy rewriting their histories so they can adjust (in their imaginations at least) the "wrong" paths taken at some point in the region's past. In other words, perhaps Jim Crow's bad history need not bar the narration of alternate, counterfactual histories with their own potentials to disclose or even actualize alternative futures.

III

What these two tacitly opposed responses to segregation in Smith's texts of the 1940s—hypocritical restraint or alternate histories—present us with are the limits within which Southern liberalism seemed thinkable at that time. Manifestly unsatisfied with the intractability of the problem as framed by her in the 1940s, Smith began in the next decade to address herself in earnest to the possibility of finding and offering new solutions to segregation. At the very least, it was in such a spirit that she undertook *The Journey* (1954), her second memoir, which is composed of a strange hybrid of genres and modes, including autobiographical writing, travel narratives, and inspirational tracts. The rhetorical gambit of the argument in *The Journey* is the sustained attempt to pass off *Killer of the Dream*'s impasses as so many ordeals waiting to be mastered. Increasingly a keyword in her work following her cancer diagnosis in 1953, "ordeal" came to denote for Smith nothing less than the conditions necessary for all distinctly human acts of creativity.[30] Against worldviews that would stress both radical contingency and the incapacity of human agents to have any sort of meaningful effect on the world, Smith's later writing presents instead a philosophy of history comfortingly rooted in evolution and developmental biology.

To this end, *The Journey* starts to develop an epochal overview of terrestrial history according to which the human species appears as the privileged and as-yet-ever-unfolding product of environmentally instigated ordeals. Human properties and capacities are said to be the hard-won artifacts of evolutionary trials met and effectively surpassed deep in our species' past, but this should not lead one to assume that all such ordeals have in fact been overcome entirely. In fact, in a case of ontogeny reliably recapitulating phylogeny, even old trials must be met anew by each individual woman and man as she/he develops physically, psychologically, and socially.[31] A prized instance of just such an ordeal for Smith in *The Journey* is the one that comes into being in the relationship between mother and child, whereby the resolution of tensions between anxiety and tenderness are understood as helping the "little human animal" to become "a human being": "Without the anxiety which comes first out of child-helplessness, we would not so desperately need tenderness; without tenderness we could not have found the miraculous talents, the powers, which have changed us into human beings; and once finding them, we would not have developed them further had we not been urged on by necessity and ordeal to dream and bring forth the dream."[32] Said to be more than merely biological matter by virtue of his/her interpersonal self-awareness, the human being comprises the evolutionarily generated result of a self-regulating economy of problems and their immanent solutions, of needs and their imminent satisfaction, and of dreams and their eventual actualization. In particular, the very existence of human beings as such is taken by Smith in *The Journey* to be an irrefutable marker or trace of difficult evolutionary trials overcome as well as an indication that all future ordeals can indeed be successfully mastered. As Smith's highly selective historical overviews and examples here aim to reveal, anthropogenesis has been and continues to be an experience in the perfectibility of nature.

To be sure, this is not a framework through which many of Smith's contemporaries sought to approach civil rights activism and desegregation. Yet the earlier vision of the South set forth by her in *Strange Fruit* and *Killers of the Dream* did indeed encompass the double bind within which many pre-*Brown* Southern liberals saw themselves more and more trapped: full of desperate hopes for the prospects of desegregation and reenfranchisement, yet increasingly driven to treat Jim Crow as the inexorable final result of Southern history to date. Smith's eventual response to this dilemma in and after *The Journey* was to develop her own philosophy of history rather than to submit to the bad outcomes of history or to offer imagined alternatives to the past, even though both options appealed to many of her fellow liberals at the time.

In order to develop this point, it is worthwhile to consider more closely Gunnar Myrdal's magnum opus *An American Dilemma: The Negro Problem and Modern*

Democracy (1944). Though not as expressly deterministic as many comparable works of the period, *An American Dilemma* nevertheless does refer often to the obdurate persistence of racialist themes in U.S. history and to the obstacles facing those who would strive to overcome them. For instance, in his chapter on the factors underlying the politics of the singular "Negro Problem," Myrdal alludes to the transhistorical efficacy of white supremacy in unifying white Southerners across regional and class differences into one solid mass of racial animus. At the very least, Myrdal assumes that something like this has been the case in the South since at least just before the Civil War: "In their poverty, ignorance, and dependence, [antebellum poor white Southerners] knew generally little about the world outside the Southern region which was gradually becoming culturally isolated. And they were offered one great and glittering solace: 'white supremacy.' They were not at the bottom, they were protected from the status of Negroes by a clear dividing line, and they were told that they could compete freely up to the very top."[33] According to Myrdal, this racial antagonism started to take on a more explicitly political cast in the first years of Reconstruction, with the freedmen being met "with a solid mistrust against them, which was crystallized into an elaborate political philosophy, powerful even in its partial disorganization."[34] On the basis of this Solid South framework, Myrdal is able to make the following incredible claim: "Negro disenfranchisement is evidently part and parcel of a much more general tendency toward *political conservatism* which stamps the entire region. The Negro is, as we shall find, a main cause of this general conservatism."[35] Though certainly a "complicated matter" subject to longer and more nuanced histories of subjugation and institutionalized oppression—as Myrdal himself demonstrates at length—white Southern attitudes toward African Americans nevertheless appear in *An American Dilemma* to have solidified into an overwhelming force around the time of the Civil War, the effects of which have been continuously operative and unavoidably felt throughout the South ever since.[36]

157

While he tends to interpret racial disenfranchisement in the South in an almost teleological manner, Myrdal still manages to insist that the 1940s presented the United States and the South with a surprisingly volatile situation. Besides the direct assaults on racial disenfranchisement posed by downward pressures on poll taxes and improving education among African Americans, he also notes that there were "*various social trends*" undermining political discrimination in the South, ranging from the exhaustion of legal defenses against disenfranchisement to the Supreme Court's increasingly critical perspectives regarding the South's segregating folkways as well as the greater "respect for the law" to be found more and more often among the region's youth.[37] As farsighted as his prognoses here may in fact be in many respects—in particular, Myrdal's hunch that the Supreme Court would soon start to take a more interventionist role in legal battles over segregation seems down-right prescient—they still carry over into their "solution" some hyperdeterministic premises. For instance, the effectiveness of "*various social trends*" in and of themselves are simply taken as given, which raises the question: why would the South's few scruple-ridden liberals need to adopt more than moderate approaches if these trends were eventually going to work their way toward a satisfactory resolution of their own accord? The situation in which the midcentury Jim Crow South found itself may seem terminally unstable in *An American Dilemma*, but underneath this superficial agitation the terrible racialist theme of Southern history appears to remain as hyperbolically determined and determining as ever.

Opposing the quasi-naturalistic reticence of liberal histories in the vein of Myrdal are the alternate, counterfactual histories that became visible in the late 1940s and early 1950s when historians began to burst open those monolithic accounts of the region that presented racial segregation as the unavoidable message of Southern history. Of these historians, C. Vann Woodward remains the figure most famously connected with the overturning of such views of the region's history, and as such his works are valuable measures by which to assess Smith's early works in terms of contemporary developments in Southern liberalism. In particular, Woodward's *Origins of the New South, 1877–1913* (1951) and *The Strange Career of Jim Crow* (1955) did much to stress the *dis*continuities between the legal institutional arrangements codified in the 1890s and the state of such arrangements immediately following the Civil War. Much like Laura Deen, Sam Perry, or Prentiss Reid in *Strange Fruit*, Woodward sought to go back in time and figure out where the wrong turns had been taken in the region's past. In *Origins of the New South*, the effort to deny segregation its implacable inevitability in Southern history manifests itself in Woodward's attacks on the misuse of the expressions "Solid South" and "Bourbon," both of which are said to be "of questionable value to the historian" because the "solidarity of the region has long been exaggerated."[38] Referring specifically to the first years of Reconstruction, Woodward observes that "disaffection had been unnaturally bottled up for a generation—first by the threat of war, then by invasion, and finally by Reconstruction. The Redeemers' plan to prolong repression by threat of Negro domination and constrain all warring factions within their Procrustean one-party system met with trouble from the start. Independent movements renouncing allegiance to the Democratic party broke out in nearly all Southern states almost as soon as they were redeemed. Boasts of white solidarity that impressed outsiders were often loudest in the presence of division."[39] Far from being the motive force of Southern history, post–Civil War white supremacy was simply another myth that latter-day historians of the region needed to interrogate more critically than they had hitherto. Instead, for Woodward the narrative of what occurred in the South between 1865 and the 1890s was full of more variable and ambiguous outcomes than Myrdal seemed willing to consider.

In many ways, *The Strange Career of Jim Crow* simply overlays Woodward's arguments about disenfranchisement in *Origins of the New South* onto the even more vexing issues raised by segregation.[40] To this end, the second chapter of *The Strange Career of Jim Crow* attempts to map out three "forgotten alternatives" to the institutionalization of racism that Woodward sees as having occurred in the 1890s: Southern radicalism, conservative philosophy, and a liberal philosophy of race relations that in his view constitute "alternative philosophies [that] rejected the doctrines of extreme racism and all three were indigenously and thoroughly Southern in origin".[41] As exemplary figures of nineteenth-century Southern liberalism, Woodward singles out George Washington Cable and Lewis Harvie Blair before admitting that "neither Harvie nor Cable attracted a following in the South. Acceptance of their doctrines had to await the development of urban liberalism, which did not arrive in any force until the second quarter of the twentieth century." Pitched somewhere between "the doctrinaire Negrophile of the left and the fanatical Negrophobe of the right," nineteenth-century Southern conservatism exerted a much more substantial influence on the region's history than did the sparse record left by its few contemporary liberals (*SC*, 47). According to Woodward, the forgotten alternatives suggested by the history of conservatism in the South merely qualified the more violent aspects of white supremacy: "The conservatives acknowledged that the Negroes belonged in a subordinate role, but denied that subordinates had to be ostracized; they believed that the Negro was inferior, but denied that it followed that inferiors must be segregated or publicly humiliated" (*SC*, 48). Not forms of white supremacy per se but rather "an aristocratic philosophy and *noblesse oblige*" were all that such conservatism necessitated (*SC*, 49). In this paternalistic view, African Americans were to have been protected, not degraded by their "superior" white neighbors and fellow citizens.

159

Given these shortcomings of both Southern liberalism and Southern conservatism in the nineteenth century, the forgotten alternative most favored by Woodward is that of Southern radicalism, best emblematized for him by the Populist movement, which presented the South with a perspective on race that went beyond "the delusions and sentimental liberalism on the one hand, and the illusions of romantic paternalism on the other." Instead, it opened up the prospect of interracial class alliances *in spite of* existing racial prejudices: "There was in the Populist approach to the Negro a limited type of equalitarianism quite different from that preached by the radical Republicans and wholly absent from the conservative approach. This was an equalitarianism of want and poverty, the kinship of a common grievance and a common oppressor" (*SC*, 61). Thus, at the end of his succinct survey of the achievements of Populism, Woodward goes so far as to contend: "It is altogether probable that during the brief Populist upheaval of the 'nineties Negroes and native whites achieved a greater comity of mind and harmony of political purpose than ever before or since in the South" (*SC*, 64). As Woodward hastens to point out, however, his reasons for exhuming these neglected alternatives to Jim Crow are not to celebrate Populism above all other political movements and tendencies in the South's past. Instead, the point here is simply "to indicate that things have not always been the same in the South." In other words, "the effort to justify them as a consequence of Reconstruction and a necessity of the times is embarrassed by the fact that they did not originate in those times. And the belief that they are immutable and unchangeable is not supported by history" (SC, 65). Racism in the South's past was therefore not so much an endlessly recurring fact as it was a contingent, albeit powerful force to which the region regrettably capitulated in the 1890s when social alternatives to it wavered in the restraints each offered (SC, 67–109). As the work of historians following in this vein has since tried to demonstrate, the region's past is filled with "might-have-beens" that could very well have been the case, and at the heart of this project has long been the tacit claim that counterfactual histories make qualitative changes in the present more (not less) possible.[42]

As we have seen, Smith's two major works of the 1940s—*Strange Fruit* and *Killers of the Dream*—provide us with a body of work narrating the transition from the overly determined assumptions of Myrdal to the alternatives opened up by the likes of Woodward.[43] Smith, therefore, is a bridge in the history of liberalism and the South, and her mediating functions in this respect are to be understood as encompassing both her fiction and her activist writing. If *Strange Fruit* seems almost implacable in the ways in which it preemptively forecloses the solutions adverted to later in *Killers of the Dream*, then the clanging shut of the doors on Jim Crow's closet does not necessarily preclude the impulse for qualitative change, an impulse that manifests itself in Smith's first novel in the form of privately expressed desires for counterfactual histories promising alternative futures. This is an impulse that quite explicitly informs Woodward's work of the early 1950s, which itself evocatively altered the ways in which Southern history was conceivable at a time when social reform was not only institutionally motivated by Supreme Court rulings such as *Brown v. Board of Education* (1954) but also collectively demanded and achieved in ways entirely unthinkable in the terms assumed by *Strange Fruit*, where mass politics means lynchings, not sit-ins or marches or freedom rides.[44] This does not detract from the significance of Smith's first novel as a missing link of sorts in the history of Southern liberalism, however, because while it abstains from offering the sorts of solutions that the first edition of *Killers of the Dream* tentatively rehearses or that civil rights activism after *Brown* later opens up, *Strange Fruit* nevertheless does do an estimable job of unveiling the deterministic premises of works like Myrdal's book. *Strange Fruit* is, as it were, a baring of the racialist device within the work of liberals faced with the problems of the South in the 1940s, liberals who nevertheless remained committed to seeing—if not necessarily to making—Jim Crow's strange career come to an end somehow.

A similar and significant distinction insinuates itself as well between the courses charted out by Woodward and the idiosyncratic one followed by Smith in the 1950s and 1960s. Whereas the clarifying functions of alternate histories allow Woodward to commit himself fully to confronting racism and its discourses in all their muddled particularity, the opening of such alternatives permits Smith in her later work to retire to somewhat rarefied heights, just as the civil rights movement propagated rapidly. Unlike Woodward, Smith in the 1950s did not go on to debunk the implacability of racialist ideologies by means of a new reading of Southern history; instead, she set out to express totalizing humanist worldviews with which to efface them. As she points out in a 1965 letter:

> I am involved with segregation that is symbol and symptom of this dehu-
> manization; but this "segregation" is bigger than race, [sic] (conformity is also
> a form of segregation); it has to do with numberless relationships that are
> necessary not only to bind men into one world but necessary for their increas-
> ing complexity of mind and spirit as they continue to evolve themselves into
> human beings. I am talking about the things Teilhard de Chardin talked about,
> not the things Walter White talked about in his day or James Baldwin and Le
> Roi [sic] Jones are talking about now.[45]

For Smith, "segregation" symptomatically and symbolically refers to a truly sublime set of associations, ranging from the localized and ephemeral matters pertaining to the prospects of desegregation in the mid-century U.S. South all the way up to the cosmic evolutionary destiny of the human being as such. Perhaps even more strikingly, however, she insists here that if the struggle for racial desegregation has any meaning at all, then that meaning must be understood to derive from the small part it plays in the further integration of man's species-being (in overcoming "dehumanization"). Pierre Teilhard de Chardin's *The Phenomenon of Man*—but not LeRoi Jones's *Dutchman* (1964)—was the key to conceptually reorganizing the repugnant contingencies of racial segregation in the United States into a totalizing and compelling whole because the stakes of Smith's writing and activism are said to be nothing less than the development or the regression of the entire species.

It is thus not in the least surprising that when she encountered *The Phenomenon of Man* in the late 1950s and early 1960s Smith did so with all the force of recogni-tion. Indelibly persuaded by (because she already shared) the promissory mood in which this Jesuit paleontologist approaches evolution, Smith attempts in her 1961 revised conclusion to *Killers of the Dream* to refigure her life's work in the mythic and reassuringly teleological terms of *Phenomenon of Man* because her work, if it meant and would continue to mean anything, is said to have done its utmost to "count in the project called *Human Being Evolving*. And as we think of what could happen to the human race, if we want it to happen, when we think of the billions of dormant seeds in our nature and culture awaiting warmth and cultivation, we find ourselves ready to pick up our little watering-pot and sacks of rich soil and start out on the million-year plan for the growing of a New Man" (*KD*, 214). Countering those who would either converse rationally with individual human beings or appeal demagogically to the masses, Smith sees her life's work as bridging the gap between myth and reason through its commitment to expressing a materialism fully compatible with faith: "For neither the faith that [our fathers] leaned on nor the doubt which drove us to overvalue science can make a future fit for men. No more than ovum or sperm alone creates the child. Faith and doubt both are needed—not as antagonists but working side by side—to take us around the unknown curve."[46] What present times urgently require, Smith argues, are new rationally presented myths capable of fostering and thereafter sustaining a sense of community among the entire human race. With its faux-scientific jargon (*hominisation, noogenesis, noosphere, psychergy*, etc.) and its invitingly inclusive views of evolution as fundamentally antientropic and human-affirming, Chardin's *Phenomenon of Man* provides Smith not only with the means for shaping such myths for her fellow Southerners but also with the missing plank necessary for finally joining together her split projects as a writer and an activist. Casting her glance back over her life, Smith discovered that she was in fact a proto–Teilhard de Chardin all along. Not civil rights but the lure of the evolutionarily elected human being spreading its integrated and integrating consciousness across the universe had been the grand mythical subject of her activism and her writing every step of the way, thus making Georgia's *Strange Fruit* just another exemplary instance of the universe's phenomenon of man.

Smith's late evolutionary evangelism accordingly makes the region's problems seem far too limited in scope to qualify as a valid case study on which to base any philosophy of history as pitilessly immobilizing as the one intimated in *Strange Fruit*. Instead, the real object of history in Smith's later important works, such as *The Journey*, becomes the millennia-spanning story of the human species, which also happens to read like a determinist narrative, albeit one with a more promisingly open ending. As Smith herself puts it in *The Journey*:

> To believe in something not yet proved and to underwrite it with our lives: it is the only way we can leave the future open. Man, surrounded by facts, permitting himself no surmise, no intuitive flash, no great hypothesis, no risk is in a locked cell. Ignorance cannot seal the mind and imagination more surely. To find the point where hypothesis and fact meet; the delicate equilibrium between dream and reality; the place where fantasy and earthly things are metamorphosed into a work of art; the hour when faith in the future becomes

knowledge of the past; to lay down one's power for others in need; to shake off the old ordeal and get ready for the new; to question, knowing that never can the full answer be found; to accept uncertainties quietly, even our incomplete knowledge of God: this is what man's journey is about, I think.[47]

Consequently, the way in which Smith seeks to open up the South to a different future is to superimpose the species' history onto that of the region ("the point where hypothesis and fact meet"), an example that none of her fellow liberals seemed all that willing to follow, though W. E. B. Du Bois appears to have been the first to anticipate Smith's later evolutionary turn. In his review of *Strange Fruit*, he prophetically notes: "On each page the reader sees how both elements (white and black) in Maxwell are caught in a skein (economic, ethnic, emotional) that only evolution can untangle or revolution break."[48] Much like the examples made by Cable and Blair in Woodward's *Origins of the New South*, Smith's opting for the former did not attract much of a following among her contemporaries; unlike them, however, it remains doubtful that it ever will, at least so long as something like an interplanetary liberalism answering to their urban liberalism remains indiscernible on our horizon. Likewise, it is a wonder that Smith's shift in focus to the species did not also produce the slightest engagement with science fiction, especially in the vein of Olaf Stapledon's *Last and First Men* (1930) or H. G. Wells's *The Shape of Things to Come* (1933).

163

Along with this consequential shift in deterministic perspective comes a perhaps even more significant modification in the capacities of words to do things to people. As we have seen, *Strange Fruit* and *Killers of the Dream* both ground Southern segregation in obscene words and their complementary silences. Smith never really forgets this troubling feature that her early work obsessively explores, even after she starts to discern a way out for the region in the alternative perspectives provided by anthropogenesis. Consequently, much of her writing in the 1950s and 1960s concerns itself with neutralizing the effects that segregation's obscene words have had by rendering those words ambiguous. Instead of speech acts, segregation becomes just another instance of polysemy, of signs indefinite enough to suggest hidden contents just below their hazy surface. In short, Smith strives to make segregation symptomatic and allegorical instead of obscene. Accordingly, the South's alternate history that Smith claims to have discovered in something "bigger than race" does not just provide her with the conceptual means of overcoming the region's "bad" determinism. It also enables her to undermine the power of segregation's obscene words by translating them into less effective ones. Segregation need not endlessly create and re-create the segregated South's closet through obscenity; instead, it can be rendered as "dehumanization," a term that in turn symbolically refers us to the ordeals—but not to the tragic fated outcomes—of the human race over the course of its epochal history on this planet. Thus, in Smith's later work, racial segregation in the region is best understood in terms of the Anthropocene, rather than the Jim Crow era. Likewise, segregation's obscene words are to be approached in other words altogether so as to conjure away their traumatic barbs, gashes, and deformations.

Smith's late philosophy of history thus attempts to invert the holistic test for obscenity described in *Commonwealth v. Isenstadt*. That is to say, instead of trying to protect the whole from its potentially overwhelming parts, she takes as her measure later in life an abstract whole (the human race) in which no present part (racialist race) can ever really hope to predominate. Smith's turn to man's evolutionary prospects does not so much indicate that she breaks with the past but rather implies an even more fundamental desire for continuity: human evolution provides a precedent for overcoming dehumanization (formerly known as "segregation") because it is the story of how humans of all generations are progressively becoming still more and more human. Therefore, if there was an authority to which Smith could refer in assessing the prospects for civil rights in the Jim Crow South in the late 1950s and early 1960s, then that authority was to be found in the stability supposedly underlying anthropocentrism itself. In other words, Smith's evolutionary turn does not totally efface the obscenity of her early writings. If anything, her leap from race and region to species and cosmos marks an even deeper (if hidden) engagement with segregation's obscenity, for she, like the South's racist politicians, cannot help making "dehumanization" an obscene word just like the obscene words of segregation. As we have seen, "sacred womanhood," "purity," and "preservers of the home" were the words that framed what white women in the South were in terms of what could and could not be done to them. They apparently did not have desires of their own because they were little more than disembodied abstractions for the region's white men. Similarly, Smith's later deployment of the language of dehumanization reduces us all to our abstract taxonomic essence: we are not lesbians, Southerners, Americans, liberals, conservatives, fascists, proles, fellow travelers, scabs, communists, or any other likely form of personal or group identity; instead, we are each of us, symptomatically and symbolically, just humans, singular but equivalent exemplars of *homo sapiens*. If we read this process of allegorical abstraction obscenely—that is, if we remain attentive to the ways in which obscenity discriminates through words—then Smith's solution to Southern segregation seems downright demagogic because what that solution appears to entail at the end of the day is the making of a white woman out of everyone everywhere always.

164

Conclusion: Off the Page

While visiting New York City in 1936 to drum up funds with which to complete his music degree at the Tuskegee Institute, Ralph Ellison was the guest of Langston Hughes at a Broadway performance of Jack Kirkland's phenomenally successful stage adaptation of Erskine Caldwell's *Tobacco Road* (1933). To the mortification of himself and Hughes, however, he caused a scene when he started to laugh uncontrollably at the antics of the poor whites depicted on stage:

> For me the shock of Caldwell's art began when Ellie May and Lov were swept up by a forbidden sexual attraction so strong that, uttering sounds of animal passion, they went floundering and skittering back-to-back across the stage in the startling action which father Jeeter, that randy Adam in an Eden gone to weed, named "horsing." For when the two went into their bizarre choreography of sexual "frustrabation" I was reduced to such helpless laughter that I distracted the entire balcony and embarrassed both myself and my host. It was a terrible moment, for before I could regain control, more attention was being directed toward me than at the action unfolding on the stage.[1]

Notably, this "extravagance of laughter" both singled Ellison out as an object of sight for the rest of the audience and indicated his own inadvertent identification with Caldwell's poor white trash, who in real life would have been anathema to him because of the threat of violence they necessarily carried with them: "But even closer to my immediate experience, wasn't Ellie May's and Lov's 'horsing' all over the stage of *Tobacco Road* embarrassingly symbolic of my own frustration as a healthy young man whose sexual outlet was limited (for the most part) to 'belly-rubbing' with girls met casually at public dances? It was and it wasn't, depending upon my willingness to make or withhold a human identification. Actually, I had no choice but to identify, for Caldwell's art had seen to that."[2] Literally split in two during this laughing fit—one half laughing wildly while the other critically dissected what this laughter might be made to mean—Ellison found that "as the unruly world of *Tobacco Road* finally returned, my divided selves were made one again by a sense of catharsis. Yes, but at the expense of undergoing what a humiliating, body-wracking conflict of emotions! Embarrassment, self-anger, ethnic scorn, and at last a feeling of comic relief. And all because Erskine Caldwell compelled me to laugh at his symbolic, and therefore non-threatening, Southern whites, and thus shocked me into recognizing certain absurd aspects of our common humanity."[3] Describing this as an embodied experience of Kenneth Burke's "perspective by incongruity," Ellison goes on to note that it was "as though I had plunged through the wacky mirrors of a fun house, to discover on the other side a weird distortion of perspective which made for a painful but redeeming rectification of vision. And in a flash, time was telescoped and the imaginary assumed the lineaments of past experiences through which Jeeter Lester's comic essence became a recognizable property of characters and events that I had known in the past."[4]

Published in 1985, Ralph Ellison's "An Extravagance of Laughter" clarifies a great deal not only about the obscene potentials of Caldwell's work in particular but also about what was at stake in early twentieth-century literary obscenity more generally. The grotesque body-rubbing performed by Lov and Ellie May on a Broadway stage failed to elicit a genitally organized response from Ellison because of what was so conspicuously withheld from sight. Not sex or nudity but strangely staged back-bumping is all that Caldwell is said to have provided, to which Ellison, still adjusting to life in the Big Apple, could not help but react with explosive hilarity. Caldwell's art of "frustrabation" is thus Ellison's way of wittily condensing the eroticized charge of laughter that is described in terms of smut by Sigmund Freud, for whom such outbursts of mirth could in fact release the built-up sexual tensions caused by a failed seduction without necessarily foreclosing sexual satisfaction of some sort eventually. The immediate frustration of a man's public attempts to seduce a woman into having sex with him does not mean that the virtualization of such an encounter in his mind and those around him will fail to offer compensatory pleasures, perhaps even aggressively pursued ones. Masturbatory self-regard may thus take place either *because of* this frustration or *in spite of* it, and what Caldwell's work powerfully demonstrated to Ellison during this laughing fit was that distinguishing the one from the other may not even be possible.[5] Are Lov and Ellie May grinding their backs together because they cannot actually couple with each other on a Broadway stage or in spite of that fact? That is to say, is their back-bumping situationally determined or is it instead an expression of an obstinate individual will capable of asserting its limited agency in defiance of such a determination? Correlatively, does Ellison's extravagant laughter confirm that he is the powerless object of Caldwell's smutty staging—"I had no choice but to identify, for *Tobacco Road*'s art had seen to that"—or does it reveal to him who he really is instead by allowing him to "recogniz[e] certain absurd aspects of our common humanity"? Is "frustrabation" an experience in objectification (in being more "done to" than "doing") or in identity formation (in figuring out who one really is among other people)?

As we have seen at length, these are precisely the questions that literary obscenity raises for James T. Farrell, Wyndham Lewis, and Lillian Smith as well, though each has abiding reservations as to what sorts of identities and readers may ultimately arise from such encounters with obscenity. For one thing, Farrell's *Studs Lonigan* trilogy tends to figure objectification as an experience in *over*identification. Studs becomes the dispossessed object of a variety of contemporary societal forces—popular culture, reactionary anti-Communism, Catholicism, and so forth—by responding too forthrightly to the contradictory stimuli and cues provided by his surroundings. The interference pattern created by these overlapping prompts constitutes who he is at any given time, and since these behaviors and identities never really synchronize, he can be made to do anything even while he himself intends to do nothing. Conversely, Lewis's Cantleman preemptively ironizes this relationship by assuming that who one is need not correlate with what one may be conspicuously compelled to do. If the Western world in the early twentieth century was indeed filling up with people who only knew how to read obscenely—that is, with their bodies rather than with their minds or in their own words—and if Watsonian behaviorism indeed provided psychology with a vulgar explanation for why this was happening and how those in power could best use it to their own advantage, then Lewis insisted upon the possibility that "to do" and "to be" do not necessarily comprise the same thing: to read obscenely is not to be an obscene reader in the end, to respond amorously to Stella does not mean Cantleman is actually in love with her, and to give in to the lure of sex in a time of war is not the same thing as being the dupe of nature or the nations of Europe. Cantleman is not an object of his milieu because of what he does but rather in spite of it. That the final sentence of "Cantleman's Spring-Mate" undercuts the adequacy of this comportment does not belie the fact that Lewis himself sought to embody it time and again in his own postwar literary career. As for Smith, she took all too seriously the possibility that "to do" is indeed the same thing as "to be" when it came to responding to the obscene words of the Jim Crow South. Otherwise, there would seem to be no rational explanation for why segregation remained the case

167

in the 1940s and 1950s when there were so many persuasive logical arguments to be made against it. The capacity of words to act in the world through the bodies of the people who encounter them is taken as given in Smith's writing, and rather than try to secure a space for one's self or identity by way of hostile irony or performative contradiction, Smith devoted the last years of her life to stripping language of its effective force instead. By abstractly recasting the civil rights movement in the allegorical terms of man's evolutionary history and destiny, Smith strove to make the obscene words of segregation turn into mere stand-ins for the irrational appeals of dehumanization, into so many ordeals to be surmounted on the path to man's eventual humanization. Forcing words to mean instead of do, Smith tried to make the world safe for the endless conversation of liberalism.

Though their political orientations do not line up at all, these authors wrote obscene works that confuse *because of* explanations with *in spite of* explanations, such that the one comes to inform the other inextricably. Having an uncontrollable bodily experience because of words on a page *and* in spite of them therefore confirms that we are indeed both "done to" *and* "doing" at the same time.[6] For Farrell, Lewis, and Smith, however, experiencing an overwhelming embodied response because of and in spite of words on a page is not something that can be merely attributed to the once-potent efficacy of the English language. For Lewis and Smith in particular, there are malign social, cultural, and ideological forces behind the susceptibility of early twentieth-century readers to literary obscenity, and this is what most notably differentiates Studs Lonigan, Cantleman, and Nonnie Anderson from that exemplary reader in European modernist obscenity, Emma Bovary, who never asks who or what in her world is pulling her strings when she tries to make words get off the page and come to life for her. For literary naturalists and those modernists—like Lewis—with a tendency to interpret cultural phenomena in terms of determinism and cooptation, obscenity was not a problem in and of itself; rather, it was problematic because of what it indexed, which was a growing vulnerability to harmful forces and trends in society by way of our susceptibility to mute words on a page. What Lewis and Smith in particular sought to do with their "obscene" writing, then, was to point fingers and name names, to flesh out what and who stood behind early twentieth-century obscenity.

Caldwell is an invaluable counterpoint here precisely because his work is more concerned with *how* words might be understood to get off the page rather than who or what stands to gain if they ever do. Of course, this is not to say that his novels of the 1930s and 1940s are bereft of such content. Eugenics discourses are all over the cyclorama novels, and like many other naturalist writers of the 1930s, his political commitments were credibly fellow-traveling. More than any other naturalistic exponent of literary obscenity in English at this time, however, Caldwell tried to account for how an unmanageable bodily response to printed words might come about in the first place, and his solution—that such a response occurs by virtue of the conspicuous failure of such words to evoke an immediate response—informed his compositional reliance on repetition and his preoccupation with powerful visual experiences that elude verbal expression. Caldwell's writing thus testifies not only to the dormant potency of words in and of themselves but also to the shift in the proscriptive focus of legal obscenity from books to visual culture that was taking place in the first half of the twentieth century.

This same shift is cannily reenacted in Ellison's essay, which is nominally in honor of Caldwell's writing, though what Caldwell actually wrote does not get mentioned at all. Instead, the scene for Ellison's appreciation of Caldwell's art is a darkened Broadway theater, not a comfortable chair in a quiet room with a lot of light by which to read. In a stunning sleight of hand, Ellison honors the octogenarian Caldwell by praising Jack Kirkland instead, insofar as the performance of a theatrical adaptation of *Tobacco Road* is made to stand in for—indeed, it wholly supersedes—the act of reading that novel itself. If the Freudian smut of Caldwell's writing translates quite well into the physical immediacy of the play's "frustrabation," then that attests to the prominence of smutty triads in Caldwell's compositional methods and to Kirkland's fidelity to those methods. Accordingly, Ellison does offer a lot of insights into Caldwell's writing in "An Extravagance of Laughter," but remarkably he manages to do so without once noting the difference between a theatrical adaptation and a book, between being wracked with smutty laughter while viewing a play with an audience and having a similar experience while reading a novel alone at home. On the one hand, Ellison would seem to be suggesting that the two experiences are equivalent, that books indeed remain a force to be reckoned with when it comes to our susceptibility to uncontrollable bodily experiences. On the other hand, Caldwell's novel at most provides the mere pretext for the encounter with an audience that the performing arts and visual culture are hereafter better equipped to satisfy. Caldwell's *Tobacco Road* may be smutty, but Jack Kirkland's *Tobacco Road* is actually smut. Extending this logic into the period in which Ellison wrote his essay, we might note that Kathy Acker's *Empire of the Senseless* (1988) may have "obscene" content, but Robert Mapplethorpe's *X Portfolio* series (1978) and Karen Finley's *We Keep Our Victims Ready* (1989) are actually obscene.[7] The demotion of writing's effective force with respect to visual culture, performance art, and new media may be something we simply take for granted today, but the proscribably "obscene" works of Lewis, Caldwell, and Smith still represent a range of exemplary responses to obscenity at a time when such a demotion was only just emergent. By respectively reducing obscene reading practices to performative contradictions, predicating the ability of obscene books to arouse readers on their ostentatious failure to actually arouse readers, and robbing obscene words of their sensory content through abstraction and allegory, each

169

wrestled with literary obscenity both because of and in spite of the bodily appeals of words on a page. Muddying the distinction between *because of* explanations and *in spite of* ones is certainly a common feature of the works of each of these authors, but it also contributed to the world we inhabit today in which legal obscenity persists *regardless of* whatever effective force words on the page may still fitfully possess here and there.

Ellison's essay thus gives us a striking reason for why this came to be the case. For him the result of Caldwell's obscene "frustrabation" is a "rectification of vision" whereby he experiences extravagantly and hilariously—that is to say, bodily—an unlikely sense of unity with a "repugnant cultural other."[8] Here the uncontrollable effects smuttily produced by Kirkland's actors on a Broadway stage—and supposedly Caldwell's words on the page as well—act to promote an unlikely sense of recognition that not only humanizes the Other but also teaches Ellison a new lesson in what it means to be human himself. Whereas it is an occasion for cutting off almost all meaningful ties to other people in the works of Lewis, and whereas it ineluctably facilitates the continuation of segregating mores in those of Smith, literary obscenity in Ellison's missed encounter with Caldwell's writing produces instead a profound sense of empathetic identification that fosters improbable interpersonal connections across lines of race and class.

In other words, Caldwell got obscene books laughed off the stage, and if this Smith-like civics lesson in humanization—and not the darker homicidal impulses of Cantleman's performative chortles—is all that is to be found in the smutty mirth that occurs when words do indeed get off the page, then how could anyone really be afraid of literary obscenity anymore?

Notes

Introduction

1. See Lukács, "Narrate or Describe?"

Chapter 1

1. *Jacobellis*, 378 U.S. at 197: "It is possible to read the Court's opinion in *Roth v. United States* and *Alberts v. California* in a variety of ways. In saying this, I imply no criticism of the Court, which in those cases was faced with the task of trying to define what may be indefinable [i.e., obscenity]. I have reached the conclusion, which I think is confirmed at least by negative implication in the Court's decisions since *Roth* and *Alberts*, that under the First and Fourteenth Amendments criminal laws in this area are constitutionally limited to hard-core pornography. I shall not today attempt further to define the kinds of material I understand to be embraced within that shorthand description; and perhaps I could never succeed in intelligibly doing so. But I know it when I see it, and the motion picture involved in this case [Louis Malle's *Les Amants* (1958)] is not that."

2. *Hicklin*, L.R. 3 Q.B. at 371.

3. *Gordon*, 66 Pa. D.&C. at 125.

4. Historical overviews of twentieth-century obscenity case law in the United States tend to begin their accounts with *Hicklin*. Emblematic here are de Grazia, *Girls Lean Back Everywhere*, and Friedman, *Prurient Interests*, 16ff. U.S. government reports have also noted this long-term impact of *Hicklin* on U.S. case and statutory law. See esp. *Report of the Commission on Obscenity and Pornography*, 348ff., and *Attorney General's Commission on Pornography and Obscenity Final Report*, 1:236–48.

5. See *Roth*, 354 U.S. at 489. It should be noted, however, that legal scholars do not necessarily consider *Roth* to be an outright rejection

of *Hicklin*. For an account of *Roth* that sees it as a "mere modification" of *Hicklin* (rather than a replacement for it), see Feinberg, *The Moral Limits of the Criminal Law*, 171–78.

6. See *Bennett*, 24 F. Cas. 1093, and *Rosen*, 161 U.S. 29.

7. *Kennerley*, 209 F. at 120.

8. For critical work that stresses the gendering at work in nineteenth-century obscenity laws in the United States and Great Britain, see Kendrick, *The Secret Museum*. For one that emphasizes instead the class composition of the audiences for pornography in nineteenth-century Great Britain, see Pease, *Modernism, Mass Culture, and the Aesthetics of Obscenity*, esp. 37–71. The single best account of how changes in obscenity laws in Great Britain, the United States, and the Commonwealth of Nations have indexed historical transformations in the way in which subjectivity has been socially organized remains Hunter, Saunders, and Williamson, *On Pornography*.

9. See Alpert, "Judicial Censorship of Obscene Literature," 51ff., and Manchester, "Lord Campbell's Act."

10. See Hunter, Saunders, and Williamson, *On Pornography*, 82–84, and Marshik, *British Modernism and Censorship*.

11. See Hunter, Saunders, and Williamson, *On Pornography*, 216.

12. See ibid., 209.

13. Tenn. Code Ann., §39–17–901. Cf. *Miller*, 413 U.S. at 24.

14. Cf. Feinberg, *The Moral Limits of the Criminal Law*, 175: "The old *Hicklin* formula had not been meant to be a definition of 'obscene,' but to be more like a litmus test or drunkometer test for determining when obscenity is present. Just as the one test says that drunkenness is present when there is a certain percentage of alcohol in the blood, so the other test says that materials are obscene when they are capable of producing

a certain effect on susceptible persons. Actually, the analogy is much closer to a test for determining when a substance is intoxicating than to a test for determining when a person is intoxicated. In each case what is being tested is the capacity of an object to produce effects of some measurable kind on a precisely defined class of subjects."

15. My gloss on Peirce's definition of lithium here owes much to Paul Grimstad's remarks during the "Pragmatism and Literature" round-table at the 2008 Modern Language Association Convention in San Francisco.

16. Peirce, *Philosophical Writings of Peirce*, 31.

17. For more on the use of academics as expert witnesses in U.S. obscenity trials, see Glass, "Redeeming Value," and Nowlin, *Judging Obscenity*, 3–84.

18. The most forceful proponent of this view remains Richard Posner. See Posner, *Sex and Reason*, esp. 371 and 381. To be sure, Posner's arguments regarding this are of a piece with the decade (1990s) in which he published them insofar as the U.S. Department of Justice under Attorney General Janet Reno actively pursued prosecutions against child pornography but did not do the same for obscenity as such. During George W. Bush's presidency, however, Attorney General John Ashcroft reversed this trend and zealously prosecuted a number of high-profile obscenity cases. For more on the resurgence of obscenity prosecutions between 2000 and 2008, see Adler, "All Porn All the Time," and Koppelman, "Reading *Lolita* at Guantánamo."

19. The conflicts between jurists over whether or not the prevention of moral harm is essential to the state's interests in contemporary obscenity doctrine and whether or not obscenity doctrine as such is a suitable instrument for pursuing these interests in the first place have become quite convoluted over the past half century. Perhaps the most striking defender of the government's interest in preventing moral harm by means of obscenity laws has been Harry M. Clor. See esp. Clor, *Obscenity and Public Morality*, and Clor, *Public Morality and Liberal Society*. Neoconservatives have likewise made the case that obscene texts corrupt morals, arrest male heterosexual development (to the extent that masturbation increasingly thereby takes the place of heteronormative sexual intercourse),

undermine marriage, and ultimately threaten civilization; see esp. Kristol, "Pornography, Obscenity, and the Case for Censorship." For an attempt to undermine the government's ability to pass laws based on moral judgments and to thereby call into question obscenity censorship itself, see Gey, "The Apologetics of Suppression." An early expression of the doubts informing such an attempt can be found in Henkin, "Morals and the Constitution." Catharine A. MacKinnon would have us dispense with the moral harm interest altogether and instead affirm the need for reframing obscenity as behavior that subjugates women. See MacKinnon, *Feminism Unmodified*, esp. 146–62. Finally, Andrew Koppelman has compellingly argued that while obscene works do indeed have the capacity to inculcate bad fixed norms in their readers or viewers (thus affirming the state's interest in preventing moral harm), obscenity doctrine as such is nevertheless a poor means of solving the problems these harms pose. See Koppelman, "Does Obscenity Cause Moral Harm?" Cf. Lindgren, "Defining Pornography."

20. For work contending that obscenity is not covered by the First Amendment because it partakes more of sexual activity than it does of communication, see Finnis, "'Reason and Passion'"; Schauer, *Free Speech*; and Schauer, "Speech and 'Speech.'" For arguments that hold that obscenity and pornography are indeed covered by the First Amendment because they possess ideational contents, see Koppelman, "Is Pornography 'Speech'?," and Redish, *Freedom of Expression*, esp. 68ff. For a pro-free speech defense of pornography that directly takes aim at the work of Catharine A. MacKinnon and Andrea Dworkin, see Strossen, "A Feminist Critique of 'the' Feminist Critique of Pornography."

21. See esp. Adler, "Post-Modern Art and the Death of Obscenity Law," and Adler, "What's Left?"

22. Notable examples of this tendency among New Modernist Studies scholars to approach "obscene modernism" in terms of censorship and transgression include Chisholm, "Obscene Modernism"; Mullin, *James Joyce, Sexuality and Social Purity*; Parkes, *Modernism and the Theater of Censorship*; Potter, *Obscene Modernism*; and Vanderham, *James Joyce and Censorship*.

23. See Mao and Walkowitz, *Bad Modernisms*, and Sherry, *Modernism and the Reinvention of Decadence*.

24. Trilling, *Beyond Culture*, xiii.

25. Ibid., 13.

26. For a notable exception that critically confronts the tendency to make an absolute value out of transgression and subversion in the study of modernism and obscenity, see Ladenson, *Dirt for Art's Sake*.

27. See Marshik, *British Modernism and Censorship*, esp. 4–10.

28. See Diepeveen, *The Difficulties of Modernism*.

29. Strauss, *Persecution and the Art of Writing*, 23.

30. Ibid., 24.

31. Dore, *The Novel and the Obscene*, 7–8.

32. Ibid., 16.

33. Ibid., 8–9.

34. Cf. Potter, *Obscene Modernism*, 12: "One could go so far as to suggest that modernist texts, in their more liberatory guises, became identified with radical and obscene transgression."

35. I have done my best here to include every book that was brought up on charges of obscenity and then defended at the district, appellate, and federal court level in the United States during this fifty-year period. Therefore, my list excludes (1) works that were charged with obscenity but were not provided with legal defense, thereby leaving no record of a judge interpreting the obscenity (or lack thereof) of the charged text; and (2) works whose title was pointedly omitted in the opinion of a given case. The former exclusion is fully in keeping with my effort to move our attention from obscenity censorship to the interpretation of obscene books, particularly as this was undertaken by judges in this country at this time. The latter exclusion is unfortunately unavoidable, as many judges went out of their way to withhold the title of the obscene work or works in their opinion so as not to help boost the sales of such items. See, for instance, *Berg*, 272 N.Y.S. at 587: "We have no purpose to excite the curiosity of the prurient by naming the book—as might be desired by those interested in its publication and sale. It is sufficient to say that it is fully and completely of the type that the language of the statute condemns in article 106 of the Penal Law

as a result of legislative effort to forbid indecency in different forms. In addition it lacks literary merit. It teaches no lesson and points no moral. It describes no period of history and the people or characters of that time and their conduct and habits of life—such, for instance, as the 'Elizabethan Age'; and no folk lore or tales of primitive people living in isolated regions. We cannot believe that the story is one even possibly true or representative of any individual or of any limited class. In our opinion it is obscene, lewd, lascivious and disgusting, and nothing more; and was so intended to be for purely mercenary purposes." Fortunately, in this particular case, Leo Alpert later let the cat out of the bag by revealing that the book at issue in *Berg* was in fact Donald Henderson Clarke's *Female*. See Alpert, "Judicial History of Obscene Literature," 62.

36. Margaret Sanger's husband was charged with illegally disseminating copies of her contraception pamphlet *Family Limitation* under §1142 ("Indecent Articles") of the New York Criminal Code, which made a criminal offense out of the distribution of contraceptive information, an obscene offense under federal law at the time. Three years later, Sanger herself was found guilty under this same statute for distributing issues of her pro–birth control journal, *The Woman Rebel*. See *Margaret H. Sanger*, 222 N.Y. 192.

37. The entirety of Judge Charles C. Nott's favorable opinion in this case can be found in Holt, *"Jurgen" and the Law*, 73–74.

38. See also Dennett's own description of this case in Dennett, *Who's Obscene?*

39. This same year, Wilson's novel also faced obscenity charges in California. See *Wepplo*, 78 Cal.App.2d Supp. 959.

40. Though Émile Zola was never successfully prosecuted for obscenity in France, his essays on naturalism frequently defended the literary mode he helped found against charges of obscenity. See Zola, *The Experimental Novel*, esp. 93, 127, 245, 283, 286, 356, 364–67, and 406. In the U.K., however, Zola's English translator and publisher, Henry Vizetelly, was successfully prosecuted for obscenity. See de Grazia, *Girls Lean Back Everywhere*, 40–53 and 700–705, and Vizetelly, *Émile Zola, Novelist and Reformer*. In Germany in 1889, there took place the *Leipziger Realistenprozess*, in which Hermann Conradi's *Adam Mensch* (1889), Konrad Alberti's *Die Alten*

173

und die Jungen (1889), and Wilhelm Walloth's *Dämon des Neides* (1889) were all proscribed on grounds of obscenity. For more on the relationship between the German Criminal Code in the late nineteenth century and German literary naturalism, see Stark, "The Censorship of Literary Naturalism, 1885–1895," and Paret, "Literary Censorship as a Source of Historical Understanding."

41. Adorno, *Aesthetic Theory*, 2.

42. Marinetti, "The Founding and Manifesto of Futurism," 49.

43. Jameson, *The Ideologies of Theory*, 72. More recently, Jameson has revised his account somewhat by noting that the attempts of modernists to cancel realism were based on a misprision. See Jameson, *A Singular Modernity*, 124: "The two terms [i.e., realism and modernism], whether considered to be concepts or categories, are drawn from two unrelated systems, and like those two well-known lines which, prolonged into infinity, never meet, they are incommensurable with each other. Modernism is an aesthetic category and realism is an epistemological one; the truth claim of the latter is irreconcilable with the formal dynamic of the former." Cf. Jameson, *Signatures of the Visible*, 158–77.

44. See Jameson, *The Ideologies of Theory*, 415–33.

45. Cf. Marin, *On Representation*, 387: "Ruptures, interruptions, and syncopes have to do, on the contrary, with the very conditions of possibility, of effectiveness, of legitimacy, of representation: they play on the aporetic features, which are the very features of the general regime of mimesis to which representation belongs."

46. *Swearingen*, 161 U.S. at 451.

47. *Kennerley*, 209 F. at 121.

48. Ibid., at 122.

49. Ibid.

50. *Anderson*, 247 F. at 384.

51. Ibid.

52. *Halsey*, 234 N.Y. at 4.

53. *Dennett*, 39 F.2d at 569.

54. *One Obscene Book Entitled "Married Love,"* 48 F.2d at 823.

55. *One Book Called "Ulysses,"* 5 F. Supp. at 184.

56. *One Book Entitled "Ulysses,"* 72 F.2d at 707.

57. *Parmelee*, 113 F.2d at 731–32.

58. *Isenstadt*, 318 Mass. at 549–50.

59. *Gordon*, 66 Pa. D.&C. at 104.

60. Ibid., at 153.

61. *The Book Named "God's Little Acre,"* 326 Mass. at 283–84.

62. See de Grazia, *Girls Lean Back Everywhere*, and Boyer, *Purity in Print*. For a useful (if far from impartial) narrative of the Supreme Court's ordeals with obscenity, told from the point of view of the attorney who defended numerous "obscene" texts before that court, see Rembar, *The End of Obscenity*. A comprehensive legal account is also given in Schauer, *Law of Obscenity*.

63. See *In re Worthington Company*, 30 N.Y.S. 361.

64. Ibid., at 362–63.

65. *One Book Entitled "Ulysses,"* 72 F.2d at 707.

66. *Isenstadt*, 318 Mass. at 554.

67. For more on Crane's relationship to the ethnographic and psychological concerns evoked by Riis, see Gandal, *The Virtues of the Vicious*. For Dreiser's account of Spencer's influence on his own development, see Dreiser, *Newspaper Days*.

68. For more on Farrell as a social critic, see Gelfant, *The American City Novel*; Douglas, "*Studs Lonigan* and the Failure of History in Mass Society"; Wald, *James T. Farrell*; and Wald, *The New York Intellectuals*. For more on the influence of early twentieth-century eugenics research on Caldwell's first cyclorama novels, see Keely, "Power, Sterilization, and Eugenics in Erskine Caldwell's *Tobacco Road*"; Holmes, "Re-examining the Political Left"; and Lancaster, "Weeding Out the Recessive Gene."

69. Hill, "The Travels of Naturalism and the Challenges of a World Literary History," 1203.

70. My gloss of New Historicism owes much to Walter Benn Michaels's remarks during the "Dating New Historicism" roundtable at the 2013 Modern Language Association Convention in Boston.

71. Clune, *American Literature and the Free Market, 1945–2000*, 7.

72. Cf. Howard, *Form and History in American Literary Naturalism*, x.

73. Cowley's essay is the final expanded version of an argument first expressed three years earlier. See Cowley, "'Not Men.'"

74. Cowley, "Naturalism in American Literature," 330–31.

75. Ibid., 331.

76. Rahv, *Image and Idea*, 133.

77. Cowley, "Naturalism in American Literature," 318.

78. Ibid., 333.

79. Ibid., 330. Cf. Rahv, *Image and Idea*, 136.

80. Norris, *Novels and Essays*, 228.

81. See Cargill, *Intellectual America*, 13.

82. See ibid., 175.

83. Cf. the dichotomous typology offered for literary naturalism as "passive documentation" on the one hand and muckraking on the other in Rahv, *Image and Idea*, 131–32. Also see the easy-to-overlook disqualifier at the end of the chapter on American Naturalism in Cargill, *Intellectual America*, 175: "It is important to note that the leaders in the American Naturalistic school are by no means *convinced* Naturalists—they betray themselves by pet schemes for human betterment, schemes in which no genuine and thorough-going pessimist has any legitimate interest. The volition to clutch at a straw is yet a manifestation of the spirit and a sign of hope."

84. Walcutt, *American Literary Naturalism, a Divided Stream*, 25.

85. Ibid., 28.

86. Ibid. The best explication of this turn in Walcutt's argument can be found in Howard, who reliably evinces skepticism toward the capacity of literary naturalism to resolve the tensions between determinism and reformism. See Howard, *Form and History in American Literary Naturalism*, esp. 38–40, 109, 116, 125–27, 131, and 140.

87. Walcutt, *American Literary Naturalism, a Divided Stream*, 28.

88. Ibid., 295. Cf. Rahv, *Image and Idea*, 137–38.

89. See Walcutt, *American Literary Naturalism, a Divided Stream*, 295.

90. Ibid., 297.

91. Caldwell, "Naturalism and the American Novel."

92. Ibid.

93. See Stovall, *American Idealism*. Underscoring the degree to which no consensus seemed to be forming as to what even counted as a naturalist work, Rahv called into question the competency of those critics who approached either Faulkner or Caldwell as naturalist writers. See Rahv, *Image and Idea*, 135–36.

94. Caldwell, "Naturalism and the American Novel."

95. Ibid.

96. Douglas, "*Studs Lonigan* and the Failure of History in Mass Society," 494.

97. Farrell, Studs Lonigan, 437. Hereafter abbreviated SL; further references provided parenthetically.

98. Douglas, "Studs Lonigan and the Failure of History," 492.

99. Cf. Adler, "The Art of Censorship," 210.

100. Cf. the discussion of Caldwell, visuality, and the covers to the paperback reprints of his work in chapter 3.

101. Gerbner, "The Social Role of the Confession Magazine," 40.

102. Watson, "Psychology as the Behaviorist Views It," 167.

103. Watson, *Behaviorism*, 303.

104. My discussion of behaviorism and Richards here is indebted to the reading developed by Gang, "Behaviorism and the Beginnings of Close Reading."

105. Richards, *Practical Criticism*, 6.

106. Fleissner, *Women, Compulsion, Modernity*, 9–10.

107. *Gordon*, 66 Pa. D.&C. at 156.

108. Ibid., at 153.

109. *Bantam Books*, 96 A.2d at 57.

110. Ibid., at 54–55.

111. Ernst and Seagle, *To the Pure . . .*, vii.

112. Ibid., 283–84.

113. See ibid., 131–68.

Chapter 2

1. *Anderson*, 247 F. at 383.

2. This was also the statute under which Joyce's "Nausikaa" episode was prosecuted in 1921, and it was somewhat notorious in contemporary writerly circles for reducing obscene literature, contraceptive devices, and instruments of abortion to identity. A shrewd discussion of this statute and the final *Ulysses/Little Review* trial can be found in Parkes, *Modernism and the Theater of Censorship*, 67–69. For Pound's apoplectic response to the statute and the suppression of the October 1917 issue of *The Little Review*, see Pound, *The Selected Letters of Ezra Pound to John Quinn, 1915–1924*, 132–35.

3. A notable recent exception to this tendency to downplay the importance of

"Cantleman's Spring-Mate" in the study of modernism and obscenity is Potter, *Obscene Modernism*, 75–91.

4. See Kenner, *Wyndham Lewis*, esp. 107.

5. See Stanfield, "'This Implacable Doctrine.'"

6. Lewis, "Cantleman's [*sic*] Spring-Mate," here 14. Hereafter abbreviated "CS-M"; further references provided parenthetically.

7. See Jameson, *Fables of Aggression*, 26–29.

8. Ibid., 27.

9. Ibid., 28.

10. For more on the formative influence of contemporary French neoclassical critiques of Romanticism on Lewis's critical thought and writing, see the insightful intellectual history offered in Wagner, *Wyndham Lewis*.

11. Watson, "The New Science of Animal Behavior," 352–53.

12. Ibid., 348.

13. Despite the stridency of the claims made by Watson and other first-wave behaviorists as to the novelty of their theories and practices, early behaviorism may nevertheless be retrospectively understood as having more continuities than discontinuities with the contemporary practice of psychology. For more on Watson, behaviorism, and their connections to early twentieth-century functional psychology, see Buckley, *Mechanical Man*, esp. 33–58.

14. For James, introspection was a privileged method in the investigation of psychology's subject matter, understood by him to consist of the dynamic interactions and relationships formed by states of consciousness, the objects of those states, and the encompassing world shared by the introspecting subject and the observing psychologist. See James, *Principles of Psychology*, 1:185. For his later skeptical reframing of the very existence of consciousness, see James, "Does 'Consciousness' Exist?"

15. Watson, *Behaviorism*, 140–43.

16. For a cogent and useful discussion of the methodological value of intersubjective agreement in behaviorist data language, see Zuriff, *Behaviorism*, esp. 13–54.

17. Lewis, *The Art of Being Ruled*, 349.

18. Ibid.

19. Ibid., 231.

20. Ibid., 232.

21. Cf. Miller, *Late Modernism*, 49–54, and Nicholls, *Modernisms*, 183–84.

22. Lewis, *Men Without Art*, 95.

23. It ought to be noted here that while Lewis does not completely disavow the utility of certain inner methods, he does limit the scope of such methods to particularized uses ("as a sort of comic relief") as well as to a restricted range of character types. See ibid., 98: "So what I think can be laid down is this: In dealing with (1) the extremely aged; (2) young children; (3) half-wits; and (4) animals, the *internal* method can be extremely effective. In my opinion it should be entirely confined to those classes of characters."

24. Ibid., 93; emphasis original.

25. Ibid., 95.

26. Ibid., 92.

27. Ibid., 93.

28. Miller, *Late Modernism*, 49.

29. Watson, "Psychology as the Behaviorist Views It," 167.

30. Indeed, Watson foregrounded this project early. For instance, see the second sentence of ibid., 158: "[Psychology's] theoretical goal is the prediction and control of behavior."

31. Watson, *Behaviorism*, 97.

32. Watson, "The New Science of Animal Behavior," 353.

33. Watson, *Behaviorism*, 11.

34. Ibid., 276.

35. Ibid., 303–4.

36. Lewis, *The Complete Wild Body*, 78. Hereafter abbreviated "B"; further references provided parenthetically.

37. Cf. Potter, *Obscene Modernism*, 78.

38. Descartes, *"Discourse on Method" and "The Meditations,"* 44.

39. Ibid., 44–45.

40. Ibid., 45.

41. Watson, *Behaviorism*, 3.

42. See ibid., 266–68.

43. Ibid., 233.

44. For Watson's Romanian nurse example, see ibid.

45. Cf. Jameson, *Fables of Aggression*, 26.

46. Lewis, *Time and Western Man*, 303; emphasis original.

47. Lewis, *The Apes of God*, 123.

48. As Ker-Orr admits at one point, "I learnt a great deal from Bestre. He is one of my masters" ("B," 84).

49. Lewis, *Blasting & Bombardiering*, 1.

50. Ibid., 5.

51. Ibid.

52. See Caillois, *The Edge of Reason*, esp. 99–103.

53. The quoted adverbs are Anderson's. See Anderson, "Judicial Opinion (Our Suppressed October Issue)," 46.

54. *Anderson*, 247 F. at 383.

55. Ibid.

56. Ibid.

57. Ibid.

58. *One Book Called "Ulysses,"* 5 F. Supp. 182.

59. For instance, see Morris L. Ernst's "Introduction" in Joyce, *Ulysses*.

60. See Vanderham, *James Joyce and Censorship*, esp. 121–28. Cf. Fiedler, "To Whom Does Joyce Belong?"

61. See Greene, "Arbitrary Tastes and Commonsense Pleasures."

62. In this regard, Hand would have us reconsider the legitimate ascription of obscenity to many of the "classics." See *Anderson*, 247 F. at 384.

63. Ibid.

64. Anderson, "Judicial Opinion," 48.

65. *One Book Called "Ulysses,"* 5 F. Supp. at 184–85.

66. *Besig*, 208 F.2d at 147.

67. *One Book Entitled "Ulysses,"* 72 F.2d at 708.

68. Ibid., at 708–9.

69. See Tischler, "A Rose Is a Pose."

70. Anderson, "Judicial Opinion," 49.

71. Ibid.

72. See Hardy, *The Trumpet-Major*, 45–61. As indicated by Cantleman's thumb-biting while reading of John Loveday's dilemma in chapter 9 of Hardy's novel, these passages involving Anne and old Mr. Derriman would have been read by Cantleman *before* those evoking his gratuitous chuckles, so the reference to mimesis or to processes of modeling here is tenable on its face.

73. Ibid., 7.

74. Joyce, *Dubliners*, 12.

75. Ibid.

76. *Hicklin*, L.R. 3 Q.B. at 371.

77. For a symptomatically critical take on Cockburn's test, see Alpert, "Judicial Censorship of Obscene Literature."

78. *One Book Called "Ulysses,"* 5 F. Supp. at 184.

79. The Supreme Court began to acknowledge something like a standard of variable obscenity (according to which obscenity determinations must take into account modes of advertising, distribution, and sale of the charged object, especially in those cases involving minors) in 1968. See *Ginsberg*, 390 U.S. 629.

80. Hunter, Saunders, and Williamson, *On Pornography*, 135.

81. See Ellmann, *James Joyce*, esp. 230, 340–42, and 364.

82. Cf. the old bookworm's final Sadean monologue in front of the narrator in Joyce, *Dubliners*, 19–20: "And if a boy had a girl for a sweetheart and told lies about it then he [i.e., the old bookworm] would give him such a whipping as no boy ever got in this world. He said that there was nothing in this world he would like so well as that. He described to me how he would whip such a boy as if he were unfolding some elaborate mystery."

83. Ibid., 18.

84. In this view, then, "An Encounter" bears comparing with Joyce's essay "Oscar Wilde: The Poet of 'Salome'" (1909). See Joyce, *Occasional, Critical, and Political Writing*, esp. 151: "Oscar Wilde's self-defence in the *Scots Observer* should be accepted as legitimate by any bench of impartial judges. Each man writes his own sin into *Dorian Gray* (Wilde's most celebrated novel). What Dorian Gray's sin was no one says and no one knows. He who discovers it has committed it."

85. Cf. Hunter, Saunders, and Williamson, *On Pornography*, esp. 12–56.

86. For a cogent critical reading of how this feature often expresses itself (sometimes tacitly, sometimes explicitly) in the form of an anti-Semitic conspiracy theory throughout Lewis's work of the 1920s and 1930s, see Ayers, *Wyndham Lewis and Western Man*.

87. See Lewis, *Time and Western Man*.

88. See Lewis, *Art of Being Ruled*, 341, and Lewis, *Time and Western Man*, 330. In the case of *Snooty Baronet*, this duplication is noted by Stanfield, "'This Implacable Doctrine.'"

89. See Lewis, *The Roaring Queen*, esp. 32–38, 63–66, 71–77, and 127–32.

90. Lewis, *Snooty Baronet*, 251.

91. Ibid., 235.

92. Caillois, *The Edge of Reason*, 91.

Chapter 3

1. *With All My Might* (1987) is Caldwell's other autobiography. He also published two autobiographical long works on race relations and Protestantism in the South: *In Search of Bisco* (1965) and *Deep South: Memory and Observation* (1968), respectively.

2. Caldwell, *Call It Experience*, 5. Hereafter abbreviated *CIE*; further references provided parenthetically.

3. For more on Caldwell's reception history, see MacDonald, *Critical Essays on Erskine Caldwell*, and McDonald, *Critical Response to Erskine Caldwell*.

4. Wagenknecht, *Cavalcade of the American Novel*, 415.

5. For a discerning, if unduly tentative attempt to trouble this consensus, see Arnold, *Erskine Caldwell Reconsidered*, 49–58. Cf. McDonald, *Critical Response to Erskine Caldwell*, 1–16, and McDonald, *Reading Erskine Caldwell*, 1–10.

6. Characteristically, Caldwell's autobiography exaggerates somewhat: it seems he did not receive a key to the city but merely "a scroll designating him an honorary member" of Kansas City. See Klevar, *Erskine Caldwell*, 278–81.

7. The relative scarcity of *Sister Carrie* is a trace of that book's censorship history. Tacitly suppressing the novel, Doubleday limited the book's initial run to one thousand copies, of which nearly half were unbound. For more on the publication and (nonexistent) advertising of Dreiser's first novel, see Lingeman, *Theodore Dreiser: At the Gates of the City*, 281–301.

8. Rainey, *Institutions of Modernism*, 76.

9. Caldwell learned the lesson (and learned it well, it would seem) of socially necessary labor time fairly early in life: "I was in my fifteenth year, the time being 1918, when I learned that under certain conditions money could be earned by work, and that labor under other circumstances did not necessarily produce pay" (*CIE*, 13). Not surprisingly, a substantial part of the experience referred to in the title of Caldwell's first autobiography concerns that of learning how to make writing pay and then continuing to make it pay.

10. All of this information derives from the page bearing the edition's copy number in Caldwell, *The Bastard*, n.p. The copy referred to throughout this chapter belongs to the University of California at Berkeley and is numbered 244.

11. Much of what follows in this paragraph owes a great deal to Rainey, *Institutions of Modernism*.

12. It should be noted that, in addition to the ten thousand copies of the novel made available in the first trade edition, Boni and Liveright also offered a luxury edition of *An American Tragedy*, autographed by Dreiser himself and priced at $12.50 per volume. For more on the mixed publication of *An American Tragedy*, see Lingeman, *Theodore Dreiser: An American Journey*, 257–80.

13. Several works in the past three decades have contributed significantly to our understanding of the institutions and market structures subtending modernist literary and cultural production. See Dettmar and Watt, *Marketing Modernisms*; Wexler, *Who Paid for Modernism?*; Turner, *Marketing Modernism between the Two World Wars*; and Rosenquist, *Modernism, the Market and the Institution of the New*.

14. Limited editions of works by modernist writers continued to appear at the beginning of the 1930s, but their frequency decreased predictably (yet significantly) because of poor sales. For a brief look at the example of the 1930 Hours Press edition of Pound's *A Draft of XXX Cantos*, see Rainey, "A Poem Including History," 212–14.

15. For more on Caldwell's royalty problems with The Heron Press, see Arnold, *Conversations with Erskine Caldwell*, esp. 270–71, and Dan B. Miller, *Erskine Caldwell*, 111.

16. For more on Caldwell's unpublished short novel entitled *The Bogus Ones*, written in response to the suppression of *The Bastard*, see Cook, *Erskine Caldwell and the Fiction of Poverty*, 17–18; Klevar, *Erskine Caldwell*, 83–99; Dan B. Miller, *Erskine Caldwell*, 95–101, 110–11; and Owen, "'The Bogus Ones.'"

17. Caldwell, "In Defense of Myself."

18. Lawrence, *Phoenix*, 172.

19. Ibid., 173.

20. Ibid., 175.

21. Ibid., 176.

22. Ibid., 175.

23. Miller, *The World of Lawrence*, 177.

24. Ladenson, *Dirt for Art's Sake*, 145. Ladenson offers her own gloss of a portion of the Miller passage I have quoted in this paragraph as well.

25. The relationship of Caldwell's work to that of Lawrence has not been adequately pursued in the study of either author, and it is unfortunately not within the scope of this project to undertake a sustained comparative analysis beyond the suggestive links indicated here. For more on Lawrence and Caldwell, see Cook, *Erskine Caldwell and the Fiction of Poverty*, 17–18, and Owen, "'The Bogus Ones,'" esp. 35–37.

26. Caldwell, *Writing in America*, 95.

27. See Marcuse, *One-Dimensional Man*, 56ff.

28. *Kingsley*, 360 U.S. 684.

29. Caldwell, "In Defense of Myself," n.p.

30. Caldwell, *The Bastard*, 15–16. Hereafter abbreviated *TB*; further references provided parenthetically.

31. In effect, Caldwell's remarks on the hooch dancer's dance in *The Bastard* anticipate developments in obscenity jurisprudence in the United States, Great Britain, and the Commonwealth by almost half a century. See the discussion of variable obscenity in Hunter, Saunders, and Williamson, *On Pornography*, 240.

32. It should be noted that in subsequent chapters, the narrator violates the novella's point of view at least three more times to give the reader access to the interiorities and life histories of John Hunter (the Lewisville Sheriff's son) and Myra Morgan. See *TB*, 59–65, 152–54, 160.

33. To underscore Potter's point once more, this time with an example drawn from Caldwell's career, I would like to point out that the Viking Press released Caldwell's *Journeyman* in a limited edition of 1,475 copies because it feared obscenity prosecutions of the kind *God's Little Acre* had faced in the state of New York upon the release of that book in 1933. *Journeyman* did not have enough artistic merit in the estimations of Viking's editors and lawyers to justify a larger initial print-run, like the one afforded *God's Little Acre*. For more on this decision by Viking, see Klevar, *Erskine Caldwell*, 147, 153, 157. For the New York City obscenity case involving *God's Little Acre*, see *Viking Press*, 264 N.Y.S. 534.

34. Potter, *Obscene Modernism*, 69.

35. Caldwell, *God's Little Acre*, 88. Hereafter abbreviated *GLA*; further references provided parenthetically.

36. Vials, "Whose Dixie?" 85.

37. Caldwell, *Journeyman*, 168–69. Hereafter abbreviated *J*; further references provided parenthetically.

38. See MacDonald, "Repetition as Technique in the Short Stories of Erskine Caldwell"; Castille, "'No More Obscene than the Truth'"; and Metress, "Repetition as Radical Critique in Erskine Caldwell's *God's Little Acre*."

39. See Freud, *Beyond the Pleasure Principle*.

40. My gloss of Freud and *Beyond the Pleasure Principle* here owes much to Green, *Time in Psychoanalysis*, esp. 75–99.

41. See Stein, *The Making of Americans*, esp. 191–98.

42. Cf. Lyotard, "Discourse Figure."

43. Cf. the replacement of visual details with statements as to the brute coordination of cause and effect in the hooch dancer episode in *TB*, 52–53.

44. For Greenberg's call for the purifying separation of artistic mediums from each other, see "Towards a Newer Laocoon" (1940), in *Clement Greenberg*, 1:23–38. For Greenberg's naturalization of vision, see *Art and Culture*, esp. 136–37 and 143.

45. Smithson's wall installation consisted of a set of mirrors constructed in such a way as to cancel planes of focus, to split the spectator's field of vision, and to make the spectator disappear altogether, depending on where she/he was positioned with respect to the mirror chambers. Duchamp's final major work is a tableau comprised of a wooden door with peepholes looking out onto a recumbent naked woman holding up a gas lamp while her legs are spread and her face is occluded.

46. For more information on the formation of the New American Library and its two signature imprints, Signet and Mentor, see especially Bonn, *Heavy Traffic and High Culture*. Cf. Bonn, *Under Cover*, esp. 48–49, 69–70. For more on Caldwell's decision to enter into the incredibly remunerative world of paperback reprints, see Klevar, *Erskine Caldwell*, 267–71 and 282.

47. For more on the critical turn against Caldwell during and after the 1940s, see the

essays collected in the second part of McDonald, *Critical Response to Erskine Caldwell*, 107–91.

48. See Klevar, *Erskine Caldwell*, 270–71.

49. Bonn, *Under Cover*, 102.

50. Though the cover to *Tragic Ground* here designates it as a Penguin Book, this edition (as well as that of the *Journeyman* cover included here) was in fact issued by Signet in the transitional period between Weybright and Enoch's move from Penguin to New American Library. Note that, contrary to branding practices associated with both companies at the time, neither the Penguin nor the Signet logos are included in the top framing bar of the cover.

51. Cf. Vials, "Whose Dixie?" esp. 85–86. Vials implicitly takes on Laura Mulvey's totalizing (and one would think warmed-over) thesis in "Visual Pleasure and Narrative Cinema" (1973/1975) far too uncritically for his remarks on the flawed sexual politics of the male gaze in Caldwell's fiction to have quite the same force his other insights into Caldwell's eccentric compositional methods tend to have.

52. Again, the resonances with Duchamp's *Étant donnés* are quite striking here.

53. Much of this information regarding the proscription of Caldwell's fiction in Great Britain and the United States appears in chronicle-like form in Haight, *Banned Books*, 106–7.

54. A richer historical reckoning of U.S. mass-market paperback publishing would start with the production methods, marketing practices, and cultural effects of such works during the first U.S. paperback revolution that took place throughout the nineteenth century. I refer the interested reader here to Denning, *Mechanic Accents*, and to Tebbel, *Between the Covers*.

55. See Bonn, *Under Cover*, 41–42.

56. Following the precedent set by the first trade edition of *Ulysses*, the first Penguin edition of *God's Little Acre* included the entirety of City Magistrate Benjamin Greenspan's favorable opinion of the novel as an appendix.

57. Qtd. in United States House of Representatives, *Report of the Select Committee on Current Pornographic Materials*, 1.

58. Ibid., 116.

59. Ibid., 117.

60. Ibid., 120.

61. Ibid., 121–22. For more on the Gathings Committee (particularly its effects on the

paperback publishing industry and its critical—derisive even—reception in contemporary public discourses), please refer to the following: Bonn, *High Culture*, 133–53; Bonn, *Under Cover*, 55, 103; Davis, *Two-Bit Culture*; and Speer, "Paperback Pornography."

62. See Haight, *Banned Books*, 109–10.

63. See Freud, *Jokes and Their Relation to the Unconscious*, 99–100.

64. Ibid., 99.

65. Ibid., 100.

66. Ibid., 99.

67. For a complementary use of Freudian smut to approach the transitive and mimetically ideational qualities that can be discerned within the formal disruptions of late modernist laughter, see Miller, *Late Modernism*, esp. 55–57.

68. Hurston, *Their Eyes Were Watching God*, 78 and 79–80.

Chapter 4

1. For more on Smith and ideology, see Jay Watson, "Uncovering the Body, Discovering Ideology." For a notable effort to situate Smith in terms of liberalism, see Haddox, "Lillian Smith, Cold War Intellectual." The relation of Smith's writing to racial conversion narratives is discussed in Hobson, *But Now I See*, 18–36. Smith likewise figures into the nuanced account of temporality in Southern fiction offered in Duck, *The Nation's Region*, 195–99. The role of the grotesque in Smith's work is accounted for in Yaeger, *Dirt and Desire*, esp. 237–48. Depictions of same-sex desire in Smith's early writing are analyzed in Johnson, "The Language of Sexuality and Silence in Lillian Smith's *Strange Fruit*," and in Gary Richards, *Lovers and Beloveds*, 94–116.

2. See Lillian Smith, *Strange Fruit*, 192: "[Nonnie Anderson] was remembering when she was eleven. [Big Henry] had met up with her on the way from school and said, swinging his books back and forth across his shoulders as he said it, 'Say,' he said and grinned, 'say, how about fuckin with me?' And as she stared the color had beat through her face and neck. 'You knows,' he grinned, 'fuckin,' and opened his pants." Hereafter abbreviated *SF*; further references provided parenthetically.

3. Most of this paragraph derives from Smith's own account in Lillian Smith, *How Am I to Be Heard?* 81–82. Cf. DeVoto, "The Decision in the *Strange Fruit* Case."

4. *Isenstadt*, 318 Mass. at 547.

5. Ibid., at 556.

6. Cf. Duhamel, *After "Strange Fruit*," and McCoy, "Banned in Boston."

7. *Isenstadt*, 318 Mass. at 548.

8. Ibid., at 549.

9. *One Book Called "Ulysses*," 5 F. Supp. at 185.

10. *Levine*, 83 F.2d at 158.

11. The remaining four pages of the *Isenstadt* opinion address and dismiss in turn the nineteen-point attack waged by Isenstadt's lawyers on the Commonwealth's obscenity statute. The court also reiterates that juries (and not literary, social, and psychological "experts") are the real authorities in obscenity cases. The opinion then closes by noting that an amendment to the state's obscenity statute is set to go into effect later in the year and that this amendment will allow obscenity proceedings to be instigated against books directly. See ibid., at 561.

12. Ibid.

13. Ibid.

14. Ibid., at 562.

15. Ibid.

16. Cf. *SF*, 1–2, 6, 14, 30, 145, 168, 193, 201, 238, 243, 267, 274. Notably, when there was talk of filming *Strange Fruit* in the early 1960s, Smith lobbied hard for Audrey Hepburn to play Nonnie. See Lillian Smith, *How Am I to Be Heard?* 280 and 289.

17. If anything, the demands that Ed makes of his sister Nonnie seem to suggest his desires are more likely incestuous (*SF*, 12, 25–29, 155–56).

18. The foundational text for this line of inquiry remains Sedgwick, *Epistemology of the Closet*.

19. By way of comparison, see Johnson, "The Language of Sexuality and Silence," 17–19.

20. Lillian Smith, *Killers of the Dream*, 106. Hereafter abbreviated *KD*; further references provided parenthetically.

21. Cf. Watson, "Uncovering the Body, Discovering Ideology," esp. 473.

22. Yaeger, *Dirt and Desire*, 246–47.

23. Cf. Jenkins, *The South in Black and White*, esp. 117.

24. Watson, "Uncovering the Body, Discovering Ideology," 491.

25. Two salient counterweights to Smith's view here are Felman, *The Literary Speech Act*, and Butler, *Excitable Speech*.

26. In the terms established by J. L. Austin, Smith confuses perlocutionary performatives with illocutionary ones, much as Catharine A. MacKinnon is said to do by Butler, for whom such a confusion implicitly necessitates greater state-sponsored censorship and oversight in place of the formation of nonsovereign agents who are able to act on behalf of their interests and to contest injurious language, in some cases by appropriating and repurposing it. See Butler, *Excitable Speech*, esp. 17–27, 39–41, 63–69, 73–74, 112.

27. See MacKinnon, *Only Words*.

28. See ibid., 29–31.

29. See White and Sugg Jr., *From the Mountain*, 116–30.

30. As Smith declares in the opening pages of *The Journey*, "only in ordeal is a man revealed at his most creative." See Lillian Smith, *The Journey*, 10.

31. Not for nothing, Smith poses birth "as the prototype of all human ordeal." See ibid., 206–7, 209.

32. Ibid., 77–78.

33. Gunnar Myrdal, *An American Dilemma*, 1:444.

34. Ibid., 1:445.

35. Ibid., 1:440.

36. Ibid.

37. Ibid., 1:514; emphasis original.

38. Woodward, *Origins of the New South, 1877–1913*, 75.

39. Ibid., 76.

40. Cf. King, *A Southern Renaissance*, 270–71.

41. Woodward, *The Strange Career of Jim Crow*, 45. Hereafter abbreviated SC; further references provided parenthetically.

42. For instance, see Barbara J. Fields, "Ideology and Race in American History."

43. For more on Smith's role in the history of Southern liberalism, see Sosna, *In Search of the Silent South*, 174–97.

44. See Mack, "Rethinking Civil Rights Lawyering and Politics in the Era Before *Brown*."

45. Lillian Smith, *How Am I to Be Heard?* 327.

46. Lillian Smith, *The Journey*, 55. Cf. Teilhard de Chardin, *The Phenomenon of Man*, 283–84.

47. Lillian Smith, *The Journey*, 256.

48. Du Bois, "Searing Novel of the South," 1.

Conclusion

1. Ellison, *Going to the Territory*, 186.

2. Ibid., 196.

3. Ibid., 193.

4. Ibid., 194. For more on Kenneth Burke's "perspective by incongruity," see Burke, *Permanence and Change*, 69ff.

5. Cf. Burke, *Permanence and Change*, 36: "Shifts of interpretation result from the different ways in which we group events in the *because of*, *in spite of*, and *regardless of* categories."

6. This is my Burkean gloss on Fleissner's cogent explication of the roles played by compulsion and embodiment in early twentieth-century U.S. literary naturalism.

7. Of those artists (Finley, Mapplethorpe, Holly Hughes, John Fleck, and Tim Miller) who found themselves deprived of NEA funding due to charges of indecency in the late 1980s and early 1990s, Mapplethorpe has received the lion's share of the critical and biographical attention: Morrisroe, *Mapplethorpe*; Danto, *Playing with the Edge*; and Patti Smith, *Just Kids*. For more on Finley and her work, see the following: Carr, *On Edge*, 121–31; de Grazia, *Girls Lean Back Everywhere*, 658–88; Hart, *Fatal Women*, 89–104; and Shank, *Beyond the Boundaries*, 199–212.

8. For more on "repugnant cultural other," see Harding, "Representing Fundamentalism."

Bibliography

Primary Texts

Anderson, Margaret. "Judicial Opinion (Our Suppressed October Issue)." *The Little Review* 4, no. 8 (December 1917): 46–49.

Caldwell, Erskine. *The Bastard*. New York: Heron, 1929.

———. *Call It Experience: The Years of Learning How to Write*. New York: Duell, Sloan and Pearce, 1951.

———. *God's Little Acre*. Athens: University of Georgia Press, 1995.

———. "In Defense of Myself." Portland, Maine: n.p., 1930.

———. *Journeyman*. New York: Duell, Sloan and Pearce, 1950.

———. "Naturalism and the American Novel." Guilford, Conn.: J. Norton, n.d.

———. *Writing in America*. New York: Phaedra, 1967.

Dreiser, Theodore. *Newspaper Days*. Edited by T. D. Nostwich. Philadelphia: University of Pennsylvania Press, 1991.

Ellison, Ralph. *Going to the Territory*. New York: Random House, 1986.

Farrell, James T. *Studs Lonigan*. New York: Penguin, 2001.

Hardy, Thomas. *The Trumpet-Major*. Edited by Richard Nemesvari. Oxford: Oxford University Press, 1991.

Hurston, Zora Neale. *Their Eyes Were Watching God*. New York: Harper, 2006.

Joyce, James. *Dubliners*. New York: Penguin, 1992.

———. *Occasional, Critical, and Political Writing*. Edited by Kevin Barry. Oxford: Oxford University Press, 2000.

———. *Ulysses*. New York: Random House, 1945.

Lawrence, D. H. *Phoenix: The Posthumous Papers of D. H. Lawrence*. Edited by Edward D. McDonald. New York: Viking, 1968.

Lewis, Wyndham. *The Apes of God*. Edited by Paul Edwards. Santa Rosa: Black Sparrow, 1981.

———. *The Art of Being Ruled*. Edited by Reed Way Dasenbrock. Santa Rosa: Black Sparrow, 1989.

———. *Blasting & Bombardiering*. Berkeley: University of California Press, 1967.

———. "Cantelman's [*sic*] Spring-Mate." *The Little Review* 4, no. 6 (October 1917): 8–14.

———. *The Complete Wild Body*. Santa Barbara: Black Sparrow, 1982.

———. *Men Without Art*. Edited by Seamus Cooney. Santa Rosa: Black Sparrow, 1997.

———. *The Roaring Queen*. Edited by Walter Allen. New York: Liveright, 1973.

———. *Snooty Baronet*. Edited by Bernard Lafourcade. Santa Barbara: Black Sparrow, 1984.

———. *Time and Western Man*. Edited by Paul Edwards. Santa Rosa: Black Sparrow, 1993.

Miller, Henry. *The World of Lawrence: A Passionate Appreciation*. London: Calder, 1985.

Norris, Frank. *Novels and Essays*. New York: Library of America, 1986.

Pound, Ezra. *The Selected Letters of Ezra Pound to John Quinn, 1915–1924*. Edited by Timothy Materer. Durham: Duke University Press, 1991.

Smith, Lillian. *How Am I to Be Heard? Letters of Lillian Smith*. Edited by Margaret Rose Gladney. Chapel Hill: University of North Carolina Press, 1993.

———. *The Journey*. New York: World Publishing, 1954.

———. *Killers of the Dream*. Garden City, N.Y.: Doubleday, 1963.

———. *Strange Fruit*. New York: Reynal & Hitchcock, 1944.

Stein, Gertrude. *The Making of Americans*. London: Dalkey Archive, 2006.

White, Helen, and Redding S. Sugg Jr., eds. *From the Mountain: Selections from "Pseudopodia" (1936), "The North Georgia Review" (1937–1941), and "South Today" (1942–1945)*. Memphis: Memphis State University Press, 1972.

Case Law

Anderson v. Patten, Postmaster, 247 F. 382 (S.D.N.Y. 1917).

Attorney General v. The Book Named "Forever Amber," 323 Mass. 302 (Mass. Sup. Ct. 1948).

Attorney General v. The Book Named "God's Little Acre," 326 Mass. 281 (Mass. Sup. Ct. 1950).

Attorney General v. The Book Named "Serenade," 326 Mass. 324 (Mass. Sup. Ct. 1950).

Bantam Books, Inc. v. Matthew F. Melko, 96 A.2d 47 (N.J. Sup. Ct. 1953).

Besig v. United States, 208 F.2d 142 (9th Cir. 1953).

Commonwealth v. Buckley, 200 Mass. 346 (Mass. Sup. Ct. 1909).

Commonwealth v. DeLacey, 271 Mass. 327 (Mass. Sup. Ct. 1930).

Commonwealth v. Feigenbaum, 70 A.2d 389 (Pa. Sup. Ct. 1950).

Commonwealth v. Friede, 271 Mass. 318 (Mass. Sup. Ct. 1930).

Commonwealth v. Gordon et al., 66 Pa. D.&C. 101 (Phil. Com. Pleas Ct. 1949).

Commonwealth v. Isenstadt, 318 Mass. 543 (Mass. Sup. Ct. 1945).

Doubleday v. New York, 335 U.S. 848 (1948).

Ginsberg v. New York, 390 U.S. 629 (1968).

Halsey v. The New York Society for the Suppression of Vice, 180 N.Y.S. 836 (N.Y. Sup. Ct. App. Div. 1920).

Halsey v. The New York Society for the Suppression of Vice, 234 N.Y. 1 (N.Y. Ct. App. 1922).

In re Worthington Company, 30 N.Y.S. 361 (N.Y. Sup. Ct. 1894).

Jacobellis v. Ohio, 378 U.S. 184 (1964).

Kingsley International Pictures Corporation v. Regents of the University of the State of New York, 360 U.S. 684 (1959).

Miller v. California, 413 U.S. 15 (1973).

Parmelee v. United States, 113 F.2d 729 (D.C. Ct. App. 1940).

People v. Berg, 272 N.Y.S. 586 (N.Y. Sup. Ct. App. Div. 1934).

People v. Brainard, 183 N.Y.S. 452 (N.Y. Sup. Ct. App. Div. 1920).

People v. Creative Age Press, Inc., 79 N.Y.S.2d 198 (N.Y. City Mag. Ct. 1948).

People v. Dial Press, 182 Misc. 416 (N.Y. City Mag. Ct. 1944).

People v. Doubleday, 71 N.Y.S.2d 736 (N.Y. Sup. Ct. App. Div. 1947).

People v. Doubleday, 297 N.Y. 687 (N.Y. Ct. App. 1947).

People v. Friede, 233 N.Y.S. 565 (N.Y. City Mag. Ct. 1929).

People v. Gotham Book Mart, Inc., 285 N.Y.S. 563 (N.Y. City Mag. Ct. 1936).

People v. Herman Miller, 279 N.Y.S. 583 (N.Y. City Mag. Ct. 1935).

People v. London, 63 N.Y.S.2d 227 (N.Y. City Mag. Ct. 1946).

People v. Margaret H. Sanger, 222 N.Y. 192 (N.Y. Ct. App. 1918).

People v. Pesky, 243 N.Y.S. 193 (N.Y. Sup. Ct. App. Div. 1930).

People v. Seltzer, 203 N.Y.S. 809 (N.Y. Sup. Ct. 1924).

People v. Vanguard Press, Inc., 84 N.Y.S. 2d. 427 (N.Y. City Mag. Ct. 1947).

People v. Viking Press, Inc., et al., 264 N.Y.S. 534 (N.Y. City Mag. Ct. 1933).

People v. Wepplo, 78 Cal.App.2d Supp. 959 (Cal. Ct. App. 1947).

People v. William Sanger, 154 N.Y.S. 414 (N.Y. Sup. Ct. App. Div. 1915).

R. v. Hicklin (1868) L.R. 3 Q.B. 360.

Rodd v. United States, 165 F.2d 54 (9th Cir. 1947).

Rosen v. United States, 161 U.S. 29 (1896).

Roth v. United States, 354 U.S. 476 (1957).

The St. Hubert Guild v. Peter J. Quinn, 118 N.Y.S.
    582 (N.Y. Sup. Ct. App. Term 1909).
Swearingen v. United States, 161 U.S. 446 (1896).
Theodore Dreiser v. John Lane Company, 171
    N.Y.S. 605 (N.Y. Sup. Ct. App. Div. 1918).
United States v. Bennett, 24 F. Cas. 1093
    (C.C.S.D.N.Y. 1879).
United States v. Dennett, 39 F.2d 564 (2d Cir.
    1930).
United States v. Kennerley, 209 F. 119 (S.D.N.Y.
    1913).
United States v. Levine, 83 F.2d 156 (2d Cir. 1936).

United States v. One Book Called "Ulysses," 5 F.
    Supp. 182 (S.D.N.Y. 1933).
United States v. One Book Entitled
    "Contraception," 51 F.2d 525 (S.D.N.Y.
    1931).
United States v. One Book Entitled "Ulysses," 72
    F.2d 705 (2d Cir. 1934).
United States v. One Obscene Book Entitled
    "Married Love," 48 F.2d 821 (S.D.N.Y.
    1931).
Walker v. Popenoe, 149 F.2d 511 (D.C. Ct. App.
    1945).

Secondary Sources

Adler, Amy M. "All Porn All the Time." *New York University Review of Law and Social Change* 31, no. 4 (2007): 695–710.
———. "The Art of Censorship." *West Virginia Law Review* 103, no. 2 (Winter 2000): 205–17.
———. "Postmodern Art and the Death of Obscenity Law." *Yale Law Journal* 99, no. 6 (April 1990): 1359–78.
———. "What's Left? Hate Speech, Pornography, and the Problem for Artistic Expression." *California Law Review* 84, no. 6 (December 1996): 1499–1572.
Adorno, Theodor *Aesthetic Theory.* Translated by Robert Hullot-Kentor. Minneapolis: University of Minnesota Press, 1997.
Alpert, Leo M. "Judicial Censorship of Obscene Literature." *Harvard Law Review* 52, no. 1 (1938): 40–76.
Arnold, Edwin T., ed. *Conversations with Erskine Caldwell.* Jackson: University Press of Mississippi, 1988.
———. *Erskine Caldwell Reconsidered.* Jackson: University Press of Mississippi, 1990.
Attorney General's Commission on Pornography and Obscenity Final Report. 2 vols. Washington, D.C.: U.S. Department of Justice, 1986.
Ayers, David. *Wyndham Lewis and Western Man.* New York: St. Martin's, 1992.
Bonn, Thomas L. *Heavy Traffic and High Culture: New American Library as Literary Gatekeeper in the Paperback Revolution.* Carbondale: Southern Illinois University Press, 1989.

———. *Under Cover: An Illustrated History of American Mass Market Paperbacks.* New York: Penguin, 1982.
Boyer, Paul S. *Purity in Print: Book Censorship in America from the Gilded Age to the Computer Age.* Madison: University of Wisconsin Press, 2002.
Buckley, Kerry W. *Mechanical Man: John Broadus Watson and the Beginnings of Behaviorism.* New York: Guilford, 1989.
Burke, Kenneth. *Permanence and Change: An Anatomy of Purpose.* Berkeley: University of California Press, 1984.
Butler, Judith. *Excitable Speech: A Politics of the Performative.* New York: Routledge, 1997.
Caillois, Roger. *The Edge of Reason: A Roger Caillois Reader.* Translated by Claudine Frank and Camille Naish. Durham: Duke University Press, 2003.
Cargill, Oscar. *Intellectual America: Ideas on the March.* New York: Macmillan, 1948.
Carr, C. *On Edge: Performance at the End of the Twentieth Century.* Middletown: Wesleyan University Press, 2008.
Castille, Philip. "'No More Obscene than the Truth': Erskine Caldwell's *God's Little Acre* and Southern Industrial Protest." *Situations* 2, no. 2 (2007): 59–79.
Chisholm, Dianne. "Obscene Modernism: Eros Noir and the Profane Illumination of Djuna Barnes." *American Literature* 69, no. 1 (March 1997): 167–206.

185

Clor, Harry M. *Obscenity and Public Morality: Censorship in a Liberal Society*. Chicago: University of Chicago Press, 1969.

——. *Public Morality and Liberal Society: Essays on Decency, Law, and Pornography*. Notre Dame: University of Notre Dame Press, 1996.

Clune, Michael W. *American Literature and the Free Market, 1945–2000*. Cambridge: Cambridge University Press, 2010.

Cook, Sylvia Jenkins. *Erskine Caldwell and the Fiction of Poverty: The Flesh and the Spirit*. Baton Rouge: Louisiana State University Press, 1991.

Cowley, Malcolm. "Naturalism in American Literature." In *Evolutionary Thought in America*, edited by Stow Persons, 300–333. New Haven: Yale University Press, 1950.

——. "'Not Men': A Natural History of American Naturalism." *Kenyon Review* 9, no. 3 (Summer 1947): 414–35.

Danto, Arthur. *Playing with the Edge: The Photographic Achievement of Robert Mapplethorpe*. Berkeley: University of California Press, 1996.

Davis, Kenneth. *Two-Bit Culture: The Paperbacking of America*. Boston: Houghton Mifflin, 1984.

De Grazia, Edward. *Girls Lean Back Everywhere: The Law of Obscenity and the Assault on Genius*. New York: Random House, 1992.

Dennett, Mary Ware. *Who's Obscene?* New York: Vanguard Press, 1930.

Denning, Michael. *Mechanic Accents: Dime Novels and Working-Class Culture in America*. London: Verso, 1987.

Descartes, René. *"Discourse on Method" and "The Meditations."* Translated by John Veitch. Amherst, N.Y.: Prometheus Books, 1989.

Dettmar, Kevin, and Stephen Watt, eds. *Marketing Modernisms: Self-Promotion, Canonization, and Rereading*. Ann Arbor: University of Michigan Press, 1996.

DeVoto, Bernard. "The Decision in the *Strange Fruit* Case: The Obscenity Statute in Massachusetts." *New England Quarterly* 19, no. 2 (1946): 147–83.

Diepeveen, Leonard. *The Difficulties of Modernism*. New York: Routledge, 2003.

Dore, Florence. *The Novel and the Obscene: Sexual Subjects in American Modernism*. Stanford: Stanford University Press, 2005.

Douglas, Ann. "*Studs Lonigan* and the Failure of History in Mass Society: A Study in Claustrophobia." *American Quarterly* 29, no. 5 (Winter 1977): 487–505.

Du Bois, W. E. B. "Searing Novel of the South." *New York Times Book Review*, March 5, 1944, 1, 20.

Duck, Leigh Anne. *The Nation's Region: Southern Modernism, Segregation, and U.S. Nationalism*. Athens: University of Georgia Press, 2006.

Duhamel, P. Albert. *After "Strange Fruit": Changing Literary Taste in Post–World War II Boston*. Boston: Trustees of the Public Library of the City of Boston, 1980.

Ellmann, Richard. *James Joyce*. Oxford: Oxford University Press, 1982.

Ernst, Morris L., and William Seagle. *To the Pure . . . : A Study of Obscenity and the Censor*. New York: Viking, 1928.

Feinberg, Joel. *The Moral Limits of the Criminal Law: Offense to Others*. New York: Oxford University Press, 1988.

Felman, Shoshana. *The Literary Speech Act: Don Juan with J. L. Austin, or Seduction in Two Languages*. Translated by Catherine Porter. Ithaca: Cornell University Press, 1983.

Fiedler, Leslie. "To Whom Does Joyce Belong? *Ulysses* as Parody, Pop, and Porn." In *Light Rays: James Joyce and Modernism*, edited by Heyward Ehrlich, 26–37. New York: New Horizon Press, 1984.

Fields, Barbara J. "Ideology and Race in American History." In *Region, Race, and Reconstruction: Essays in Honor of C. Vann Woodward*, edited by J. Morgan Kousser and James M. McPherson, 143–77. New York: Oxford University Press, 1982.

Finnis, John M. "'Reason and Passion': The Constitutional Dialectic of Free Speech and Obscenity." *University of*

186

Pennsylvania Law Review 116, no. 2 (December 1967): 222–43.

Fleissner, Jennifer. *Women, Compulsion, Modernity: The Moment of American Naturalism.* Chicago: University of Chicago Press, 2004.

Freud, Sigmund. *Beyond the Pleasure Principle.* Translated by James Strachey. New York: Norton, 1989.

———. *Jokes and Their Relation to the Unconscious.* Translated by James Strachey. New York: Norton, 1960.

Friedman, Andrea. *Prurient Interests: Gender, Democracy, and Obscenity in New York City, 1909–1945.* New York: Columbia University Press, 2000.

Gandal, Keith. *The Virtues of the Vicious: Jacob Riis, Stephen Crane, and the Spectacle of the Slum.* New York: Oxford University Press, 1997.

Gang, Joshua. "Behaviorism and the Beginnings of Close Reading." *English Literary History* 78, no. 1 (Spring 2011): 1–25.

Gelfant, Blanche Housman. *The American City Novel.* Norman: University of Oklahoma Press, 1954.

Gerbner, George. "The Social Role of the Confession Magazine." *Social Problems* 6, no. 1 (Summer 1958): 29–40.

Gey, Steven G. "The Apologetics of Suppression: The Regulation of Pornography as Act and Idea." *Michigan Law Review* 86, no. 7 (June 1988): 1564–634.

Glass, Loren. "Redeeming Value: Obscenity and Anglo-American Literary Modernism." *Critical Inquiry* 32, no. 2 (Winter 2006): 341–61.

Green, André. *Time in Psychoanalysis: Some Contradictory Aspects.* Translated by Andrew Weller. London: Free Association, 2002.

Greenberg, Clement. *Art and Culture: Critical Essays.* Boston: Beacon Press, 1961.

———. *Clement Greenberg: The Collected Essays and Criticism.* Edited by John O'Brian. 4 vols. Chicago: University of Chicago Press, 1986.

Greene, Jody. "Arbitrary Tastes and Commonsense Pleasures: Accounting for Taste in Cleland, Hume, and Burke." In *Launching Fanny Hill: Essays on the Novel and Its Influence,* edited by Patsy S. Fowler and Alan Jackson, 212–66. New York: AMS Press, 2003.

Haddox, Thomas F. "Lillian Smith, Cold War Intellectual." *Southern Literary Journal* 44, no. 2 (Spring 2012): 51–68.

Haight, Anne Lyon. *Banned Books: Informal Notes on Some Books Banned for Various Reasons at Various Times and in Various Places.* New York: R. R. Bowker, 1955.

Harding, Susan. "Representing Fundamentalism: The Problem of the Repugnant Cultural Other." *Social Research* 58, no. 2 (Summer 1991): 373–93.

Hart, Lynda. *Fatal Women: Lesbian Sexuality and Marks of Aggression.* London: Routledge, 1994.

Henkin, Louis. "Morals and the Constitution: The Sin of Obscenity." *Columbia Law Review* 63, no. 3 (March 1963): 391–414.

Hill, Christopher. "The Travels of Naturalism and the Challenges of a World Literary History." *Literature Compass* 6, no. 6 (October 2009): 1198–210.

Hobson, Fred C. *But Now I See: The White Southern Racial Conversion Narrative.* Baton Rouge: Louisiana State University Press, 1999.

Holmes, Sarah C. "Re-examining the Political Left: Erskine Caldwell and the Doctrine of Eugenics." In *Evolution and Eugenics in American Literature and Culture, 1880–1940: Essays on Ideological Conflict and Complicity,* edited by Lois A. Cuddy and Claire M. Roche, 240–58. Lewisburg: Bucknell University Press, 2003.

Holt, Guy, ed. *"Jurgen" and the Law: A Statement with Exhibits, Including the Court's Opinion, and the Brief for the Defendants on Motion to Direct an Acquittal.* New York: Robert M. McBride, 1923.

Howard, June. *Form and History in American Literary Naturalism.* Chapel Hill: University of North Carolina Press, 1985.

Hunter, Ian, David Saunders, and Dugald Williamson. *On Pornography: Literature, Sexuality, and Obscenity Law.* London: Macmillan, 1993.

187

James, William. "Does 'Consciousness' Exist?" *Journal of Philosophy, Psychology, and Scientific Methods* 1, no. 18 (1904): 477–91.

———. *Principles of Psychology*. 2 vols. New York: Henry Holt, 1918.

Jameson, Frederic. *Fables of Aggression: Wyndham Lewis, the Modernist as Fascist*. Berkeley: University of California Press, 1979.

———. *The Ideologies of Theory*. London: Verso, 2008.

———. *Signatures of the Visible*. London: Routledge, 1990.

———. *A Singular Modernity: Essays on the Ontology of the Present*. London: Verso, 2002.

Jenkins, McKay. *The South in Black and White: Race, Sex, and Literature in the 1940s*. Chapel Hill: University of North Carolina Press, 1999.

Johnson, Cheryl L. "The Language of Sexuality and Silence in Lillian Smith's *Strange Fruit*." *Signs* 27, no. 1 (Autumn 2001): 1–22.

Keely, Karen A. "Power, Sterilization, and Eugenics in Erskine Caldwell's *Tobacco Road*." *Journal of American Studies* 36, no. 1 (April 2002): 23–42.

Kendrick, Walter. *The Secret Museum: Pornography in Modern Culture*. Berkeley: University of California Press, 1987.

Kenner, Hugh. *Wyndham Lewis*. Norfolk, Conn.: New Directions, 1954.

King, Richard H. *A Southern Renaissance: The Cultural Awakening of the American South, 1930–1955*. New York: Oxford University Press, 1980.

Klevar, Harvey L. *Erskine Caldwell: A Biography*. Knoxville: University of Tennessee Press, 1993.

Koppelman, Andrew. "Does Obscenity Cause Moral Harm?" *Columbia Law Review* 105, no. 5 (June 2005): 1653–79.

———. "Is Pornography 'Speech'?" *Legal Theory* 14, no. 1 (March 2008): 71–89.

———. "Reading *Lolita* at Guantánamo: Or, This Page Cannot Be Displayed." *Dissent* 53, no. 2 (Spring 2006): 64–71.

Kristol, Irving. "Pornography, Obscenity, and the Case for Censorship." *New York Times Magazine* (March 28, 1971): 24.

Ladenson, Elisabeth. *Dirt for Art's Sake: Books on Trial from "Madame Bovary" to "Lolita."* Ithaca: Cornell University Press, 2007.

Lancaster, Ashley Craig. "Weeding Out the Recessive Gene: Representations of the Evolving Eugenics Movement in Erskine Caldwell's *God's Little Acre*." *Southern Literary Journal* 39, no. 2 (Spring 2007): 78–99.

Lindgren, James. "Defining Pornography." *University of Pennsylvania Law Review* 141, no. 4 (April 1993): 1153–275.

Lingeman, Richard. *Theodore Dreiser: An American Journey, 1908–1945*. New York: Putnam's Sons, 1990.

———. *Theodore Dreiser: At the Gates of the City, 1871–1907*. New York: Putnam's Sons, 1986.

Lukács, György. "Narrate or Describe?" In *Writer and Critic*, edited and translated by Arthur D. Kahn, 110-48. London: Merlin Press, 1971.

Lyotard, Jean-François. "Discourse Figure: The Utopia Behind the Scenes of the Phantasy." Translated by Mary Lydon. *Theatre Journal* 35, no. 3 (October 1983): 333–57.

MacDonald, Scott, ed. *Critical Essays on Erskine Caldwell*. Boston: G. K. Hall, 1981.

———. "Repetition as Technique in the Short Stories of Erskine Caldwell." In *The Critical Response to Erskine Caldwell*, edited by Robert L. McDonald, 208-20. Westport, Conn.: Greenwood Press, 1997.

Mack, Kenneth W. "Rethinking Civil Rights Lawyering and Politics in the Era before *Brown*." *Yale Law Journal* 115, no. 2 (November 2005): 256–354.

MacKinnon, Catharine A. *Feminism Unmodified: Discourses on Life and Law*. Cambridge, Mass.: Harvard University Press, 1987.

———. *Only Words*. Cambridge, Mass.: Harvard University Press, 1993.

Manchester, Colin. "Lord Campbell's Act: England's First Obscenity Statute." *Journal of Legal History* 9, no. 2 (September 1988): 223–41.

Mao, Douglas, and Rebecca L. Walkowitz, eds. *Bad Modernisms*. Durham: Duke University Press, 2006.

Marcuse, Herbert. *One-Dimensional Man: Studies in the Ideology of Advanced Industrial Society*. Boston: Beacon Press, 1991.

Marin, Louis. *On Representation*. Stanford: Stanford University Press, 2001.

Marinetti, F. T. "The Founding and Manifesto of Futurism." In *Futurism: An Anthology*, edited by Lawrence Rainey, Christine Poggi, and Laura Wittman, 49–53. New Haven: Yale University Press, 2009.

Marshik, Celia. *British Modernism and Censorship*. Cambridge: Cambridge University Press, 2006.

McCoy, Ralph E. "Banned in Boston: The Development of Literary Censorship in Massachusetts." PhD diss., University of Illinois, 1956.

McDonald, Robert L., ed. *The Critical Response to Erskine Caldwell*. Westport, Conn.: Greenwood Press, 1997.

———, ed. *Reading Erskine Caldwell: New Essays*. Jefferson, N.C.: McFarland, 2006.

Metress, Christopher. "Repetition as Radical Critique in Erskine Caldwell's *God's Little Acre*." In *Reading Erskine Caldwell: New Essays*, edited by Robert L. McDonald, 165–82. Jefferson, N.C.: McFarland, 2006.

Miller, Dan B. *Erskine Caldwell: The Journey from "Tobacco Road."* New York: Knopf, 1995.

Miller, Tyrus. *Late Modernism: Politics, Fiction, and the Arts between the World Wars*. Berkeley: University of California Press, 1999.

Morrisroe, Patricia. *Mapplethorpe: A Biography*. New York: Random House, 1995.

Mullin, Katherine. *James Joyce, Sexuality, and Social Purity*. Cambridge: Cambridge University Press, 2003.

Myrdal, Gunnar. *An American Dilemma: The Negro Problem and American Democracy*. 2 vols. New York: Harper and Brothers, 1944.

Nicholls, Peter. *Modernisms: A Literary Guide*. Basingstoke: Palgrave Macmillan, 2009.

Nowlin, Christopher. *Judging Obscenity: A Critical History of Expert Evidence*. Montreal: McGill-Queen's University Press, 2003.

Owen, Guy. "'The Bogus Ones': A Lost Erskine Caldwell Novel." *Southern Literary Journal* 11, no. 1 (Fall 1978): 32–39.

Paret, Peter. "Literary Censorship as a Source of Historical Understanding: A Comment." *Central European History* 18, nos. 3–4 (September–December 1985): 360–64.

Parkes, Adam. *Modernism and the Theater of Censorship*. New York: Oxford University Press, 1996.

Pease, Allison. *Modernism, Mass Culture, and the Aesthetics of Obscenity*. Cambridge: Cambridge University Press, 2000.

Peirce, Charles. *Philosophical Writings of Peirce*. Edited by Justus Bucher. New York: Dover, 1955.

Posner, Richard. *Sex and Reason*. Cambridge, Mass.: Harvard University Press, 1992.

Potter, Rachel. *Obscene Modernism: Literary Censorship and Experiment, 1900–1940*. Oxford: Oxford University Press, 2013.

Rahv, Philip. *Image and Idea: Fourteen Essays on Literary Themes*. Norfolk, Conn.: New Directions, 1949.

Rainey, Lawrence. *Institutions of Modernism: Literary Elites and Public Culture*. New Haven: Yale University Press, 1998.

———. "A Poem Including History: The Cantos of Ezra Pound." *Paideuma* 21 (Spring/Fall 1992): n.p.

Redish, Martin H. *Freedom of Expression: A Critical Analysis*. Charlottesville, Va.: Michie, 1984.

Rembar, Charles. *The End of Obscenity: The Trials of "Lady Chatterley," "Tropic of Cancer," and "Fanny Hill."* New York: Random House, 1968.

Report of the Commission on Obscenity and Pornography. New York: Bantam, 1970.

Richards, Gary. *Lovers and Beloveds: Sexual Otherness in Southern Fiction, 1936–1961*. Baton Rouge: Louisiana State University Press, 2005.

Richards, I. A. *Practical Criticism: A Study of Literary Judgment*. London: Kegan Paul, 1930.

Rosenquist, Rod. *Modernism, the Market, and the Institution of the New*. Cambridge: Cambridge University Press, 2009.

189

Schauer, Frederick F. *Free Speech: A Philosophical Enquiry*. Cambridge: Cambridge University Press, 1982.

———. *The Law of Obscenity*. Washington, D.C.: Bureau of National Affairs, 1976.

———. "Speech and 'Speech'—Obscenity and 'Obscenity': An Exercise in the Interpretation of Constitutional Language." *Georgetown Law Journal* 67 (1979): 899–933.

Sedgwick, Eve Kosofsky. *Epistemology of the Closet*. Berkeley: University of California Press, 1990.

Shank, Theodore. *Beyond the Boundaries: American Alternative Theatre*. Ann Arbor: University of Michigan Press, 2002.

Sherry, Vincent. *Modernism and the Reinvention of Decadence*. Cambridge: Cambridge University Press, 2015.

Smith, Patti. *Just Kids*. New York: Ecco, 2010.

Sosna, Morton. *In Search of the Silent South: Southern Liberals and the Race Issue*. New York: Columbia University Press, 1977.

Speer, Lisa K. "Paperback Pornography: Mass Market Novels and Censorship in Post-War America." *Journal of American and Comparative Cultures* 24, nos. 3–4 (Fall/Winter 2001): 153–60.

Stanfield, Paul Scott. "'This Implacable Doctrine': Behaviorism in Wyndham Lewis' *Snooty Baronet*." *Twentieth-Century Literature* 47, no. 2 (Summer 2001): 241–67.

Stark, Gary D. "The Censorship of Literary Naturalism, 1885–1895: Prussia and Saxony." *Central European History* 18, nos. 3–4 (September–December 1985): 326–43.

Stovall, Floyd. *American Idealism*. Port Washington, N.Y.: Kennikat Press, 1965.

Strauss, Leo. *Persecution and the Art of Writing*. Glencoe, Ill.: Free Press, 1952.

Strossen, Nadine. "A Feminist Critique of 'the' Feminist Critique of Pornography." *Virginia Law Review* 79, no. 5 (August 1993): 1099–190.

Tebbel, John. *Between the Covers: The Rise and Transformation of Book Publishing in America*. New York: Oxford University Press, 1987.

Teilhard de Chardin, Pierre. *The Phenomenon of Man*. Translated by Bernard Wall. New York: Harper and Row, 1965.

Tischler, Alyson. "A Rose Is a Pose: Steinian Modernism and Mass Culture." *Journal of Modern Literature* 26, nos. 3–4 (Summer 2003): 12–27.

Trilling, Lionel. *Beyond Culture*. New York: Viking, 1965.

Turner, Catherine. *Marketing Modernism between the Two World Wars*. Amherst: University of Massachusetts Press, 2003.

United States House of Representatives. *Report of the Select Committee on Current Pornographic Materials, House of Representatives, Eighty-Second Congress Pursuant to H. Res. 596: A Resolution Creating a Select Committee to Conduct a Study and Investigation of Current Pornographic Materials*. Washington, D.C.: United States Government Printing Office, 1952.

Vanderham, Paul. *James Joyce and Censorship: The Trials of "Ulysses."* London: Macmillan, 1998.

Vials, Chris. "Whose Dixie? Erskine Caldwell's Challenge to *Gone with the Wind* and Dialectical Realism." *Criticism* 48, no. 1 (Winter 2006): 69–94.

Vizetelly, Ernest. *Émile Zola, Novelist and Reformer: An Account of His Life and Work*. New York: John Lane, 1904.

Wagenknecht, Edward. *Cavalcade of the American Novel*. New York: Holt, Rinehart and Winston, 1952.

Wagner, Geoffrey. *Wyndham Lewis: A Portrait of the Artist as the Enemy*. New Haven: Yale University Press, 1957.

Walcutt, Charles Child. *American Literary Naturalism, a Divided Stream*. Minneapolis: University of Minnesota Press, 1956.

Wald, Alan M. *James T. Farrell: The Revolutionary Socialist Years*. New York: New York University Press, 1978.

———. *The New York Intellectuals: The Rise and Decline of the Anti-Stalinist Left from the 1930s to the 1980s*. Chapel Hill: University of North Carolina Press, 1987.

Watson, Jay. "Uncovering the Body, Discovering Ideology: Segregation and Sexual

Anxiety in Lillian Smith's *Killers of the Dream.*" *American Quarterly* 49, no. 3 (September 1997): 470–503.

Watson, John B. *Behaviorism.* 2nd ed. Chicago: University of Chicago Press, 1930.

———. "The New Science of Animal Behavior." *Harper's Monthly Magazine* 120 (February 1910): 346–53.

———. "Psychology as the Behaviorist Views It." *Psychological Review* 20 (1913): 158–77.

Wexler, Joyce Piell. *Who Paid for Modernism? Art, Money, and the Fiction of Conrad, Joyce, and Lawrence.* Fayetteville: University of Arkansas Press, 1997.

Woodward, C. Vann. *Origins of the New South, 1877–1913.* Baton Rouge: Louisiana State University Press, 1951.

———. *The Strange Career of Jim Crow.* New York: Oxford University Press, 1974.

Yaeger, Patricia. *Dirt and Desire: Reconstructing Southern Women's Writing, 1930–1990.* Chicago: University of Chicago Press, 2000.

Zola, Émile. *The Experimental Novel and Other Essays.* New York: Cassell, 1893.

Zuriff, G. E. *Behaviorism: A Conceptual Reconstruction.* New York: Columbia University Press, 1985.

Index

REFIGURING MODERNISM   ARTS

LITERATURES

SCIENCES

(A Series Edited By)
Jonathan Eburne

Refiguring Modernism features cutting-edge interdisciplinary approaches to the study of art, literature, science, and cultural history. With an eye to the different modernisms emerging throughout the world during the twentieth century and beyond, we seek to publish scholarship that engages creatively with canonical and eccentric works alike, bringing fresh concepts and original research to bear on modernist cultural production, whether aesthetic, social, or epistemological. What does it mean to study modernism in a global context characterized at once by decolonization and nation-building; international cooperation and conflict; changing ideas about subjectivity and identity; new understandings of language, religion, poetics, and myth; and new paradigms for science, politics, and religion? What did modernism offer artists, writers, and intellectuals? How do we theorize and historicize modernism? How do we rethink its forms, its past, and its futures?

(Other Books in the Series)